W9-DDL-000

# THE ANIMAL RIGHTS MOVEMENT IN THE UNITED STATES, 1975–1990
## An Annotated Bibliography

by
**BETTINA MANZO**

**The Scarecrow Press, Inc.**
**Metuchen, N.J., & London**
**1994**

British Library Cataloguing-in-Publication data available

**Library of Congress Cataloging-in-Publication Data**

Manzo, Bettina, 1943–
    The animal rights movement in the United States,
    1975–1990 : an annotated bibliography / by Bettina Manzo.
        p.   cm.
    Includes index.
    ISBN 0-8108-2732-8 (acid-free paper)
    1. Animal rights movement—United States—Bibliography.
    2. Animal rights—United States—Bibliography.   3. Ani-
    mal experimentation—United States—Bibliography.
    I. Title.
    Z7164.C45M38    1994
    [HV4764]
    016.179′3′0973—dc20                                    94-19622

For my mother and father,
Jean and Dominick Manzo

# CONTENTS

Acknowledgments, vii
Introduction, ix
Periodical Abbreviations, xi
I    The Animal Rights Movement, 1
        General, 3
        Activists and Organizations, 26
II   Philosophy, Ethics, and Religion, 39
III  Law and Legislation, 68
IV   Factory Farming and Vegetarianism, 77
        General, 77
        Philosophy, Ethics, and Religion, 92
        Law and Legislation, 96
V    Trapping and Fur Industry, 99
        General, 99
        Law and Legislation, 109
VI   Companion Animals, 112
VII  Wildlife, 123
        General, 123
        Hunting, 129
VIII Circuses, Zoos, Rodeos, Dog and Horse Racing, Pigeon
        Shoots, Aquatic Theme Parks, and Other Recreational
        Use of Animals, 136
IX   Animal Experimentation, 147
        General, 147
        Philosophy, Ethics, and Religion, 181
        Law and Legislation, 185
        Agency Rules, Regulations, and Policies, 202
        Animal Liberation Front, 207
        Important Cases:
            Silver Spring Monkeys, 217
            University of Pennsylvania Baboon Studies, 225
            Other, 229

Military Experiments, 236
Genetic Experiments, 239
Consumer Product and Toxicity Tests, 241
Animal Use in Educational Settings, 246
Alternatives to Animal Experimentation, 252
Scientific Validity of Animal Experimentation, 261
Animal Researchers' Response, 265
Author and Editor Index, 273
Subject Index, 282
About the Author, 297

# ACKNOWLEDGMENTS

Thanks to Swem Library's fine collection at the College of William and Mary, I was able to obtain nearly all the titles I needed in order to compile this bibliography. For those titles not available at the college library, I'd like to thank John Lawrence, Carol Linton, and Gerry Lopez of the Interlibrary Loan Department at Swem Library, who borrowed a number of materials for me from other institutions. Their efforts insured the bibliography included essential titles. My gratitude also goes to Alan Zoellner, Linda Templeman, and Cynthia Della-Posta in the Documents Department of Swem Library for helping me to identify and locate relevant U.S. government publications and for allowing me free access to their stacks. And finally, many thanks to Chip Roberson who encouraged me to have this bibliography published.

# INTRODUCTION

This bibliography lists materials that address the issues, philosophy, organizations, and activities of the animal rights movement in the United States between 1975 and 1990. The choice of 1975 as the year marking the start of the animal rights movement is arbitrary, because in this country, organized interest in the protection of animals has existed to a greater or lesser extent for more than 150 years. Beginning in 1975, however, perhaps triggered by the publication of Peter Singer's *Animal Liberation: A New Ethic for Our Treatment of Animals*, individuals and organizations interested in the problem of animal abuse became more articulate, more focused, and more organized than ever before in the identification of their issues and pursuing their goals.

The proliferation of printed materials on the subject has kept pace with this new activism and also reflects the growing popularity of the movement as well as the controversy it has provoked. Because of the abundance of information, however, I have had to be selective and include only representative pieces rather than attempt an all-inclusive bibliography. The citations are accompanied by an annotation, except in the case of self-explanatory titles and those I have not had the opportunity to read.

I have drawn from a variety of publications in collecting citations—newspapers, magazines, journals, books, government publications, and reports that cover a wide array of disciplines—law, business, the sciences, philosophy, ethics, religion, psychology, politics and government, and current affairs. Publications from the animal rights movement itself often provide the best insight into the movement, but because of their overwhelming number, I have cited only two on a comprehensive basis—*Animals Agenda* and *Animals Voice*. Both of these magazines cover the spectrum of animal rights issues, activities, and goals, and, I believe, provide good representation of the character of the animal rights movement in America.

The animal rights movement in the United States is part of a larger, global animal rights movement, and the international exchange of ideas is often facilitated by newspapers, books, and journal articles. For that reason, I have included foreign publications written in English, especially relevant philosophical works.

It is not the purpose of this bibliography to define the position of those who oppose the animal rights movement, but I have included a number of articles and books that do so. They provide context for the controversy and demonstrate the animal rights movement's success in provoking debate and response.

Citations are divided by major animal rights issues and, when necessary, subdivided within each division. A subject index is also included to provide greater access to individual citations by topic.

Bettina Manzo
1994

# PERIODICAL ABBREVIATIONS

| | |
|---|---|
| *AA* | *Animals Agenda* |
| *AV* | *Animals Voice* |
| *Chron H Ed* | *Chronicle of Higher Education* |
| *CSM* | *Christian Science Monitor* |
| *LAT* | *Los Angeles Times* |
| *NYT* | *New York Times* (Late Edition) |
| *WP* | *Washington Post* |
| *WSJ* | *Wall Street Journal* (Eastern Edition) |

# I THE ANIMAL RIGHTS MOVEMENT

The animal rights movement in the United States is composed of individuals and organizations working aggressively on local, state, and national levels to eliminate the abuse of animals in a variety of settings. The movement's goals and activities are based on the ethical propositions that animals have a right both to their own lives and to a purpose of their own and that to use, abuse, or kill them in the service of man is unacceptable. Included within the activists' circle of concern are animals used by the biomedical industry in medical research, consumer product safety testing, and academic settings; animals bred, raised, and slaughtered for food, especially in factory-farm environments; fur-bearing animals trapped or bred for their pelts and skins; animals used or killed in recreational activities such as rodeos, circuses, zoos, dog fights, and hunting; and the millions of stray or abandoned dogs and cats who are euthanized in animal shelters and pounds each year.

The animal rights movement has borrowed many of its techniques and strategies from other major reform movements in the United States, such as the civil rights and womens' rights movements. Tactics include legal initiatives and legislative lobbying, educational and public awareness activities, economic boycotts, protests, demonstrations, sit-ins, rallies, and, in some well-publicized cases, acts of civil disobedience that involve the freeing of animals and the vandalism of property.

Animal rights organizations have proliferated greatly in the United States in the past fifteen years, and although the battle against the abuse of animals is a common denominator among them, they can and do vary significantly in their specific individual goals. Some are interested in reducing and regulating the use of animals within a particular setting; others wish to eliminate the setting itself. For instance, regulationists might work for legislation to improve housing and methods of slaughtering of food animals

1

while abolitionists are promoting vegetarianism as the ultimate solution to factory-farming abuses and the unnecessary killing of animals. As a practical matter, however, abolitionists often work for regulatory measures in the belief that at this time it is unrealistic to eliminate many of the well-entrenched uses of animals in this country.

Animal rights organizations also differ in the specific abuses they each choose to target. Some, such as People for the Ethical Treatment of Animals, the Fund for Animals, and the Humane Society of the United States, have a broad mission and extend their energies to end animal mistreatment in many arenas, from factory farming to pet overpopulation to fur animals. Others, such as the American Anti-Vivisection Society and the Committee to Abolish Sport Hunting focus primarily on the elimination of one specific form of animal cruelty or abuse. And still others, such as Farm Sanctuary and Primarily Primates, spend much of their time rehabilitating or caring for formerly abused animals. In addition to these types of organizations, a number of groups have joined together around a particular type of activity. The Animal Legal Defense League, for instance, is a collection of lawyers who work to initiate legislation or use the courts to defend animals and activists. The Culture and Animals Foundation, another example, encourages the development of intellectual and artistic endeavors and sponsors an annual Spoletto Festival for the Animals in North Carolina.

Although the call for better treatment of animals dates back as far as the time of the ancient Greek philosophers, it is only in the past fifteen to twenty years that the concept of animal rights has become an issue entertained by mainstream America. The publication in 1975 of *Animal Liberation: A New Ethics for Our Treatment of Animals,* by Australian philosopher Peter Singer, which defined the exploitation of animals as speciesism and which chronicled the many abuses against animals, galvanized those already involved in animal welfare work, educated and inspired many new recruits, and spawned dozens of national and grass roots organizations.

Another phenomenon of the animal rights movement has been the impact it has had on traditional animal welfare organizations. Groups that once were concerned primarily with protecting domestic animals such as dogs and cats now have become as interested in confronting nontraditional issues such as animal experimentation and factory farming.

The animal rights movement in the United States should not be considered in isolation but as part of a larger, global reform movement. Canada, Western Europe, Great Britain, and Australia all have an active and vigorous animal rights movement, and animal rights organizations are also starting to form in other areas of the world. The reasons why the animal rights message has met with such a receptive audience at this time in our global history still have not been studied, but no doubt those reasons have to do with a complex set of ethical, economic, psychological, and sociological factors. Documentation of the movement's evolution awaits the attention of a future historian or sociologist.

Only the future, too, will determine what ultimate impact the animal rights movement will have on the relationship between human society and animals. Although the movement has had great success in riveting the public's attention to its cause, as well as some success in eliminating some mistreatment of animals, in the past few years, those who oppose the goals of the animal rights movement, especially those in the biomedical industry, have launched an aggressive campaign to stop such activism in its tracks. It is too early to know whether the movement will survive this counterattack or whether, as many animal rights activists hope, the '90s will prove to be the decade of radical and positive change in the ways human society treats animals.

## General

1. "Animal Rights Nonsense," *Nature* 305 (October 13, 1983):562.

    Animal rights taken to its logical conclusion is absurd and leads to remarkable consequences. If animals can have rights, they must also have responsibilities, which they can't or won't fulfill. Middle ground is animal welfare, not animal rights.

2. *Animal Rights: Opposing Viewpoints.* San Diego: Greenhaven Press, 1989.

    Reprint of essays that look at pros and cons of animal experimentation, wildlife protection, vegetarianism, and animal rights philosophy and ethics.

3.  Barker, Leigh. "Violence, Infiltration, and Sabotage: What
    We Can Learn from Other Movements," *AA* 9 (July/August
    1989):26–29.
    All reform movements have had infiltrators in their midst
    who instigated violence and illegal acts. Animal rights move-
    ment must avoid that fate by discouraging violence and in-
    trigue at every opportunity.

4.  Bartlett, Kim. "The Politics of Animal Liberation," *AA* 7
    (November 1987): 12–3+.
    At the first national convocation of Green Party in the
    United States, most Greens thought animal rights a fringe
    issue. Undaunted, the Animal Liberation caucus drafted a
    12-point plank that addressed issues of animal experimenta-
    tion, vegetarianism, factory farming, banning of predator
    control, trapping and hunting on public lands.

5.  Behar, Richard. "Meet the Meatless," *Forbes* 143 (March 20,
    1989):43–44.
    Animal rights movement is not nearly as large nor as influ-
    ential as media has portrayed it to be, nor should it be called
    "terrorist," because there is not one recorded instance in which
    any animal rights group has hurt anyone. There are signs the
    novelty of animal rights is beginning to wane, although
    Americans may have to endure a bit more before the move-
    ment burns out. Profiles Ingrid Newkirk, cofounder of People
    for the Ethical Treatment of Animals, and her organization.

6.  Bishop, Katherine. "Growing Militancy for Animal Rights Is
    Seen," *NYT* 19 January 1988:A14.
    In San Francisco, the FBI has begun to investigate arson
    cases involving research labs and meat companies.

7.  Bleiberg, Robert M. "Animal Worship–I," *Barron's* 69
    (February 13, 1989):11.
    Those who would protect endangered species and other
    animals are nuts and kooks. The animal rights movement is
    deeply irrational, but nevertheless it is gaining too much in-
    fluence and threatening agriculture, science, and even tradi-
    tional animal welfare societies.

8. Bleiberg, Robert M. "Animal Worship–II," *Barron's* 69 (November 13, 1989):9.

   Condemns animal rights movement, focusing on the Animal Liberation Front and journalists who give the front's headline-grabbing activities too much attention.

9. Brebner, Sue, and Debbie Baer. *Becoming an Activist: PETA's Guide to Animal Rights Organizing.* Washington, DC: People for the Ethical Treatment of Animals, 198?.

   Fourteen-chapter guide to channeling concern for animals into activism. Includes topics such as making and distributing leaflets, starting an animal rights group, lobbying, fundraising, working with the media, and researching an issue.

10. Breedy, Kevin J. "The Politics of Animal Rights," *AA* 10 (March 1990):17–21.

    Philosophical arguments are the foundation of the animal rights political movement. Discusses use of media by both animal rights activists and their opponents.

11. Brooks, S. "Animal Rights: Front Page News," *Editor & Publisher* 117 (June 23, 1984):48+.

    The animal rights movement has become front-page news during the past few years. The *Wall Street Journal*, the *New York Times*, and the *Christian Science Monitor* have included articles on topics ranging from factory farming to animal experimentation. The movement is being taken seriously by the media, but animal rightists feel that much more attention is needed to expose many well-entrenched practices of cruelty to animals.

12. Browne, Malcolm W. "How Terribly Sensible Man Is About Animals," *NYT* 7 October 1980:C3.

    Humans have a double standard. In our anthropocentric view of the world with humans as the center, we feel free to experiment on animals and eat them. Yet as humans overpopulate the earth, driving both our own and other species to extinction, nobody talks about culling our herds. Our future extinction as a species might be tragic to us, but for animals who may survive, our passing will not be mourned.

13. Callen, Paulette. "The Winds of Change," *AV* 3,1 (1990):44–47.

    Examines reform movements of the past. Success for animals' cause may be hardest and longest to obtain, but animal rights is the logical result of evolution of human consciousness and expanding compassion.

14. Cantor, Aviva. "The Club, the Yoke, and the Leash: What We Can Learn from the Way a Culture Treats Animals," *MS* 12 (August 1983):27–30.

    Patriarchal model of oppression of animals serves as a model and training ground for all forms of oppressing certain groups of humans, including women. Three strategies are used: the club uses brute force, the yoke imposes control and restrictions, and the leash demands helplessness and dependency.

15. Carlsen, Spence. "Animals Are Victims of Vast Human-Regulated System of Slavery," *LAT* 22 April 1987:II,5.

    The idea that animals can have rights is ridiculous only if we believe animals are radically different from us. By dehumanizing them, calling them research tools, hamburgers, or resources, we mask the fact that they can suffer, feel pain, and have emotional lives.

16. Carone, Jack, and Mary McDonald-Lewis. "Civil Disobedience in the Movement," *AV* 2 ( June 1989):64.

    Discusses civil disobedience in theory and practice as it relates to animal rights movement and its goals.

17. Carone, Jack, and Mary McDonald-Lewis. "Putting It on the Line—And in Front of the Camera: Staging Civil Disobedience Today," *AV* 2,5 (1989):73.

    Since the first tea party in Boston, civil disobedience has proved an effective weapon in bringing about reform, but today it must be refurbished by imagination, dedication, and determination to attract news media and get the message of animal rights across to the public.

18. Carone, Jack, and Mary McDonald-Lewis. "Taking the

First Step: Staging Your Own Civil Disobedience," *AV* 2,6 (1989):75.

How-to for participating in civil disobedience. Read everything you can on the subject, especially the classics by Thoreau and King. Adhere to the six golden rules of behavior: (1) don't engage in violence, (2) carry no weapons, (3) never run—such behavior triggers the police to respond aggressively, (4) never damage property, (5) never show up inebriated or on drugs, and (6) keep appearance clean and attitude polite. Follow-up activities include cleaning up the action site, ferrying injured activists to hospital, and obtaining bond or legal counsel if necessary.

19. Carson, Gerald. *Men, Beasts, and Gods: A History of Cruelty and Kindness to Animals.* New York: Charles Scribner's Sons, 1972.

History of relationship between humans and lower animals dating from prehistoric eras. Chapters on rodeo, fur, animal experimentation, vegetarianism.

20. Chase, Marcelle P. "Animal Rights: An Interdisciplinary, Selective Bibliography," *Law Library Journal* 82 (Spring 1990):359–91.

More than 300 entries of books and journal articles relating to legal and ethical aspects of animal welfare.

21. Clarke, Paul A. B., and Andrew Linzey, eds. *Political Theory and Animal Rights.* London: Pluto Press, 1990.

Demonstrates long and continuing relationship between political theory and the status of animals in society. Essayists include Aristotle, Hobbes, Marx, John Stuart Mill, Locke, Kant, Albert Schweitzer, James Madison, Montaigne, Peter Singer, and Tom Regan.

22. Clifton, Merritt. "Animal Welfare Information Center in Operation," *AA* 9 (March 1989):24.

Information Center at National Agricultural Library created by the "Improved Standards for Laboratory Animals" collects materials relating to welfare of laboratory animals, but it also holds literature dealing with farm animals and wild animals as well.

23.   Clifton, Merritt. "Out of the Cage: The Movement in Transition," *AA* 10 (January/February 1990):26–30.
      Animal rights movement is starting to make a difference. Public opinion is shifting and the opposition is starting to launch counterattack campaigns. Looks at animal rights movement in relation to Bill Moyer's model of the evolution of social movements.

24.   Clifton, Merritt. "To Life," *AA* 10 (April 1990):15–20+.
      Examines link between animal rights and environmental and other life-affirming movements.

25.   Darlin, Damon. "Company Sticks to Its Rats and Mice, but Animal Welfarists Object," *WSJ* 16 November 1982:B35.
      Animal rights groups protest manufacture of a mousetrap that catches its prey with glue. Mice die of starvation and thirst.

26.   Davidoff, Donald [Donna] J. "Animal Rights: Selected Resources and Suggestions for Further Study," *Reference Services Review* 17,3 (1989):71–77.
      Bibliographies, books, government publications, and other basic readings on animal rights. Also includes selected list of animal rights organizations.

27.   Davis, Karen. "What's Wrong with Pain Anyway?" *AA* 9 (February 1989):50–51.
      Pain is not always evil. It differs in degree, duration, cause, and kind. Today's society has little tolerance for pain, yet the mental anguish we feel for environmental destruction and suffering animals could lead ultimately to our own deliverance.

28.   Dawkins, Marian Stamp. *Animal Suffering: The Science of Animal Welfare.* New York: Chapman & Hall, 1980.
      Addresses issue of how to recognize animal suffering scientifically. The inability on the part of scientists and animal welfarists to agree on what constitutes animal suffering also prevents agreement on proper and humane way to treat animals. Collecting information on how animals are treated

nowadays and learning more about animal behavior may represent the first steps in resolving differences between animal welfarists and those whom they criticize.

29.  Dawkins, Marian Stamp. "From An Animal's Point of View: Motivation, Fitness, and Animal Welfare," *Behavioral and Brain Sciences* 13,1 (1990):1–9.

Animal behaviorist at University of Oxford makes the case that animal suffering exists, and she discusses how it can be defined and measured in a scientific, objective way. Environments for captive animals in labs, farms, and zoos can be designed in a way that is based on assessment of their needs. (Article is followed by forty short essays written by scientists and philosophers responding to Dawkins.)

30.  DeCapo, Thomas A. "Challenging Objectionable Animal Treatment with the Shareholder Proxy Proposal Rule," *University of Illinois Law Review* 1988 (Winter 1988):119–49.

Considers whether shareholder proxy proposals present a viable method for protesting and changing abusive treatment of animals by publicly owned corporations.

31.  Donahue, Thomas J. "The Moral Case for Animal Rights," *CSM* 1 October 1990:18.

Philosopher from Mercyhurst College says if we treated humans the way we treat most animals, we would be accused of "atrocities" against humanity. We justify our behavior by saying animals do not have souls and are not rational, but neither of these arguments holds water. The animal rights movement confronts us with a dilemma. We must find legitimate justification of current practices toward animals or abandon them as immoral.

32.  Donnelly, William L., and Cynthia Erber. "Investing for Animal Rights," *AA* 9 (September 1989):46–47.

Finding companies to invest in that don't exploit animals directly or indirectly isn't easy. Strategies include identifying companies that don't use animals in their products or in testing, and supporting shareholder actions protesting company policies that exploit animals.

33. Donovan, Josephine. "Animal Rights and Feminist Theory," *Signs: Journal of Women in Culture and Society* 15 (Winter 1990):350–75.

    Looks at feminist thought about animals from early suffragettes to present feminism. Proposes a feminist ethics toward animals based on natural rights, utilitarianism, and emotional and spiritual conversation with nonhuman life forms.

34. Elshtain, Jean Bethke. "Why Worry About the Animals?" *Progressive* 54 (March 1990):17–23.

    Why has concern for animals become popular now with so many other issues clamoring for attention? Surveys proliferation of animal rights organizations, their goals, and specific issues, with special attention to animal experimentation. Change in this area is obstructed by scientists' defensive and secretive attitudes.

35. Fallows, James. "Lo, the Poor Animals: What Did Noah Save Them For?" *Atlantic Monthly* 238 (September 1976): 58–65.

    Our traditional belief that man is often kinder than nature is now being questioned by animal rights movement. Points to worst abuses of factory farming and says that although animal rights activists will not have much effect on turning us all into vegetarians, they may reduce some of the brutality of factory farming. In the laboratory, where many animal experiments are done not because anyone really wants answers but because grants have been awarded and research contracts let, reform will have to come from the scientists themselves.

36. Finsen, Lawrence. "Animal Rights People May Not Be So 'Misguided' After All," *LAT* 3 June 1985:II,5.

    Assistant professor of philosophy at the University of Redlands says only a small portion of the 60 million animals in U.S. laboratories are used in serious research. Most die for frivolous reasons in testing new cosmetics, shampoos, household cleaners, and radiator fluid. The idea that humans are inherently superior no longer seems a rational conclusion but a prejudice.

37. Fox, Michael W. *Returning to Eden: Animal Rights and Human Responsibility.* New York: Viking, 1980.

    Human salvation depends upon our success in eliminating exploitation of the earth and its nonhuman animals and returning to the time of Eden, when man and nature were in tune. Looks at common abuses of animals in the laboratory, on the factory farm, and in the wild, examining each as both a veterinarian and an environmentalist.

38. Friedman, Ruth. "Animal Rights: Periodicals for Libraries," *Serials Librarian* 15 (1988):155–61.

    List of magazine and journal titles published by or for animal welfare/rights movement.

39. Godlovitch, Stanley and Rosalind, and John Harris, eds. *Animals, Men, and Morals: An Inquiry into the Maltreatment of Non-Humans.* New York: Taplinger, 1972.

    Early collection of essays by prominent animal rights thinkers who survey and critique use of animals in agriculture, science, and fashion. History of moral attitudes toward animals and an analysis of cultural and social habits that lead to subjugation of animals.

40. Greanville, David Patrice. "Environmentalists and Animal Rightists—The New Odd Couple," *AA* 9 (October 1989):22–24.

    Environmentalists thus far have not shown much sympathy for animal rights causes, but it's in the interest of the animal rights movement to bridge the gap and win them over. The two groups have much in common, although differences exist that must be addressed.

41. Greanville, David Patrice. "The Greening of Animal Rights," *AA* 8 (September/October 1988):36–37.

    Animal rights movements needs to adopt a more sophisticated political perspective of its activism in relation to other social issues, such as feminism, ecology, world hunger, and the Green Party.

42.   Greanville, David Patrice. "Media Diary (1)," *AA* 9 (April 1988):44–46.

Media is starting to pay more attention to animal rights issues since mid-1987. Examines some of the reasons why, using a focus on specific cover stories in *Newsweek, Harpers, New York Times,* and *The Reader's Digest.*

43.   Greanville, David Patrice. "Media Diary (2)," *AA* 9 (May 1989):46–48.

Survey of how the animal rights movement and its issues are treated by the media. Discusses such T.V. shows as PBS's nature programs, TBS's environmental programs, Donahue, Sally Jessy Raphael, Morton Downey, CBS's "48 Hours," and ABC's "20/20."

44.   Greanville, David Patrice. "The Myopic Tube: Media Diary 3," *AA* 9 ( July/August 1989):44–46.

Nature shows on television, while informative, are gravely flawed, since they rarely discuss political and social forces that are destroying wildlife. Examines "National Geographic," Audubon, TBS programs, "Wildlife America" with Marty Stouffer, and "Nature" with George Page.

45.   Greenfield, Meg. "In Defense of the Animals," *WP* 11 April 1989:A19.

Greenfield says the animal rights people are starting to get to her. Although she doesn't agree with most of their goals or that animals are as important as humans, she finds some of their arguments compelling.

46.   Groller, Ingrid. "Do Animals Have Rights," *Parents* 65 (May 1990):33.

According to a national public opinion poll, 80% of the public think animals have rights, 63% said killing animals for fur should be illegal, and 60% disapprove of hunting.

Other questions addressed the use of leather, food animals, zoos, and medical research.

47. Harriston, Keith, and Avis Thomas-Lester. "Animal Rights Activists' Day in the Sun," *WP* 11 June 1990:E1+.

    Twenty-four thousand animal rights activists rallied at the Ellipse in Washington and marched down Pennsylvania Avenue to the U.S. Capitol to show their support for the end of animal abuse in all its forms.

48. Harvard University's Office of Government and Community Affairs, based on research by Phillip W. D. Martin. *The Animal Rights Movement in the United States: Its Composition, Funding Sources, Goals, Strategies, and Potential Impact on Research,* September 1982.

    Early attempt to assess animal rights movement, its organizations, and its effect on the use of animals in research.

49. Hitchens, Christopher. "Minority Report," *Nation* 240 (February 2, 1985):102.

    Remembers German revolutionary Rosa Luxembourg, who while witnessing great inhumanity to humans, could also feel concern at the mistreatment of animals. The real crime in our abuse of animals is that it degrades the perpetrator as well as the victim.

50. "Investing for Animals," *Vegetarian Times* 139 (March 1989):24.

    Faria Clark, a broker for a Tucson Prudential-Bache Securities office, invests her animal welfare organization clients' money in areas that earn a profit but don't violate their ethical and political views.

51. Jackson, Christine M. "The Fiery Fight for Animal Rights," *Hastings Center Report* 19 (December 1989):37–39.

    People for the Ethical Treatment of Animals staff member explains the difference between animal rights and animal welfare and identifies forms of animal exploitation and modes of activism employed by animal advocates.

52. "Just Like Us," *Harpers* 277 (August 1988):43–52.

     A conversation about the philosophical, legal, and constitutional ramifications of animal rights with Jack Hitt, a *Harpers* editor; Arthur Caplan, director of the Center for Biomedical Ethics at the University of Minnesota; Gary Francione, professor at the University of Pennsylvania Law School; Roger Goldman, professor at St. Louis University School of Law; and Ingrid Newkirk, director of People for the Ethical Treatment of Animals.

53. Kahrl, William. "Animal Rights People Are Gaining on Us," *LAT* 27 August 1984:II,5.

     Today's issues of animal welfare are the same as they have always been, but today's activists are more articulate and professional than those of yesteryear. Yet if they're so smart, why have they chosen to campaign against use of animals in medicine and science, instead of targeting the cosmetic industries or factory farms where they'd be more likely to gain public sympathy and support?

54. Kislak, Paula. "On Choosing a Vet," *AV* 3 (March/April 1990):31.

     It's difficult and often impossible to find a veterinarian who supports animal rights position against trapping, hunting, and animal experimentation.

55. Krawiec, Richard. "Dealing with the Media: Advice from a Journalist," *AA* 10 (September 1990):16–17.

     Tips for animal activists in dealing with the media. Treat reporters as allies, be prompt and concise, don't sound like a misanthrope or be self-righteous. Don't parrot weak arguments or focus on issues you can't win.

56. Leepson, Marc. "Animal Rights," *Editorial Research Reports* (August 8, 1980):563–80.

     Discusses opposition to animal experimentation, historically and today, saying most Americans today accept the use of animals in scientific research. Arguments for and against LD-50 and Draize tests. Describes conditions for factory-farm animals and looks at vegetarianism as a moral issue. Bibliography of books, articles, reports, and studies for further reading on the subject are included.

57. Macauley, David. "Political Animals: A Study of the Emerging Animal Rights Movement in the United States: Strategies and Concerns of the Movement," *Between the Species* 3 (Summer 1987):119–27.

58. Macauley, David. "Political Animals: A Study of the Emerging Animal Rights Movement in the United States," *Between the Species* 3 (Spring 1987):66–75.

59. Magel, Charles R. *A Bibliography on Animal Rights and Related Matters.* Washington, DC: University Press of America, 1981.

    With its 1989 companion, *Keyguide to Information Sources in Animal Rights*, represents the most comprehensive bibliography available on animal rights, covering full range of issues from BC to 20th century. Includes 2,718 citations of books, monographs, journal articles, and government documents.

60. Magel, Charles R. *Keyguide to Information Sources in Animal Rights.* Jefferson, NC: McFarland & Co., 1989.

    With its 1981 companion, *A Bibliography on Animal Rights and Related Matters*, represents the most comprehensive bibliography available on animal rights. Overview of literature on philosophy and animals, science and medicine and animals, education and animals, law and animals, religion and animals, and vegetarianism and animals. Also included are over 300 annotated citations summarizing books and journal articles that address a wide range of animal rights topics.

61. Maggitti, Phil. "The Opposition Motion," *AA* 10 (June 1990):17–20+.

    Groups that traditionally profit from use of animals such as the fur industry, farm bureau federations, biomedical research, cosmetics associations, safari organizations, hunting groups, and some universities, are taking notice of animal rights movement and starting to counterattack.

62.    Maggitti, Phil. "Veterinarians: For or Against Animal Rights?" *AA* 9 (February 1989):12–16+.

Veterinarians often support all the things animal rights activists condemn: animal experimentation, hunting, trapping, factory farming. Differences stem from both economic and philosophical reasons. Vets believe that owners who provide them with a livelihood are their first consideration; activists say the animal's well-being should come first. A few veterinarians, however, are stepping forward as leaders in animal rights movement.

63.    McCarthy, Coleman. "Animal Rights: Not a Crank Cause," *WP* 21 April 1984:A21.

Banning steel-jaw leghold traps would be progress of a minor kind, but what's really needed is a recognition of the full range of animal rights. Animal rights movement is growing as a national force whose strength can be judged by the intellectual depth of its philosophers.

64.    McCarthy, Coleman. " 'Terrorists' for Animal Rights," *WP* 16 June 1990:A23.

Twenty-four thousand "terrorists," as Health and Human Services Secretary Louis Sullivan called them, gathered at the Capitol to support animal rights. Sullivan's smear of the group is part of a counteroffensive launched by those in animal experimentation and the meat industry, whose profits are based on the use of animals. The public, however, is becoming more educated on the issues and sees the uselessness of animal slaughter to satisfy human greed.

65.    Midgley, Mary. "Practical Solutions," *Hastings Center Report* 19 (December 1989):44–45.

Bringing about improvement in the treatment of animals requires both outrage at the conditions that need change and a practical plan to effect change. Challenge is to be realistic and at the same time not lose the indignation that provides power and motivation.

66. Moore, Mary Tyler. "Please Help Me Stop Cruelty to Animals," *Good Housekeeping* 182 (June 1976):80+.

    Inspired by a film made by Cleveland Amory and Fund for Animals about slaughter of baby seals, Moore joined the organization and became its national chairperson. She asks readers to join with her in fight to promote animal welfare.

67. Moran, Victoria. "Compassionate Entrepreneurs," *AA* 9 (January 1989):47.

    Businesspeople bring morality to the marketplace by starting up companies that promote reverence for life. Examples include a mail order company supplying non-leather accessories, a vegetarian Montessori school, a vegetarian bakery/restaurant, and a home-cleaning agency that uses only cleaning products not tested on animals.

68. Moran, Victoria. "Lights, Camera, Activism," *AA* 10 (April 1990):51.

    How animal advocates can use public access television stations to get the animal rights message out.

69. Moran, Victoria. "The Nonviolent Way," *AA* 9 (June 1989):53.

    The vast majority of animal rights supporters are nonviolent. Boycotting a cruel product, letters of protest, and peaceful demonstrations are all part of an approach to change and to the incorporation of "principled action" into our lives. With violence the strong win, with nonviolence the righteous win.

70. Moran, Victoria. "Those Who Know Can Teach," *AA* 10 (July/August 1990):50.

    Noncredit adult education classes are perfect forums for teaching about animals and ethics. All that's needed is to know the subject well.

71. Moretti, Laura A. "Because We Must!" *AV* 2 (August 1989):112.

    Recalls Martin Luther King's famous march on

Washington and other social protest marches on the Capitol and reflects that when humans suffer injustice, they can protest and bring change for themselves. Animals cannot, so we must do it for them.

72.    Moretti, Laura A. "Distorted Priorities," *AV* 2,6 (1989):80.
       The litany of human suffering is endless: homelessness, AIDS, drug addiction, rape, suicide, child abuse. These issues are not separate from animal rights, but are interconnected. Violence begets violence, whether against animals or humans. We cannot personally solve many of the world's problems, but we can eliminate violence from our own lives. Remove your connection both from the slaughterhouse by not eating animals and from the suffering of fur animals by not wearing their skins.

73.    Morris, Desmond. "Animal Contract," *AV* 3 (August 1990):24–5+.
       Relationship between animals and man has changed over the course of the years. Where once we shared the earth on equal footing, now humans are exploitative and persecutorial, driving many species to extinction.

74.    Morse, Mel. *Ordeal of the Animals*. Englewood Cliffs, NJ: Prentice-Hall, 1968.
       Published in 1968, this book reflects abuses that animals still face today. Discusses animals' plight in laboratories, on the farm, and in circuses, rodeos, horse races, and shows. The needless, senseless suffering of animals won't end until more people take an active interest in changing things.

75.    Mouras, Belton P. *I Care About Animals: Moving from Emotion to Action*. New York: Barnes, 1977.
       Founder of the Animal Protection Institute draws up a plan of action for animal activists to follow in fighting animal abuse. Strategies include letter-writing campaigns, education of the public, lobbying for changes in the law, demonstrations, petitions, and organizing broad-based support groups.

76. Mouras, Belton P. "Protecting Animals: The New American Reality," *USA Today* 113 (November 1984):38–42.

    President of Animal Protection Institute says when humane groups act together, animal abuse can be challenged and eliminated. Cites saving of dolphins from tuna fishermen as an example.

77. Newkirk, Ingrid. *Save the Animals! 101 Easy Things You Can Do.* New York: Warner Books, 1990.

    Guide to making consumer and life-style choices that will help to end abuse of animals in our society. Suggestions range from choosing correct veterinarian to going vegetarian, from not wearing leather to boycotting products tested on animals.

78. "Now It's Civil Rights for Animals: Latest Target of a New Group of Activist Crusaders: People Who Inflict Needless Pain or Abuse on Farm Animals, Pets or Creatures in the Wild," *U.S. News & World Report* 89 (December 22, 1980):55–56.

79. Park, Ava. "Animals: Casualties of the Me Generation," *AV* 2 (August 1989):58.

    Animals are just fodder for individuals of the self-centered Me Generation, who see everything as something to be purchased and consumed. Animals are to wear, eat, or provide entertainment.

80. Paterson, David, and Richard D. Ryder. *Animals' Rights: A Symposium.* Proceedings held under auspices of Royal Society for the Prevention of Cruelty to Animals at Trinity College, Cambridge, on the Ethical Aspects of Man's Relationships with Animals, August 18 and 19, 1977. New York: Centaur Press, 1979.

81. "Public Opinion," *AA* 10 (May 1990):35–36.

    Opinion polls reveal Americans' attitude toward fur coats, testing of cosmetic and household products on animals, medical research with animals, vegetarianism, and question of whether animals have rights.

82. Regan, Tom. *The Struggle for Animal Rights*. Clarks Summit, PA: International Society for Animal Rights, 1987.

    "We are what we do," states Regan, and what he does and has been doing for a number of years is defining and defending animal rights. One of the most prominent leaders in the movement brings together several essays written over three years that identify and explain the major animal rights issues.

83. Regan, Tom. "The Torch of Reason," *AV* 1 (September/October 1988):12–17.

    Speech given at gathering of animal rights activists on World Day for Lab Animals, refuting opposition's charges that the movement is made up of ignorant misanthropes and terrorists.

84. Rollin, Bernard E. *Animal Rights and Human Morality*. Buffalo, NY: Prometheus Books, 1981.

    Four-part book dealing with moral theory and animals, animal rights and legal rights, use and abuse of animals in research, and pet animals.

85. Rollin, Bernard E., and James R. Simpson. "Economic Consequences of Animal Rights Programs," *Journal of Business Ethics* 3 (August 1984):215–25.

86. Ryder, Richard D. *Animal Revolution: Changing Attitudes Toward Speciesism*. Oxford, England: Basil Blackwell, 1989.

    Coiner of the word "speciesism" and prominent leader of animal rights movement in Great Britain examines evolution of the movement and its influence on attitudes. Focuses on developments in Great Britain but devotes a chapter to international activities, including those in U.S.

87. Salt, Henry. "Restrictionists and Abolitionists," *AV* 7 (November 1987):42–43.

    A reprint of a 1900 article by Henry Salt, nineteenth-century humanitarian, who argued for and wrote about an-

imal rights. Discusses the positions of those who would reform institutions where animal abuse takes place and those
who would abolish them.

88. Sammut-Tovar, Dorothy, and Kim Sturla. *Do Animals Have
    Rights? Teacher's Packet*. San Mateo, CA: Peninsula Humane
    Society, 1983. Available from (ERIC, ED239947.)
    Activities designed to sensitize students in grades 4–6 to
    the needs of animals and the injustices many species suffer.
    Covers trapping, dogfighting, hunting, factory farming, an-
    imal experimentation, exotic pets, and animal habitat de-
    struction.

89. Schwartz, Sheila. "Humane Education: Collaborating for
    Pro-Animal School Programming," *AA* 9 (October
    1989):12–13.
    Strategy for animal rights advocates to gain access to
    schools where they can present information on animal wel-
    fare.

90. Seligman, Daniel. "The Next Big Cause," *Fortune* 119
    (March 27, 1989):163.
    Pushing vegetarianism looks like a winner for animal
    rights groups because of the nation's increasing concern
    with health, but activists need to look at economic reality of
    reducing animal suffering whether in animal research or
    food or fur production if they're to make any further
    progress.

91. "A Shadow Cast on a Good Cause," *Nature* 339 ( June 15,
    1989):491.
    Animal rights terrorism—extremism among the ex-
    treme—is an issue that should command our attention, not
    only in the academic community but everywhere. Such ter-
    rorists are undermining an otherwise good cause.

92. Shenon, Philip. "A Meeting Seeks Ways to Aid Animal
    Rights," *NYT* 8 August 1983:B2.

Four-day conference on animal rights at Montclair State College was attended by 250 people who heard lectures on wildlife conservation, vivisection, and vegetarianism. Participants included lawyers, teachers, writers, and groups such as National Anti-Vivisection Society, Attorneys for Animal Rights, People for the Ethical Treatment of Animals, and Association for the Prevention of Cruelty to Animals.

93. Siegel, Steve. "Grass Roots Opposition to Animal Exploitation," *Hastings Center Report* 19 (December 1989):39–41.

Director of Trans Species Unlimited says his organization's goal is to build a grass roots animal rights movement. Discusses difference between his group and more traditional animal protection organizations. Defines objectives of the struggle and its stages. One goal is to win agreement and support of the public by educating them to widespread animal abuse.

94. Singer, Peter. "Animal Liberation: A Personal View," *Between the Species* 2 (Summer 1986):148–54.

Personal essay documenting Singer's evolution from Oxford student to one of the animal rights movement's best-known philosophers and activists.

95. Singer, Peter. "Ten Years of Animal Liberation," *New York Review of Books* 31 (January 17, 1985):46–51.

Ten years before, *New York Review of Books* published Singer's revolutionary essay "Animal Liberation." The author looks back at the decade to review animal liberation movement and the literature it has generated. Concludes the movement has come through with its foundations intact and continues to grow in strength and make significant gains. Reviews some of the books published in the previous ten years: Michael Fox's *Farm Animals: Husbandry, Behavior, and Veterinary Practice*; Andrew Rowan's *Of Mice, Models, and Men*; Tom Regan's *All That Dwell Therein*; Mary Midgley's *Animals and Why They Matter*; and R. G. Frey's *Rights, Killing, and Suffering*.

96. Singer, Peter, ed. *In Defense of Animals.* New York: Harper & Row, 1986.
    Collection of essays by international leaders and activists in animal rights movement. Topics range from vivisection to factory-farm animals, from zoos to endangered species. Essayists include Tom Regan, Jim Mason, Alex Pacheco, Donald Barnes, Henry Spira, and Richard Ryder.

97. Singer, Sidney. "The Neediest of All Animals," *AA* 10 (June 1990):51.
    A medical student says it's easy for animal rights activists to become hostile to humankind for its abuse of animals, but as a healer he rejects that attitude and wants to help people find and nurture the kindness inside themselves. Animal liberation is human liberation.

98. Sperling, Susan. *Animal Liberators.* Berkeley, CA: University of California, 1988.
    Evolutionary anthropologist interviews nine animal rights activists, including an attorney, a college student, a feminist, and a psychologist from the San Francisco Bay Area primarily about the issue of animal experimentation. Concludes they want a new definition of relationship with animals, not just better treatment for them. Sees them as people highly critical of science and medicine with a fear of ecological disaster tied to use of animals in science.

99. Spickard, J. W. "Animal Rights Language and the Public Polity," *Between the Species* 3 (Spring 1987):76–80.

100. Spiegel, Marjorie. "Blinded by the Light," *AV* 3,1 (1990):33–39.
    Comparison of human slavery and the oppression of animals.

101. Spiegel, Marjorie. *The Dreaded Comparison: Race and Animal Slavery.* Philadelphia: New Society Pub., 1988.
    The arguments and rationale used to hold blacks in bondage and treat them badly are basically the same as

those used to exploit animals. One difference is that while slavery no longer exists, oppression of animals continues unabated.

102. Starr, Douglas. "Equal Rights," *Audubon* 86 (November 1984):30–35.
Overview of the philosophy, goals, activities, organizations, and individuals of the animal rights movement.

103. "State of the Movement," *AV* 3 (October 1990):60–61.
Review of animal rights activities: media exposure, formation of National Foundation for Animal Law as a civil liberties union for animal rights movement, establishment of Animal Rights Law Clinic at Rutgers University Law School, recent activities of Animal Liberation Front, scholarships and competitions sponsored by National Anti-Vivisection Society, and demonstrations and protests at Tule Elk hunt in California and at Procter and Gamble.

104. Stein, Benjamin J. "And Animals as Victims," *WP* 24 April 1984:A13.
Americans say they love animals, but their behavior belies it. President Ronald Reagan should appoint a special assistant for animal rights, someone who would create a federal policy on ethical and humane treatment of animals and an agency to enforce it.

105. Stinnet, Caskie. "Live and Let Live," *Atlantic Monthly* 238 (December 1976):27–28.
Personal essay addressing man's obligation to respect the lives of animals, to do them no harm not only for their sake but for our own. Cites Rachel Carson, author of *The Silent Spring* as a positive role model and heart surgeon Michael DeBakey as a negative one.

106. Sunlin, Mark. "In the Beginning Was the Word Anthropocentricity," *AV* 3,1 (1990): 17.
Discussion of anthropocentricity, or the belief that humans are the most significant entities in the universe. Human and nonhuman animals have many things in com-

mon, and we should not be too embarrassed to dispense compassion beyond human lines.

107. "Tag Sales," *AA* 10 (March 1990):22.
How to make money for your animal rights group by holding yard sales.

108. "The 'Terrorist' Label: How to Neutralize It," *AA* 9 (September 1989):39–42.
Tips from leaders in animal rights movement on how to fight "terrorist" label. Comments are from Donald Barnes, National Anti-Vivisection Society; Dona Spring, Disabled and Incurably Ill for Alternatives to Animal Research; Wayne Pacelle, Fund for Animals, Henry Spira, Animal Rights International; and Bradley Miller, Humane Farming Association.

109. "Thousands March for Animals," *AA* 10 (September 1990):38–39.
Twenty-five thousand attend March for Animals in Washington, D.C., but while exhilarating for attendees, media gives it scant attention.

110. Troiano, Linda. "Home Sweet Planet: Owl Connections," *American Health* 8 (March 1989):90–92.
Animal rights and environmental issues start to mesh.

111. Tyrrell, R. Emmett, Jr. "Save the Chickens," *American Spectator* 22 (February 1989):10–11.
Animal rights movement resembles Colonial bigots who persecuted Baptists and Quakers as opposed to resembling a reform movement in the American tradition of suffragettes and slavery abolitionists.

112. "The White Award," *AV* 3 (December 1990):55.
The White Award, named after monkey-brain transplanter Robert White, is given each year to worst abuser of other-than-human beings. This year's award goes to the organization Research! America, whose purpose is to promote the virtues of vivisection.

113. Wright, Robert. "Are Animals People Too?" *New Republic* 202 (March 12, 1990):20–22.

   Author finds himself drawn reluctantly into animal rights logic that if humans enjoy rights, so too should animals. Identifies problems that animal rights movement may have in achieving its goals but hopes that civilization is moving in the right direction and things for animals will improve in fits and starts over time.

114. Wynne-Tyson, Jon, ed. *The Extended Circle: A Commonplace Book of Animal Rights.* New York: Paragon House, 1989.

   Anthology of the views of writers, philosophers, scientists, churchpeople, and other public figures who see the underlying unity of life and our obligation to extend the boundary of our compassion to nonhuman animals.

115. Zak, Stephen. "Ethics and Animals," *Atlantic* 263 (March 1989):68–74.

   Examines philosophy of animal rights, present status of animals under the Animal Welfare Act, and ethics of animal experimentation.

## Activists and Organizations

116. Adams, Brook. "The Coldest Cut: Sue Coe's Porkopolis," *Art in America* 78 ( January 1990):127–28.

   Positive critique of New York exhibition of Sue Coe's drawings of slaughterhouse scenes from the animals' viewpoint.

117. Anderson, Christopher. "Activist Group Under Fire," *Nature* 343 (February 15, 1990):580.

   People for the Ethical Treatment of Animals is planning to sue author Katie McCabe for malicious and business libel. In an article appearing in the *Washingtonian*, she accused People for the Ethical Treatment of Animals (PETA) of tax evasion and PETA cofounder Alex Pacheco of staging an experiment done on the Silver Spring monkeys for publicity purposes.

118. "Animal Rights Group 'Blows Whistle' on Cronies,"
     *Archery World* 34 (October/November 1985):81.
     Mobilization for Animals publishes exposé on financial
     status of top animal welfare organizations. Wildlife
     Legislative Fund of America, a group that opposes animal
     rights, is pleased, believing it will cause dissension and di-
     vision in the animal rights community.

119. Astor, Gerald. "Doris Day's Surprizing New Life,"
     *McCall's* 105 (September 1978):120+.
     Profile of Doris Day and her organization, Doris Day
     Pet Foundation.

120. Bartlett, Kim. "An Interview with Coleman McCarthy,"
     *AA* 8 (September/October 1988):7–11.
     Interview with Coleman McCarthy, syndicated colum-
     nist for *Washington Post* Writers Group and animal rights
     activist.

121. Bauston, Lorri. "Children of a Lesser God," *AV* 2
     (February 1989):22–23.
     Describes Farm Sanctuary, the only animal shelter in
     this country devoted to abused and neglected farm ani-
     mals. Residents include turkeys, pigs, cows, and sheep
     abandoned on "dead piles" at stockyards, injured in trans-
     portation to slaughterhouses, or victimized by abusive fac-
     tory-farm practices. In addition to rescue and rehabilita-
     tion work, Farm Sanctuary also promotes investigations
     and campaigns against cruel factory-farm practices.

122. Bishop, Katherine. "Animal Rights Battle Gaining
     Ground: Influence Is Felt from Fur Shop to Laboratory,"
     *NYT* 14 (January 1989):1.
     Animal rights organizations run gamut from main-
     stream American Society for the Prevention of Cruelty to
     Animals, which encourages better treatment of animals, to
     shadowy Animal Liberation Front, which FBI recently
     classified as a terrorist group. Membership in animal rights
     organization has grown dramatically in past eight years
     along with their funding. Visibility has also been increased

by the support of well-known celebrities like Berke Breathed of "Bloom County" comic strip fame and clothes designer Bill Blass.

123.   "Champions of Synthetic Fiber, Angry Human Stars Make the Fur Fly at a Benefit for Animal Rights," *People Weekly* 31 (March 6, 1989):266–67.

People for the Ethical Treatment of Animals throws a rock-against-fur fund-raiser featuring Go-Go Jane Wiedlin, River Phoenix, and Lene Lovich.

124.   "Change at Humane Society Prompts Debate," *NYT* 19 August 1986:A20.

Dr. John E. McArdle resigned or was fired from the Humane Society of the United States (HSUS) as director of animal welfare over what seems a split between the old guard and the new. McArdle is more in tune with new animal rights philosophy, but the HSUS board are conservative and wish to be seen as animal welfare proponents.

125.   Clifton, Merritt. "ASPCA Board Chairman Apologizes for Pro-Hunting Statements," *AA* 9 (March 1989):24.

Board chairman of the American Society for the Prevention of Cruelty to Animals (ASPCA) Thomas McCarter III admits to hunting and shooting captive birds. The ASPCA opposes all sport hunting and may ask for his resignation.

126.   Clifton, Merritt. "A Cheer for Donaldson," *AA* 9 (March 1989):21.

Profile of James Donaldson, top professional basketball player, vegetarian, and animal welfare advocate.

127.   Clifton, Merritt. "Tony LaRussa: Going to Bat for the Animals," *AA* 10 (March 1990):10–11.

How Tony LaRussa, manager of the Oakland Athletics, and his wife, Elaine, became involved in the animal rights movement and life-style.

128.   "Cock and Bull Awards for Animal Oppressors," *USA Today* 113 (April 1985):11–12.

Animal Protection Institute gives Cock and Bull awards to individuals and groups responsible for the most ill-conceived, least excusable, and most devastating animal abuse. Among this year's recipients are Alaska, for installing radio collars on individual wolves so they could be tracked to their pack and shot from the sky; Ann Landers's unquestioning support for animal experimentation, people who put poison in Mars bars in Britain to call attention to animal rights; and the French, for blowing up penguins and their nests in Antarctica.

129. "Connecticut Humane Plans No Change," *AA* 9 (July/August 1989):22–23.

Connecticut Humane Society, one of the six richest animal protection groups in the country, is charged with poor service, mismanagement, and dubious fund-raising techniques. A statewide reform group calls for the director's resignation.

130. Cornell, Marly. "Culture for Animals," *AA* 9 (January 1989):27.

Triangle Animal Awareness Week in North Carolina, sponsored by the Culture and Animals Foundation, uses dance, poetry, theater, and painting to promote animal rights.

131. Cornell, Marly. "Sue Coe: Rebel with Many Causes," *AA* 9 (February 1989):7–9.

Profile of artist Sue Coe, who has done several paintings with laboratory and factory-farming animals as her subjects.

132. Davis, Karen. "A Peaceable Kingdom for Farm Animals," *AA* 9 (January 1989):17.

Author talks about her experiences as a volunteer at the Farm Sanctuary in Avondale, Pennsylvania, a place where farm animals are offered permanent shelter from factory farms, stockyards, and slaughterhouses.

133. Deats, Paula. "Save the Animals!" *Cosmopolitan* 183 (November 1977):170+.

Profiles of activists Eileen Chivers of Greenpeace; Louise Roberts, Sandy Rowland, and Virginia Handley of Fund for Animals; and Linda Pfieffer of Chimp Rehabilitation Program and their efforts to expose and correct cases of animal abuse.

134.  DeSilver, Drew. "Natalie Merchant: One in 10,000," *Vegetarian Times* (March 1989):54–6+.
      Profile of vegetarian, animal rights activist and rock singer.

135.  Echenbarger, William. "The Guru of Animal Rights," *Esquire* 103 (February 1985):66.
      Tom Regan, philosophy professor at North Carolina State University, has become the intellectual leader of the animal rights movement with the publication of his book *The Case for Animal Rights*. Animals should be treated well not out of kindness, he says, but as a matter of right. Regan suggests a good first step toward becoming involved in animal rights movement is to become a vegetarian.

136.  Flick, Larry. "PETA Mounts Anti-Fur Concert, Album," *Billboard* 102 (March 31, 1990):34.
      People for the Ethical Treatment of Animals will sponsor its second annual anti-fur rock concert and album.

137.  Forbes, Dana. "Where Animals Come First," *AA* 9 (September 1989):26–8+.
      In 1979, Cleveland Amory, animal rights activist, had on his hands 577 burros from the Grand Canyon, which he'd saved from death. He opened Black Beauty Ranch, a refuge in Texas for animals like the burros, who needed a home. Feral goats, pigs, coyotes, chimpanzees, bears, lions, and an elephant also live there now.

138.  Garment, Suzanne. "Holiday Vow, Don't Take Human Lives Lightly," *WSJ* 28 November 1986:10.
      Describes visit to headquarters of People for the Ethical Treatment of Animals (PETA) in Washington, DC. Says PETA wants all animals out of the lab and that their cause

is making progress in both legal and illegal channels. They see in the eyes of a marmoset a fellow creature who has the same moral essence as a human child. This attitude goes chillingly well beyond the lab animal issue and has serious implications.

139. Hampton, Aubrey. "George Bernard Shaw and the Animals," *AA* 3 (May 1990):20–23.

Glimpse of the famous playwright's thoughts on the abuse of animals through a study of his plays and other writings. A vegetarian and antivivisectionist, Shaw often spoke out publicly on animal rights issues.

140. Hogshire, Jim. "Sam La Budde: Earth Activist," *AA* 9 (October 1989):8–9.

Profile of the activist responsible for videotaping driftnet fishermen killing dolphins, which led to successful boycott of tuna.

141. Holden, Constance. "Animal Rights Advocate Urges New Deal," *Science* 201 (July 7, 1978):35.

English-born veterinarian, psychologist, and director of Humane Society Institute for the Study of Animal Problems Michael Fox says we have to be ethically responsible toward animals because they exist, not simply because they are sentient. He cites inhumaneness to animals in research laboratories, factory farms, and high school science fairs and offers some solutions to the problem.

142. Iacobbo, Karen and Michael. "DJ of Animal Rights: Shelton Walden," *AA* 9 (November 1989):10+.

Profile of New York City radio show host of Walden's Pond, a program dedicated to animal rights issues.

143. Iacobbo, Karen and Michael. "Ken Shapiro and PSYETA: Changing Psychology," *AA* 9 (March 1989):8–9.

Profile of Ken Shapiro, a psychotherapist at Bates College in Maine and cofounder of Psychologists for the Ethical Treatment of Animals.

144. Iacobbo, Karen and Michael. "Sandy Larson: Humane Educator," *AA* 10 (May 1990):9–10.
Profile of Sandy Larson, education coordinator for the New England Anti-Vivisection Society.

145. Jones, Arthur. "Apostle of the Four-Legged," *National Catholic Reporter* 19 (March 25, 1983):1.
Profile of Brother Victorian Maltison, head of Lazarian Society for Animals in Lake Huntington, New York, who believes animals have souls and finds nothing in Catholic doctrine that refutes his belief.

146. Kelling, Vanessa. "In the Wake of a Dolphin," *AV* 3 (October 1990):62.
Profile of the late Dexter Cate, protector of dolphins and other marine animals.

147. Kelling, Vanessa. "One Person: Many Lives," *AV* 3 (December 1990):18.
Profile of Bobbi Lazare, public relations director at Living Free, an animal sanctuary in California.

148. Lauer, Margaret. "A Champion of Animal Rights," *Progressive* 48 (April 1984):14–15.
Profile of Henry Spira, animal rights activist and former schoolteacher, who led the fight against the LD-50 and Draize tests.

149. Maggitti, Phil. "Marian Probst: In the Shadow of the Curmudgeon," *AA* 9 ( June 1989):7–8.
Profile of Marian Probst—unsung, behind-the-scenes heroine at the Fund for Animals and editorial assistant to Cleveland Amory.

150. Maggitti, Phil. "Marv Levy: Buffalo Coach Tackles the Issues Head On," *AA* 9 (November 1989):8–9.
Profile of Buffalo Bills' head coach, who has come out against fur trapping and hunting and for humane treatment of all living creatures.

151. Maggitti, Phil. "Nancy Burnet: On a Wing and a Prayer and Perseverance," *AA* 9 (March 1989):6–7.
     Profile of Nancy Burnet, founder of United Activists for Animal Rights and the Coalition to Protect Animals in Entertainment.

152. Maggitti, Phil. "Peggy McCay: Days of Her Life," *AA* 10 (January/February 1990):10.
     Profile of animal rights activist Peggy McCay, well-known actress of the daytime drama "Days of Our Lives."

153. Maggitti, Phil. "Peter Falk: And Mrs. Colombo, She'd Agree, Too," *AA* 9 (June 1989):9.
     Peter Falk outlaws fur coats and cosmetics tested on animals on the set of the Detective Colombo mystery series.

154. Maggitti, Phil. "Priscilla Feral: In for the Long Haul," *AA* 10 (January/February 1990):11–12.
     Profile of animal rights activist Priscilla Feral, president of Friends of Animals.

155. Maggitti, Phil. "Standing up for Student Rights," *AA* 10 (December 1990):14.
     Three million frogs and thousands of cats, dogs, mice, rabbits, and pigs end up in high school biology dissection labs. Students who want to opt out of the exercise on ethical grounds now have an organization they can turn to for support and tactical advice: Student Action Corps for Animals (SACA). SACA maintains student helpline, publishes newsletter written by high schoolers, provides information on animal rights issues, and gives educational presentations.

156. Maggitti, Phil. "Susan Rich: Compassion Begins in the Home," *AA* 10 (May 1990):8–9.
     Profile of Susan Rich, national volunteer coordinator and director of the Compassion Campaign for People for the Ethical Treatment of Animals.

157. Marcotte, Paul. "More Than a Pet Project: Chicago

Attorney Works for Expansion of Animal Rights," *American Bar Association Journal* 75 (January 1989):26+.

Profile of Chicago attorney Kenneth Ross, secretary and board member of the Animal Legal Defense League, a group of lawyers who specialize in cases involving animal abuse.

158. McCarthy, Coleman. "Philosopher of Animal Rights," *WP* 9 June 1990:A23.

Peter Singer's *Animal Liberation* gives the animal rights movement intellectual shape. The author took a fringe issue in 1975 and made it mainstream. Explores Singer's thoughts on animal rights and says after all these years no one has yet been able to refute his argument.

159. McFarland, Cole. "The Last Leg of Lamb: A Profile of Linda McCartney," *AV* 2,6 (1989):72–73.

Profile of vegetarian, animal rights activist, and musician Linda McCartney, wife of ex-Beatle Paul McCartney.

160. McFarland, Cole. "Phoenix Rising," *AV* 2 (February 1989):89.

Profile of River Phoenix—teen actor, environmentalist, vegan, and animal rights activist.

161. Moretti, Laura A. "The Best People," *AV* 2,6 (1989):15.

Profile of Luke Dommer—ex-marine, vegetarian, and founder of the Committee to Abolish Sport Hunting.

162. Moretti, Laura A. "Donald Barnes: Change of Heart," *AV* 2 (June 1989):16–17.

Ex-researcher and present director of the National Anti-Vivisection Society tells why he stopped experimenting on animals and joined animal rights movement.

163. Moretti, Laura A. "The Final Frontier," *AV* 9 (October 1990):26–27.

Profile of activist Sam La Budde, who recorded on video the indiscriminate slaughter of dolphins caught in driftnets set to catch tuna.

164. Nevin, David. "Scientist Helps Stir New Movement for Animal Rights," *Smithsonian Magazine* 11 (April 1980): 50–58.
Profile of Michael W. Fox—veterinarian, animal ethologist, scientist, and crusader for animal rights.

165. "Of Plaster and Poster Paste," *AV* 2 (August 1989):98.
Anonymous animal rights group pastes antivivisection posters on sidewalks, walls, bridges, and bus benches in an effort to publicize World Laboratory Animal Liberation Week.

166. "On Earth as It Is in Heaven," *AV* 2 (February 1989):92.
Gentle World, an organization that seeks to encourage others to experience the benefits of the vegan life-style, employs educational materials, seminars, and community service projects to get its message across.

167. Pacelle, Wayne. "Animal Rights in Bloom: An Interview with Berke Breathed," *AA* 9 (July/August 1989):7–11.
Creator of "Bloom County" comic strip explains his newly emerging attitudes on animal rights issues.

168. Pacelle, Wayne. "An Interview with Luke Dommer," *AA* 9 (January 1989):6–9.
Luke Dommer, head of the Committee to Abolish Sport Hunting, talks about why and how he has dedicated his life to defending wildlife and fighting sport hunting.

169. Pacelle, Wayne. "Spotlighting Creative Ideas for Animals," *AA* 7 (November 1987):4–5.
Profiles individuals and groups that are working for animal rights through educational and legislative projects within their professions or communities.

170. "PETA Sues Washington Writer," *AV* 3 (March/April 1990):54.
People for the Ethical Treatment of Animals (PETA) files a lawsuit against a *Washingtonian* columnist, who alleges PETA staged a photograph of the Silver Spring monkeys held in a restraining device.

171.  "PETA's Music Festival Attracts Thousands," *AA* 8 (September/October 1988):22.

Music festival in support of animal rights at the Washington monument includes performers Howard Jones, Lene Lovich, Natalie Merchant, Guadalcanal Diary, Exene of X, Betty, Big Bang Theory, and the B-52s.

172.  Pritzker, Karen. "Bernstein for the Defenseless," *McCall's* 114 (July 1987):62.

Profile of Madeline Bernstein, senior legal counsel and vice president for Humane Law Enforcement for the American Society for the Prevention of Cruelty to Animals.

173.  Regan, Susan. "Ned Buyukmihci," *AV* 2 (June 1989): 20–21.

Associate professor of ophthalmology at University of California School of Veterinary Medicine and cofounder of Association of Veterinarians for Animal Rights disapproves of killing and harming healthy animals to learn how to heal. This attitude has led academic colleagues and administrators to call for his dismissal .

174.  Regan, Tom. "A Fierce Meditation: A Profile of Gwenyth Snyder," *AV* 2,5 (1989):46–48.

Interview with Beverly Hills, senior citizen animal rights activist.

175.  Regan, Tom. "One Day a Great Pitcher: An Interview with Cleveland Amory," *AV* 2 (February 1989):16–17.

Interview with veteran animal rights activist and founder of the Fund for Animals and the Black Beauty Farm.

176.  Regan, Tom. "The Tiny Seed: An Interview with Margaret Owings," *AV* 1 (September/October 1988): 18–20.

Interview with California activist who has worked forty years in animal protection to save mountain lions, otters, and sea lions.

177. Robbins, William. "Animal Rights: A Growing Movement in U.S.," *NYT* 15 June 1984:A1.
     Brief survey of animal rights movement, specific organizations and individuals, and their positions on various issues.

178. Rottenberg, Dan. "He Fights for the Animals," *The Reader's Digest* 119 (December 1981):59+.
     Profile of Cleveland Amory—satirical social historian, animal rights activist, and founder of Fund for Animals.

179. "Sacred Cows," *AV* 2 (February 1989):33–34.
     Artist Brad Hicks reflects on dairy cattle, the subject of many of his paintings. Accompanied by five reproductions of his work.

180. Sherman, Jeffrey. "Radical Chic," *Vogue* 179 (January 1989):38.
     Profile of Martha Plimpton—actress and animal rights advocate, with emphasis on her fashion and style preferences.

181. Sommer, Mark. "Animal Rhythms: Rocking for Animal Rights," *AA* 9 (July/August 1989):14–8+.
     People for the Ethical Treatment of Animals sponsors rock concerts for animal rights in New York City and Washington, D.C., featuring Lene Lovich, Mink Stole, Jane Wiedlin, River Phoenix, Larry "Bud" Melman, Natalie Merchant, and the B-52s.

182. Unti, Bernard. "John McArdle," *AV* 2 (June 1989):18–19.
     McArdle talks about his experience in graduate school, where lab animals were treated with indifference and neglect and how that triggered his participation in animal rights movement.

183. Valentine, Paul W. "U.S. Accused of Trying to Smear Animal Rights Groups," *WP* 7 December 1989:A17.
     Alex Pacheco, cofounder of People for the Treatment of Ethical Treatment of Animals, and Carol Lyn Burnett of

the same group were arrested, tried, and acquitted on felony assault charges brought against them in demonstration at National Institutes of Health headquarters in Washington, D.C. The two say they were singled out in order to discredit animal rights movement and undermine their organization's membership and fund-raising capabilities.

184.  Walker, Alice. "Am I Blue? Ain't These Tears in These Eyes Tellin' You?" *MS* 15 (July 1986):29–30.

Personal essay from prominent contemporary writer, describing her empathy with animals and their ability to suffer.

# II PHILOSOPHY, ETHICS, AND RELIGION

Philosophy and ethics have played a major role in the rise of the animal rights movement in the United States. Beginning in 1975 with Peter Singer's classic *Animal Liberation: A New Ethics for Our Treatment of Animals* and sustained by the numerous writings of Tom Regan—activist and philosophy professor at North Carolina State University—a vigorous school of thought has evolved that defines and examines the status of animals. Many concepts, especially the legitimacy of animals having rights and the interests and the moral status of animals, have ignited far-reaching debate not only among philosophers but also among scientists, psychologists, businesspeople, elected public officials, lawyers, and the general public.

Theological debate regarding animal rights has not kept pace with the philosophical, but even within religious circles, there is a burgeoning interest in the need to readdress humankind's relations with animals. Rev. Andrew Linzey, a British Episcopalian cleric, has had significant influence in the movement through his activism and his interpretation of Christian doctrine at the same time as some elements in the Jewish, Buddhist, Hindu, and Moslem communities are also promoting more ethical treatment of animals based on the traditional sources of their individual religions.

185.   Ahlers, Julia. "Thinking Like a Mountain: Toward a Sensible Land Ethic," *Christian Century* 107 (April 25, 1990): 433–34.

   Animal rights activists and some environmentalists don't understand the relation between nature and man. Their attitudes and behavior reflect more of an alienation from nature than a oneness with it.

186. Armstrong, Susan B. "The Rights of Non Human Beings: A Whiteheadian Study." Ph.D. dissertation, Bryn Mawr College, 1976.
   Examines Whitehead's theory of intrinsic value and other aspects of his metaphysics and applies them to human responsibility toward nonhuman beings.

187. Bartlett, Kim. "A Conversation with Andrew Linzey: On Christianity and Animals," *AA* 9 (April 1988):7–20+.
   Rev. Dr. Andrew Linzey, Church of England theologian, is one of the few clergy who support and work for animal rights. Discusses church's traditional indifference to animal abuse, how that can change, and the attempt to develop a Christian theology about animals.

188. Benson, John. "Duty and the Beast," *Philosophy* 53 (October 1978):529–49.
   Compares and assesses Peter Singer's and Stephen Clark's ideas on the moral status of animals.

189. Boyce, John R., with Christopher Lutes. "Animal Rights: How Much Pain Is a Cure Worth?" *Christianity Today* 29 (September 6, 1985): 35–38.
   Christian researcher shares his reaction to a conference he attended on "Religious Perspectives on the Use of Animals in Science." The idea animals have rights much as humans do should cause immediate uneasy feelings, since it eliminates the idea humans are unique. Such thinking leads to pantheism and away from Christianity. Scripture shows humans are superior to animals and more valued. We should emphasize animal welfare, not animal rights.

190. Burch, Robert W. "Animals, Rights, and Claims," *Southwest Journal of Philosophy* 8 (Summer 1977): 53–59.

191. Callicott, J. Baird. "Animal Liberation: A Triangular Affair," *Environmental Ethics* 2 (Winter 1980):311–38.
   Comparison of ethical foundations of animal liberation movement and Aldo Leopold's "land ethic." Concludes a

society in which animals hold rights is better suited to satire than philosophical discussion.

192. Cave, George P. "Animals, Heidegger, and the Right to Life," *Environmental Ethics* 4 (Fall 1982):249–54.
Attempts to resolve the conflicts of interest between animals and humans. As a solution, suggests the idea of "Care" as Heidegger interprets word. Because animals care or are concerned with their own existence, humans have a moral obligation or duty not to kill them.

193. Cave, George P. "On the Irreplaceability of Animal Life," *Ethics and Animals* 3 (December 1982):106–16.

194. Cave, George P. "Rational Egoism, Animal Rights, and the Academic Connection," *Between the Species* 1 (Spring 1985):21–27.

195. Cebik, L. B. "Can Animals Have Rights: No and Yes," *Philosophical Forum* 12 (Spring 1981): 251–68+.

196. "A Changing Roman Catholic Perspective," *AA* 9 (April 1989):9.
Excerpt from Item 34, Section IV, "Authentic Human Development" from Pope John Paul II's encyclical addressing nature, including animals, and human responsibility to them.

197. Clark, Stephen R. L. "Animals, Ecosystems, and the Liberal Ethic," *Monist* 70 ( January 1987):114–33.
It is within the context of libertarianism or liberal political theory that the concept of animals' having rights has significance. The concept gains plausibility from a vision of cosmic democracy in which duties go beyond rights of self-ownership.

198. Clark, Stephen R. L. "Animal Wrongs," *Analysis* 38 ( June 1978):147–49.
Disagrees with R. G. Frey's argument that babies and

imbeciles should be treated as having rights, but nonhumans should not. Explains why it is wrong to injure sentient, appetitive, partially communicative beings whether they be human or nonhuman.

199.  Clark, Stephen R. L. *The Moral Status of Animals.* New York: Oxford University Press, 1977.

Scholarly examination of past and present philosophical arguments that allow humans to continue dominion and exploitation of animals, with special emphasis on the immorality of eating animals. We shouldn't cause unnecessary suffering, and on that basis alone we might all become vegetarians. Discusses animals' place in the natural order.

200.  Clingerman, Karen J. *Ethical and Moral Issues Relating to Animals: January 1979–March 1990,* Quick Bibliography Series, QB 90–48. Beltsville, MD: Animal Welfare Information Center, National Agricultural Library, 1990, A17.18/4:90–48.

Approximately 380 citations from AGRICOLA database covering a broad range of animal welfare/rights issues, including vegetarianism, farm animals, circus animals, seal hunts, horse riding, animal experimentation, and alternatives.

201.  Close, Sandy. "Biological Advances Make Animal Rights Vital," *Los Angeles Daily Journal* 22 September 1983:4.

Premise that human life is unique is now being threatened by biological breakthroughs showing animals are less different from humans than we once thought. Animal rights may help to keep ethical considerations apace with biological ones.

202.  Cottingham, John. " 'A Brute to the Brutes?': Descartes' Treatment of Animals," *Philosophy* 53 (October 1978): 551–59.

Argues that Descartes did not hold the "monstrous view" toward animals often attributed to him.

203. Davis, Michael. "The Moral Status of Dogs, Forests, and Other Persons," *Social Theory and Practice* 12 (Spring 1986):27–59.
     Only animals with whom humans can empathize can have rights, but even then only as "persons third class."

204. Dombrowski, Daniel A. "The Ancient Mariner, God, and Animals," *Between the Species* 2 (Summer 1986): 111–15.

205. Dombrowski, Daniel A. *Hartshorne and the Metaphysics of Animal Rights.* Albany, NY: State University of New York Press, 1988.
     Justification of vegetarianism and animal rights based on the broader respect-for-nature arguments of Charles Hartshorne, American philosopher.

206. Donnelley, Strachan. "Speculative Philosophy, the Troubled Middle, and the Ethics of Animal Experimentation," *Hastings Center Report* 19 (March/April 1989):15–21.
     Describes dilemma of the troubled middle who see inherent goodness in life and concrete value in individual animals but also believe humans are superior to animals. Our final duty is to the overall goodness or well-being of organic life. This attitude does not always favor humans over animals, but when it does, as in the use of animals in research, it's important to follow very strict behavior in seeing animals are respected and treated humanely.

207. Donnelley, Strachan and Kathleen Nolan, eds. "Animals, Science, and Ethics," *Hastings Center Report* 20 (May/June 1990; Suppl. 8–13): 1–32.
     Proposes to take a fresh look at complex ethical issues that arise in scientific use of animals in a nonideological and nonadversarial forum. Collection of essays on the topic by laboratory and field researchers, veterinarians, philosophers, lawyers, and scientists interested in animal welfare.

208. Dunkerly, Rick. "Re-Examining the Christian Scriptures," *AV* 2 (August 1989):46.
     Christians who believe the Bible is the word of God

must reexamine it for its teachings about animals. The Bible mentions animals quite often, in many roles, and with purpose. For instance, Christ was not born in a stable surrounded by animals by accident. We must treat animals now as they will be treated at the Second Coming as part of all creation.

209. Elliot, Robert. "Moral Autonomy, Self-Determination, and Animal Rights," *Monist* 70 (January 1987):83–97.

210. Elliot, Robert. "Regan on the Sorts of Beings That Can Have Rights," *Southern Journal of Philosophy* 16 (Spring 1978):701–5.

    Examines Tom Regan's arguments against Joel Feinberg's interpretation of interest and goodness principles. Argues sentience is a necessary condition for possessing interests and inherent good.

211. Fisher, John A. "Taking Sympathy Seriously: A Defense of Our Moral Psychology Towards Animals," *Environmental Ethics* 9 (Fall 1987):197–215.

    Although sympathy is disreputable to many thinkers when considering moral concern for animals, it has a definite place in the discussion and can be placed on an objective basis. Even as sympathy is appropriate for humans, so, too, is it for animals.

212. Fox, Michael A. " 'Animal Liberation': A Critique," *Ethics* 88 (January 1978):106–18.

    Criticism of arguments found in Peter Singer's *Animal Liberation: A New Ethics for Our Treatment of Animals* and Tom Regan's "The Moral Basis of Vegetarianism." Concept of moral rights cannot be extended to include animals, and concept of animal rights is a bogus issue. We must be concerned about treatment of animals because they are sentient, not because they have rights.

213. Fox, Michael A. "Animal Rights: Misconceived Humaneness," *Dalhousie Review* 58 (Summer 1978): 230–39.

Animal rights movement requires examination of the nature of rights. Criticizes "Universal Declaration of Rights of Animals," a document presented to UNESCO, which states all animals are born with an equal claim upon life and equal rights to existence. This document and others like it are philosophically and legally sloppy. Humans have a moral obligation to avoid mistreating animals, but this has to do with duty, not rights.

214. Fox, Michael A. "Animal Suffering and Rights," *Ethics* 88 (January 1978): 134–38.
Responds to criticism by philosophers Peter Singer and Tom Regan.

215. Francis, Leslie Pickering, and Richard Norman. "Some Animals Are More Equal Than Others," *Philosophy* 53 (October 1978):507–27.
Takes issue with Peter Singer's principle of equal consideration of interests. Greater weight should be given to human interests, because humans have relations with other humans that they cannot have with animals. Animals should not be treated cruelly, but this shouldn't depend upon animals' having rights. Nor should calling for their better treatment be considered a liberation movement.

216. Frey, R. G. "Animal Rights," *Analysis* 37 (June 1977): 186–89.
Explains ways to argue why mentally enfeebled humans can have rights, but nonhuman animals cannot: (1) babies are potentially rational; (2) mentally enfeebled, except in rationality, are similar to the rest of us; (3) babies and mentally enfeebled possess immortal souls.

217. Frey, R. G. "Autonomy and the Value of Animal Life," *Monist* 70 (January 1987):50–63.
Frey disagrees with Tom Regan's argument that animals can be accorded equal value and equal rights by the same criteria that humans are accorded equal value. Not all human life has equal value; quality of life is an important factor. Humans can make their lives a thing of value by

way of the capacity for critical evaluation, assessment, and ordering of first-order desires. Animals, or humans who cannot do this, are slaves to their first-order desires and therefore suffer inferior quality of life.

218.  Frey, R. L. "Interests and Animal Rights," *Philosophical Quarterly* 27 ( July 1977):254–59.

Frey challenges some of Tom Regan's arguments about whether animals can have interests and therefore rights. If animals have interests (rights) only if humans are there to say so, then humans have them only if humans are there to say so. This, Frey says, yields an unwelcome result or else requires additional argumentative support.

219.  Frey, R. G. *Interests and Rights: The Case Against Animals.* New York: Oxford University Press, 1980.

Challenges view that animals have moral rights or that vegetarianism has a moral base. Examines linkage between these claims and the idea that animals have interests. Specifically addresses arguments of philosophers Peter Singer and Tom Regan.

220.  Frey, R. G. "Rights, Interests, Desires, and Beliefs," *American Philosophical Quarterly* 16 ( July 1979):233–39.

The question is not which rights animals may or may not possess or whether their rights are on a par with those possessed by humans, but rather can animals be the logical subject of rights at all?

221.  Giraud, Raymond. "Rousseau and Voltaire: The Enlightenment and Animal Rights," *Between the Species* 1 (Winter 1984/85):4–9.

222.  Gleason, Sean J., and Janice C. Swanson, comps. *An Annotated Bibliography of Selected Materials Concerning the Philosophy of Animal Rights.* Beltsville, MD: Animal Welfare Information Center, National Agricultural Library, 1988, A17.18/2:An5.

Forty-one citations arguing philosophically for and against animal rights.

223. Goodpaster, Kenneth E. "On Being Morally Considerable," *Journal of Philosophy* 75 (June 1978):308–25.
What sort of beings deserve moral consideration? Looks at four philosophers' thoughts.

224. Griswold, Charles, Jr. "The Immorality of Animals' Rights," *WP* 5 January 1986: D7.
Philosophy professor at Howard University says adhering to the animal rights philosophy would change every aspect of our lives, including the way we eat, dress, do science, farm, and learn medicine. Following the animal rights philosophy to its logical conclusion would have enormous and damaging consequences for human life.

225. Gunn, Alastair S. "Traditional Ethics and the Moral Status of Animals," *Environmental Ethics* 5 (Summer 1983):133–53.
Discussion of the moral status of animals has been within the framework of traditional ethics, rights theory, and utilitarianism. This is inappropriate. Instead, it should be examining concepts of stewardship and trusteeship in consideration of our relationship to animals.

226. Hartshorne, Charles. "The Rights of the Subhuman World," *Environmental Ethics* 1 (Spring 1979):49–60.
Do subhuman creatures have rights? The goal is to demonstrate treatment and attitudes toward animals with an ethic that can appeal to religious convictions, scientific principles, and a philosophical system. Even though a whole subhuman species may be worth more than a human life, an individual of that species probably isn't. Nevertheless, nonhuman forms have intrinsic and instrumental value, which humans are obligated to safeguard.

227. Haworth, Lawrence. "Rights, Wrongs, and Animals," *Ethics* 88 (January 1978):95–105.
There are strong and weak rights. Which, if either, are animals entitled to?

228. Hershaft, Alex. "Vegetarianism and Animal Rights (letter)," *Humanist* 37 (September/October 1977):59.
     Criticism of Michael Levin's position against animal rights.

229. Hoch, David. "Environmental Ethics and Nonhuman Interests: A Challenge to Anthropocentric License," *Gonzaga Law Review* (Winter 1988):331–47.
     What moral responsibility does a government, a corporation, a community, or an individual have to the natural environment and its indigenous animal habitants? Hoch looks at this question from both utilitarian and rights viewpoints and concludes it is anthropocentric to blindly deny rights to nonhuman animals, who are capable of pain, pleasure, and communication.

230. Hunt, Mary, and Mark Juergensmeyer, comps. *Animal Ethics: An Annotated Bibliography*. Berkeley, CA: Graduate Theological Union, 1977.
     Approximately 160 citations of books and monographs covering animal society and ethics, animal/human relationships, and the rights of animals.

231. Husack, Douglas N. "On the Rights of Non-Persons," *Canadian Journal of Philosophy* 10 (December 1980):607–22.
     There are no good reasons showing animals have moral rights and many to show they do not. Summarizes premises of other philosophers who allow animals moral standing and rights and points out fallacies: (1) not all wrong actions violate someone's rights; (2) that which violates rights is not always worse than that which is merely wrong. We can express everything we want to about how nonpersons should be treated without appealing to the rights argument.

232. Jacobs, Sidney J. "A Jewish Voice for Animals," *AV* 2 (August 1989):48–49.
     Hebrew Scriptures and postbiblical writings support many animal rights positions, from vegetarianism to anti-

fur activism. Some areas of conflict exist, however, and one is the ritual slaughter of food animals. Halacha, a body of rabbinic laws, also seems to condone use of animals in research, although for many non-Orthodox Jews, the Halacha does not necessarily determine their life-style. At present, large numbers of rabbis have been unreceptive to animal rights arguments, yet it is encouraging to hear so many Jewish voices in leadership and membership roles in animal rights organizations.

233. Jacobs, Sidney J. "Who Shall Live? Who Shall Die?" *AA* 9 (October 1989):26–33+.
     Rabbi Jacobs examines link between Judaism and animal rights issues.

234. Jamieson, Dale. "Rational Egoism and Animal Rights," *Environmental Ethics* 3 (Summer 1981):167–71.
     Argues that Jan Narveson's "rational egoism" would end in principled indifference to fate of animals and possibly human infants and idiots. Protection from suffering would depend upon the rational egoists' decision about who falls within or without the circle of morality.

235. Jamieson, Dale. "Rights, Justice, and Duties to Provide Assistance: A Critique of Regan's Theory of Rights," *Ethics* 100 (January 1990):349–62.

236. Jamieson, Dale, and Tom Regan. "Animal Rights: A Reply to Frey," *Analysis* 38 (January 1978):32–36.
     Frey argues animal rights philosophy depends on idea that the criteria banning animals from having rights also ban the mentally retarded and babies from rights. Regan and Jamieson deny this interpretation of animal rights argument but explain that even if it were correct, Frey's response to it would be unconvincing.

237. Johnson, Edward. "Animal Liberation vs. the Land Ethic," *Environmental Ethics* 3 (Fall 1981):265–73.
     J. Baird Callicott misinterprets why pain is important to

animal liberationists. Addresses the "land ethic" issue in relation to animal liberation.

238.  Johnson, Edward. *Species and Morality.* Ph.D. dissertation, Princeton University, 1976.
Examines moral status of humans and animals and their interests. There is no good reason to suppose that humans have any special moral status, and it is wrong to do to animals what we would not think of doing to humans.

239.  Johnson, Lawrence E. "Can Animals Be Moral Agents?" *Ethics and Animals* 4 (June 1983):50–61.

240.  Jones, Gary E. "Singer, Animal Rights, and Consistency," *International Journal of Applied Philosophy* 1 (Fall 1983):67–70.

241.  Jones, Gary E., and Clifton Perry. "Equal Consideration and Animal Rights," *International Journal of Applied Philosophy* 1 (Spring 1983): 87–88.

242.  Lamb, David. "Animal Rights and Liberation Movements," *Environmental Ethics* 4 (Fall 1982):215–33.
Examines Singer's analogy between human liberation and animal liberation and concludes the former is more serious than the latter. Says improving treatment of animals is a reform movement not a liberation movement and discusses blacks' and women's liberation movements to show why.

243.  Lehman, Hugh. "The Case for Animal Rights," *Dialogue* 23 (December 1984):669–76.
Examines Tom Regan's *Case for Animal Rights.*

244.  Lesco, Philip A. "To Do No Harm: A Buddhist View on Animal Use in Research," *Journal of Religion and Health* 27,4 (1988):307–12.

245.  Levin, Michael E. "All in a Stew About Animals: A Reply to Singer," *Humanist* 37 (September/October 1977):58.

Levin responds to Peter Singer's criticism of his earlier article arguing against animal rights.

246. Levin, Michael E. "Animal Rights Evaluated," *Humanist* 37 (July/August 1977):12+.

Too many people, including highly respected philosophers, are taking animal rights too seriously. Animals can't have rights, and meat eating and animal experimentation are not wrong.

247. Linzey, Andrew. *Animal Rights: A Christian Assessment of Man's Treatment of Animals.* London: SCM Press, 1976.

A scholarly study of man's treatment of animals within the framework of Christianity.

248. Linzey, Andrew. *Christianity and the Rights of Animals.* New York: Crossroad Pub., 1987.

Christian theology as it has developed over hundreds of years militates against taking animal rights seriously and is based on four points: animals have no mind or reason, animals have no immortal soul, animals are not sentient, and animals have no moral status. There is also a positive tradition in Christian thought, however, that has not received adequate attention: animals are God's creatures, animals have intrinsic value, humans have responsibility to animals, and human and animal life are interdependent. The triumph of negative theology has led us to treat animals as things. Emphasis on positive theology about animals forces us to change our life-style and leads to the one moral principle—"it is wrong to be the cause of avoidable injury."

249. Linzey, Andrew. "Christianity and the Rights of Animals," *AV* 2 (August 1989): 43–45.

250. Lowry, Jon. "Natural Rights: Men and Animals," *Southwestern Journal of Philosophy* 6 (Summer 1975):109–22.

251. Magel, Charles R. "Animals: Moral Rights and Legal Rights," *Between the Species* 1 (Spring 1985):9–14.

252.  Margolis, Joseph. "Animals Have No Rights and Are Not the Equal of Humans," *Philosophical Exchange* 1 (Summer 1974):119–23.

253.  Martin, Rafe. "Buddhism and Animals," *AV* 2 (August 1989):55–56.
      The first precept that all Buddhists strive to uphold is "Not to kill, but to cherish all life." All is interconnected, and to mistreat any part of it is to mistreat one's own self.

254.  Masri, Al-Hafiz B. A. "A Glimpse of Islam on Animals," *AV* 2 (August 1989):50–51.
      Islamic law from the Hadith or Qur'an does not offer direct guidance to resolving animal abuse practices of today. Through inference and analogy, however, these sources teach the interest of one being should not annul that of another, and the prevention of damage takes priority over the fulfillment of one's needs. The Qur'an focuses on environmental and ecological balance and speaks of an animal's life on par with a human's. "There is not an animal on earth or bird that flies on its wings, but are communities like you."

255.  McDonald, Jay. "The Liberation of Life," *AV* 2 (August 1989):46–47.
      The World Council of Churches, the world's largest Christian ecumenical organization, has issued "The Liberation of Life," a report that promises a more enlightened attitude from the church toward animals. The report specifically criticizes abuse of animals in research testing labs, in the fashion industry, on factory farms, in entertainment, and in education, concluding that apart from their usefulness to humans, animals have value for themselves and for God.

256.  McFarland, Cole. "The Conservation of Moral Energy," *AV* 2 (August 1989):52.
      Doctrine of karma addresses the rule of conservation of moral energy in the universe. Every evil or good action

reaps an appropriate reaction. Those who believe in karma try to live lives of ahimsa—the principle of noninjury or nonviolence—and this has great significance in the treatment of animals. Karmic retribution is inevitable even if it occurs in another lifetime.

257. McFarland, Cole. "The Secrets of Santeria," *AV* 2 (August 1989):84–87.

Author infiltrates a religious cult in the U.S. that practices animal sacrifice of white chickens, roosters, opossums, monkeys, goats, bulls, oxen, and white mice.

258. Midgley, Mary. *Animals and Why They Matter*. Athens, GA: University of Georgia Press, 1983.

Addresses the evolution of philosophical thought about interests and rights of animals and humans, anthropomorphism, and the subjectivity and consciousness of animals. Expands the discussion of animal rights/welfare and demonstrates the interconnectedness of animals and humans.

259. Midgley, Mary. "Brutality and Sentimentality," *Philosophy* 54 (July 1979):385–89.

Being sentimental is misrepresenting the world in order to indulge our feelings, but the charge of sentimentality is often leveled against those who feel or express sympathy when the occasion actually warrants it. Assumptions and tradition affect our attitudes and behavior toward animals, and it is time to question them. For instance, one extraordinary assumption, justified badly by Spinoza and Descartes, is that one can recognize the claim of another species only if it somehow benefits humans.

260. Miller, Harlan, and William H. Williams, eds. *Ethics and Animals*. Clifton, NJ: Humana, 1983.

Collection of essays by various authors addressing animal rights philosophy and ethics and the appropriate relationship between man and animals.

261.   Miller, Peter. "Do Animals Have Interests Worthy of Our Moral Interest," *Environmental Ethics* 5 (Winter 1983): 319–33.

262.   "Ministries for Animals," *AV* 2 (August 1989):51.

Ministries for Animals offers nonspeciesist pastoral services to local societies for the prevention of cruelty to animals and invites shelter animals into the spiritual community by acknowledging their souls/spirits. Future services will include baptism of animals and commitment to an animal's care by the human "parent proxy." Also encourages celebrations of birthdays for living animals and remembrance days for dead ones.

263.   Monticone, George T. "Animals and Morality," *Dialogue* 17 (December 1978):683–95.

Evolutionists have affirmed our physiological and anatomical kinship with animals. Behavioral kinship, too, should be recognized. But what about morality? One cannot account for our moral obligation to animals without recourse to the well-being or rights of animals. Examines ten arguments against animals' having rights and offers rebuttals.

264.   Moseley, Ray Edward. *Animal Rights: An Analysis of the Major Arguments for Animal Rights.* Ph.D. dissertation, Georgetown University, 1984.

Identifies and discusses flaws in four arguments used to support contention animals have rights.

265.   Narveson, Jan. "On a Case for Animal Rights," *Monist* 70 (January 1987):31–49.

Examines Tom Regan's *Case for Animals Rights* and its arguments. Concludes that commitment to animals is comparable to religious belief rather than a convincing philosophical argument. It's a moral theory of life that will impress only those who need something to feel guilty about.

266. Nelson, James A. "Recent Studies in Animal Ethics," *American Philosophical Quarterly* 22 (January 1985):13–24.
Study of animals and ethics is on the increase. Interest in the topic was initiated by Peter Singer and Tom Regan and followed by arguments of other thinkers who have supported, attacked, or modified the position of those two. A summary of the evolution of animal rights philosophy accompanied by a bibliography of more than eighty pro and con animal rights essays.

267. Nelson, James A. "Review of Sapontzis' Recent Work on Animal Rights," *Ethics and Animals* 3 (December 1982): 117–23.

268. Nelson, John O. "Brute Animals and Legal Rights," *Philosophy* 62 (April 1987):171–77.
Explains why animals can't have legal rights.

269. Newkirk, Ingrid E. "Glaringly Supremacist Piece (letter)," *WP* 21 January 1986:A14.
Director of People for the Ethical Treatment of Animals responds to Charles Griswold's article ("The Immorality of Animal Rights," Jan. 5). He writes not as a philosopher interested in reasonable discourse but as a supremacist bent on scaring people away from discussion.

270. Norton, Bryan G. "Environmental Ethics and Nonhuman Rights," *Environmental Ethics* 4 (Spring 1982):17–36.
Giving animals rights merely increases demands upon the environment and causes more conflict between rights-holders. It does not help decide which demands take priorities over others. An environmental ethic needs a holistic framework, and this cannot be maintained or provided for on an individual basis no matter how much the basis is expanded.

271. Ost, David E. "The Case Against Animal Rights," *Southern Journal of Philosophy* 24 (Fall 1986):365–73.
The position that animals have rights is ultimately inco-

herent and dangerous. There is no serious rational ground for the claim, and it is in conflict with the concept and function of rights in ethical theory. Using the argument of rights to protect animals is like using a howitzer to swat a fly. Examines Tom Regan's *Case for Animal Rights* and notes what he considers flawed arguments.

272. Partridge, Ernest. "Three Wrong Leads in Search for an Environmental Ethic: Tom Regan on Animal Rights, Inherent Values, and 'Deep Ecology,' " *Ethics and Animals* 5 (September 1984):61–74.

273. Paterson, R. W. K. "Animal Pain, God, and Professor Geach," *Philosophy* 59 ( January 1984):116–20.
Explores Peter Geach's conclusion that God is indifferent to animal pain and suffering.

274. Peppu, S. S. Rama Rao. "Unity of Life in Hinduism," *AV* 2 (August 1989):52–54.
Hindus believe in the Unity of Life, a doctrine that recognizes the brotherhood of all creatures. Life forms differ not in kind but in degree of evolution. Humans are not God's favorites nor his chosen creatures. Hinduism adds to the Western precept "Love thy neighbor" the precept "And every living creature is thy neighbor."

275. Pierce, Christine. "Can Animals Be Liberated?" *Philosophical Studies* 36 ( July 1979):69–75.
Challenges Peter Singer's idea of animal liberation and contends that animals, allegedly the victims of speciesism, cannot be liberated as can women and blacks, the victims of sexism and racism.

276. Povilitis, Anthony J. "On Assigning Rights to Animals and Nature," *Environmental Ethics* 2 (Spring 1980):67–71.
Argues against R. A. Watson's belief that living entities do not have intrinsic and primary rights unless they are capable of reciprocal duties. Questions Watson's anthropocentrism and his emphasis on the differences between

man and other living entities, contending he should be
looking at their evolutionary and ecological relatedness instead.

277. Rachels, James. "Darwin, Species, and Morality," *Monist*
70 (January 1987):98–113.

278. Regan, Tom. *All That Dwell Therein: Animal Rights and
Environmental Ethics.* Berkeley, CA: University of California
Press, 1982.
Collection of papers and lectures examining vegetarianism, animal experimentation, Native American relationship with nature, animals and the law, and humans' obligations to nonhumans and nature.

279. Regan, Tom. "Animal Rights, Human Wrongs,"
*Environmental Ethics* 2 (Summer 1980):99–120.
Explores moral foundations of the treatment of animals
and schools of thought on the subject: Kantian, cruelty-is-
wrong theory, and utilitarian theory. All these views are inadequate. Animals have an inherent value, and for that
reason we can attribute to them basic moral rights, including the right not to be harmed. Those who would treat
them otherwise have the onus of justifying their actions.

280. Regan, Tom. *The Case for Animal Rights.* Berkeley, CA:
University of California Press, 1983.
Major animal rights work with comprehensive philosophical defense of what it means to ascribe rights to animals, why we should recognize such rights, and what it
means if we do.

281. Regan, Tom. "Cruelty, Kindness, and Unnecessary
Suffering," *Philosophy* 55 (October 1980):531–41.
To advance anticruelty as a basis for appropriate treatment of animals is inadequate, because that means that as
long as we do not enjoy or are indifferent to animals' suffering, it's all right to cause them to suffer. Admonition to
be kind to animals is equally inadequate, because it doesn't
capture the idea we owe certain treatment to animals and

it is their due. Both kindness and cruelty, however, have a place when used in reference to the idea of "the obligatoriness of preventing unnecessary suffering."

282. Regan, Tom. "The Dog in the Lifeboat: An Exchange," *New York Review of Books* 32 (April 25, 1985):56–57.
    Tom Regan's side of a philosophical exchange with Peter Singer. Both philosophers are preeminent proponents of improving our treatment of animals, but they have differences in the arguments they use to support their position. Regan bases his on a rights approach; Singer employs utilitarian principles. The dog in a lifeboat is an example Regan used to discuss the comparative value of life, with a response from Singer following.

283. Regan, Tom. "Fox's Critique of Animal Liberation," *Ethics* 88 (January 1978):126–33.
    Response to Michael A. Fox's criticism of Regan's "Moral Basis of Vegetarianism."

284. Regan, Tom. "Frey on Interests and Animal Rights," *Philosophical Quarterly* 27 (October 1977):335–37.
    Regan says R. G. Frey misinterprets his position in comparing the interests of human babies with those of animals.

285. Regan, Tom. "McCloskey on Why Animals Cannot Have Rights," *Philosophical Quarterly* 26 (July 1976):251–57.
    Argues against H. J. McCloskey's idea that animals cannot have rights, because they cannot possess things, and beings who cannot possess things cannot possess rights. Regan says animals can possess things, although he sees this argument as unimportant. More important is that animals have an interest in what happens to them.

286. Regan, Tom. "Narveson on Egoism and the Rights of Animals," *Canadian Journal of Philosophy* 7 (March 1977): 179–86.
    Answers Jan Narveson's arguments on why animals can't have rights. Concludes pain is an evil in itself, and just as humans, including the mentally enfeebled and ba-

bies, have the right not to suffer gratuitously, so, too, do animals. Narveson's rational egoism would lead to rejection of relevance of suffering by nonhumans and some humans (such as morons). Their protection would depend upon the "sentimental interest" of others.

287. Regan, Tom. "On the Right Not to Be Made to Suffer Gratuitously," *Canadian Journal of Philosophy* 10 (September 1980):473–78.

Regan defends his definition and criteria of gratuitous suffering imposed on animals and rejects notion his arguments are utilitarian. He questions raising and slaughtering animals, not because it has been shown this violates an animal's rights and is morally wrong, but because it has not been shown it does not. Justification is demanded of those who eat animals, not of those who don't.

288. Regan, Tom. "Pigs in Space," *Philosophica* 39 (1987): 11–12.

289. Regan, Tom. "The Promise and Challenge of Religion," *AV* 2 (August 1989):40–42.

Some in the religious community are beginning to take notice of animal rights issues and to oppose them. Was it better when they went unnoticed? No, "healthy seeds wisely planted may not fall on barren soil." Some in Catholic, Jewish, and Protestant circles are basing animal rights issues on alternative interpretations of sacred texts. We are witnessing the beginning of a serious involvement of religion in the animal rights movement, and this should be encouraged.

290. Regan, Tom. "Religion and Animal Rights," *AV* 2 (August 1989):24–7+.

Animal rights is considered an extreme position by some, but extremeness is not necessarily a sign of incorrectness. When an injustice is absolute, one must oppose it absolutely. Neither reason nor intuition can confirm the belief man is superior to animals except in one way: God has chosen man as the one species capable of moral responsibility and love toward his creation and all in it.

291. Regan, Tom, and Peter Singer, eds. *Animal Rights and Human Obligations*. Englewood Cliffs, NJ: Prentice-Hall, 1976.

    Collection of more than thirty essays by philosophers such as Darwin, Voltaire, Aquinas, Aristotle, Schweitzer, Kant, and Schopenhauer that address the question Do animals have rights and do humans have obligations toward them?

292. Rollin, Bernard E. "How I Put the Horse Before Descartes: An Autobiographical Fragment," *Between the Species* 1 (Winter 1984/85):44–50.

    Veterinary professor and ethicist tells how he became interested and active in animal welfare issues.

293. Rosen, Steven. "Ahimsa: Animals and the East," *AA* 10 (October 1990):21–25.

    Respect for animals is an integral part of Eastern religions, although practice sometimes strays from principle. Discusses Hinduism, Buddhism, Zoroastrianism, Sikhism, and Jainism.

294. Russow, Lilly-Marlene. "Why Do Species Matter?" *Environmental Ethics* 3 (Summer 1981):101–12.

    Arguments for animal rights also provide a justification for differential treatment of endangered or rare species as well as for individual animals. When we value a species, we really value the existence of one animal and the existence of those, present or future, who are like it.

295. Sapontzis, Steve F. "Are Animals Moral Beings?" *American Philosophical Quarterly* 17 ( January 1980):45–52.

    Some philosophers argue animals are not moral beings, because only rational beings can be moral and animals are not rational. Asks and answers three questions: to what does rational refer, why is rationality necessary for morality, and do animals really lack the rationality necessary for morality?

296. Sapontzis, Steve F. "Everyday Morality and Animal Rights," *Between the Species* 3 (Summer 1987):107–27.

297. Sapontzis, Steve F. "The Evolution of Animals in Moral Philosophy," *Between the Species* 3 (September 1987):61–65.

298. Sapontzis, Steve F. "Moral Community and Animal Rights," *American Philosophical Quarterly* 22 (July 1985): 251–57.

    Many believe animals have no moral rights because they lack a fundamental moral worth. Addresses three interpretations of moral worth in relation to requirements that must be fulfilled if animals can have rights in the sense humans do.

299. Sapontzis, Steve F. "The Moral Significance of the 'Innocence' of Animals," *Between the Species* 3 (Winter 1987):12–18.

300. Sapontzis, Steve F. *Morals, Reason, and Animals.* Philadelphia: Temple University Press, 1987.

    Examination of animal liberation, vegetarianism, and animal experimentation, with a focus on the pivotal philosophical issues involved and responses to objections that have been raised.

301. Sapontzis, Steve F. "Must We Value Life to Have a Right to It?" *Ethics and Animals* 3 (March 1982):2–11.

302. Sapontzis, Steve F. "On Being Morally Expendable," *Ethics and Animals* 3 (September 1982):58–72.

303. Schall, James V. "On the Christian Love of Animals," *Vital Speeches* 43 (November 15, 1976): 81–86.

    What are the implications of Christianity within the context of animal liberation? Animals are for human use and enjoyment of life, and it is all right to sacrifice animals to the Lord and for our needs. Sees animal rights movement and activists as idolators who worship animals and nature as false gods. When man tries to save an endangered species, he is interfering with evolution. Concludes that one human baby is worth the whole of the animal kingdom.

304.  Shepard, Paul. "Animal Rights and Human Rites," *North American Review* 259 (Winter 1974):35–42.

Humans trying to cope with extinction of species have adopted various strategies, such as providing sanctuaries and refuges. Yet in a world of 2 million different species, this is obviously not the answer, nor is adoption of the philosophy of nonkilling. Emphasis should be placed on the food chain and each species' place in it.

305.  Sikora, R. I. "Morality and Animals," *Ethics and Animals* 2 (September 1981):46–59.

306.  Singer, Peter. *Animal Liberation*, rev. ed. New York: Avon Books, 1990.

Revised and updated edition of ground-breaking *Animal Liberation: A New Ethics for Our Treatment of Animals*. Includes a new preface that looks at growth of animal rights movement, its successes and failures.

307.  Singer, Peter. "Animal Liberation or Animal Rights?" *Monist* 70 (January 1987):3–14.

Singer explains why he does not philosophically accept the theory of "animal rights," as espoused by Tom Regan. He thinks acknowledging animals have interests, albeit different ones from humans', and giving those interests equal consideration are sounder principles upon which to base improved treatment of animals. The rights arguments are too inflexible to respond to real and imaginary circumstances.

308.  Singer, Peter. *Animal Liberation: A New Ethics for Our Treatment of Animals*. New York: New York Review of Books, 1975.

One of the most important books written on animal rights. Outlines traditional practices of abuse toward animals and presents philosophical arguments calling for a new ethics toward them. Considers animal liberation as the latest in a long line of needed social reform movements. The central point of his argument focuses on speciesism— a prejudice or attitude of bias toward the interest of one's own species and against the interests of others.

309. Singer, Peter. "Animals and the Value of Life," in *Matters of Life and Death*, Tom Regan, ed. Philadelphia: Temple University Press, 1980, pp. 218–59.

    Criticizes the argument humans have a unique value far beyond that of animals, because they alone are conscious, have an immortal soul, have been given by God dominion over animals, and are ends in themselves.

310. Singer, Peter. "A Comment on the Animal Rights Debate," *International Journal of Applied Philosophy* 1 (Spring 1983): 89–90.

311. Singer, Peter. "The Dog in the Lifeboat: An Exchange: Peter Singer Replies," *New York Review of Books* 32 (April 25, 1985):57.

    (*See* Regan, Tom, "The Dog in the Lifeboat: An Exchange.")

312. Singer, Peter. "The Fable of the Fox and the Unliberated Animals," *Ethics* 88 (January 1978):119–25.

    Responds to Michael A. Fox's criticism of Singer's *Animal Liberation: A New Ethics for Our Treatment of Animals*.

313. Singer, Peter. "Not for Humans Only: The Place of Nonhumans in Environmental Issues," in *Ethics and Problems of the 21st Century*, Kenneth E. Goodpaster and Kenneth M. Sayre, eds. Notre Dame, IN: University of Notre Dame Press, 1979, pp. 191–206.

    Discusses the importance of individual animals as well as species when examining human/animal relations.

314. Singer, Peter. " 'A Reply to Professor Levin's Animal Rights Evaluated,' " *Humanist* 37 (June/August 1977): 13+.

    Singer maintains Levin doesn't understand philosophical vegetarianism and defends his belief that it is wrong to eat animals when they are raised inhumanely.

315. Singer, Peter. "The Significance of Animal Suffering," *Behavioral and Brain Sciences* 13,1 (1990):9–12.

Animals can suffer, but Singer asks does it matter? Discusses the moral status of human and nonhuman animals. Salutes animal behaviorist Marian Dawkins Stamp, whose article appears in the same issue for helping humans understand in an objective way the subjective experiences of animals. (Forty essays by scientists and philosophers commenting on both Singer and Dawkins follow.)

316. Sitomer, Curtis J. "Animal Rights," *CSM* 26 January 1989:13.
    Brief survey of the global animal rights movement. In U.S., the issue has become a theological as well as a political, social, and moral one. Quotes theologian Andrew Linzey; Rev. James Wall, editor of *Christian Century*; and Coleman McCarthy, newspaper columnist, who all believe in the inherent value of animals.

317. Sprigge, T. L. S. "Metaphysics, Physicalism, and Animal Rights," *Inquiry* 22 (Summer 1979):101–143.

318. Squadrito, Kathy. "A Note Concerning Locke's View of Property Rights and the Rights of Animals," *Philosophia* 10 (July 1981):19–24.

319. Stafford, Tim. "Animal Lib," *Christianity Today* 34 (June 18, 1990):19–20.
    Neither animal rights activists nor scientists have the high ground in explaining their positions on animal rights, so perhaps it's time for religion to enter the debate and sort out what our attitudes and treatment of animals should be. Here, too, however, answers will vary, from those who quote Genesis and its mandate of dominion over land and oceans to Karl Barth, who sees the whole earth and all its creatures as belonging to God, not to man.

320. Steinbock, Bonnie. "Speciesism and the Idea of Equality," *Philosophy* 53 (April 1978):247–56.
    If nonhumans are different from humans in some ways, then these differences could be morally relevant. Challenges Peter Singer's view that sentience is the only

relevant consideration of interests and introduces some level of intelligence as a criterion as well. Human lives are more valuable than animals' lives.

321. Sternberg, Mary. "Give Animals a Break," *National Catholic Reporter* 21 (March 15, 1985):29.
Takes Catholic religion to task for its indifference to animal suffering and abuse. It's time for Christians to realize having dominion over animals also means having responsibility for their welfare.

322. Stockwell, John. "For the Sake of Souls," *AV* 2 (August 1989):47.
The summer 1990 Walk to Rome for Animal Rights and the Souls of Animals makes an appeal to Catholic and Protestant theologians to reverse their long-standing doctrine, maintaining animals have no soul.

323. Stott, John R. W. "Christians and Animals," *Christianity Today* 22 (February 10, 1978):38–39.
Today's animal rights movement is just a modern form of animal worship. Bible passages teach what human/animal relationship should be: (1) humans can learn from animals; (2) humans may use animals for food, clothes, etc.; (3) humans must be kind to animals. In practical terms, this means it's all right to eat animals, but factory farming should be outlawed if found to be a frustration of animals' natural behavior and needs. Vivisection is morally justifiable if necessary for medical progress.

324. Sujithammaraksa, Roongtham. *Agent-Based Morality in the Ethics of Our Treatment of Animals.* Ph.D. dissertation, University of California, Santa Barbara, 1987.
Is it possible to be humane and just to animals without holding they have moral rights and claims against us?

325. Taylor, Paul W. "Inherent Value and Moral Rights," *Monist* 70 (January 1987):15–30.
Tom Regan has presented a most powerful case for an-

imal rights, but the author explains why he still has misgivings.

326.  Tobias, Michael. "Ahimsa," *AV* 2 (August 1989):56–57.
      Jainism has one fundamental precept: ahimsa or nonviolence, noninjury. The 10 million Jains in India represent only 1 percent of the population, but their income provides 50 percent of the tax base. They contribute an overwhelming amount to philanthropy, and they support hospitals, schools, and animal sanctuaries throughout the country. Strict vegetarians, they are obsessive about their belief in not interfering with any form of life, feeling every organism is capable of salvation and happiness.

327.  Van De Veer, Donald. "Animal Suffering," *Canadian Journal of Philosophy* 10 (September 1980):463–71.
      Examines three of Tom Regan's arguments for animal rights and shows where he thinks they miss the mark.

328.  Wall, James. "An Uncaged Vision of Nonhuman Creation," *Christian Century* 106 (October 25, 1989): 947–48.
      Examines Rev. Andrew Linzey's position on animal rights, ethics, and religion. Rooted in part in the thought of Karl Barth, Linzey also borrows from Albert Schweitzer's reverence-for-life ethic as well. Christians need to acknowledge all creation shares God's love. Treatment of animals is not just another moral issue but an inseparable part of the Christian message.

329.  Watson, Richard A. "Self-Consciousness and the Rights of Nonhuman Animals and Nature," *Environmental Ethics* 1 (Summer 1979):99–129.
      Argues against Peter Singer's *Animal Liberation: A New Ethics for the Treatment of Animals*. An entity can have rights only if it is able to fulfill reciprocal duties and act as a moral agent. Under this reciprocity framework, few animals can have rights or duties in an intrinsic or primary sense, with the exception of some animals, such as dogs, chimpanzees, and gorillas.

330. White, James E. "Are Sentient Beings Replaceable?" *Ethics and Animals* 3 (December 1982):91–95.

331. Willard, L. Duane. "About Animals 'Having Rights,' " *Journal of Value Inquiry* 16 (1982):177–87.
    To talk about rights of animals is to use Jeremy Bentham's metaphor "nonsense on stilts." Humans have rights only as they decide to ascribe them to themselves. No fact or set of facts, such as having interests or being able to suffer pain, gives rights to any creature, nor do they dictate, establish, or necessarily imply rights. We may owe animals humane treatment and put great value on their life and well-being, but this is not the same as saying they have rights.

332. Williams, Meredith. "Rights, Interest, and Moral Equality," *Environmental Ethics* 2 (Summer 1980):149–61.
    Argues against Peter Singer's notion that the interests of animals merit the same consideration as those of humans. The utilitarian concept of morality as espoused by Singer does not address well the morally relevant difference between humans and animals.

333. "World Council of Churches Report," *AA* 9 (April 1989):10+.
    World Council of Churches approved a report in 1988 called "The Liberation of Life." Section Four, Respect for Individual Animals, addresses man's abusive treatment of some animals and recommends reforms.

334. Young, Thomas. "The Morality of Killing Animals: Four Arguments," *Ethics and Animals* 5 (December 1984): 88–101.

# III LAW AND LEGISLATION

The animal rights movement has recognized the need to redefine the status of animals under the law. Efforts have been made to reform or enforce existing legislation and to create new laws that will better protect animals. On national, state, and local levels, activists have endeavored to abolish the use of leghold traps in the fur industry, restrict hunting and overturn hunter harassment laws, regulate the use of animals in research, improve living conditions for factory-farm animals, protect wildlife, and generally move toward the legal concept of animals as sentient creatures with rights protected by law.

335.  Allen, Don W. "The Rights of Nonhuman Animals and World Public Order: A Global Assessment," *New York Law School Law Review* 28 (Spring 1983):377–429.
       Belief in animal rights has led to a global, social, and political movement that demands codification of basic being rights. Includes text of the "Universal Declaration of Nonhuman Animal Rights," approved on October 15, 1985, by the International League for Animal Rights.

336.  Barnes, Fred. "Pet Causes," *New Republic* 202 (March 12, 1990):23.
       Animal rights alliances produce strange bedfellows. Conservative congressmen Robert Smith of New Hampshire and Robert Dornan of California are working to release Silver Spring monkeys but are wary of some of their animal rights allies. Looks at animal rights legislation and key players in Washington.

337.  Bennon, Rhonda. "Research Guide for Animal Welfare and Animal Rights," *Legal Reference Services Quarterly* 4 (Fall 1984):3–31.

Review of animal welfare/rights legislation and relevant sections of the code of federal regulations. The author notes there have been no landmark cases yet but cites representative animal welfare cases reaching the court from different jurisdictions. Short list of books, journal and newspaper articles, and legal experts who have written on animal rights.

338.   Clingerman, Karen J., comp. *Animal Welfare Legislation: Bills and Public Laws, 1990*, AWIC Series #4. Beltsville, MD: Animal Welfare Information Center, National Agricultural Library, January 1991, A17.26:990/4.

Lists thirty-six pieces of legislation introduced in 101st Congress covering agricultural animals, assistive animals, exhibition animals, marine mammals, wildlife, and pets.

339.   Clingerman, Karen, Sean Gleason, and Janice Swanson. *Animal Welfare Legislation: Bills and Public Laws, 1980–1988*. Beltsville, MD: Animal Welfare Information Center, National Agricultural Library, October 1988, A17.26: 988/1.

Lists fifty-nine pieces of legislation relating to animal welfare, its sponsors, and status.

340.   "Court Calendar," *AA* 10 (September 1990):35.

Pending legislation and court cases affecting wide range of animal rights issues.

341.   Daniel, Michelle D. "Air Transportation of Animals: Passengers or Property?" *Journal of Air Law and Commerce* 51 (Winter 1986):497–529.

342.   Dichter, Anita. "Legal Definitions of Cruelty and Animal Rights," *Boston College Environmental Affairs Law Review* 7 (1978):147–64.

The law must recognize interest of the animal in abuse and cruelty cases, not interest of its human owner whose property has been damaged. In a definition of cruelty to animals, two concepts should be considered: natural entities have intrinsic value and certain rights, and the capacity to suffer is an appropriate consideration in determining basic rights.

343. Fabiano, Franco. "Miscellaneous: Limits on Rabbit Drives," *Idaho Law Review* 21 (Spring 1985):511-12.
Looks at outcome of Fund for Animals vs. Mud Lake Farmers Rabbit Committee, which placed some restrictions on how rabbit drives in Idaho could be conducted.

344. Favre, David S., and Murray Loring. *Animal Law.* Westport, CT: Quorum Books, 1983.
Focuses on law relating to animals from 1960 to 1980. Includes discussion of classification of animals under the law, ownership of animals, animals as personal property, bailment of animals, agistment contracts, sale of animals, animals within wills and trusts, medical care of animals, humane and cruelty laws, limitations on ownership, recovery for injury, and federal wildlife statutes. Footnotes provide references for further legal research.

345. Francione, Gary. "Harassment and Terrorism," *AV* 3 (October 1990):53.
Attorney and professor of law discusses biomedical industry's accusation that animal rights activists are terrorists. Explains how the right of free speech differs from harassment and how the charge of terrorism is an empty one that should be rebutted at every opportunity.

346. Galvin, Robert W. "What Rights for Animals? A Modest Proposal," *Pace Environmental Law Review* 2,2 (1985): 245-54.
A truly just society respects all life, and that entails recognition of legal rights for animals and correlative legal duties such rights confer.

347. Gerson, Ben. "Unleashing Animal Rights: The Movement to Give New Legal Rights to Man's 'Servants,' " *National Law Journal* 4 (January 4, 1982):1+.
First legal conference on animal rights meets in New York to discuss litigation in test cases, develop a fund for

legal defense, and draft model legislation. Looks at specific legislation as it relates to farm and lab animals.

348. Goodkin, Susan L. "The Evolution of Animal Rights," *Columbia Human Rights Law Review* 18 (Spring 1987): 259–88.
Animal rights is a logical progression in evolution of natural rights theories. Lab animals have the right to be free from pain inflicted for research purposes regardless of possible human advantage. Looks at historical legal treatment of animals and concludes establishment of rights for them promises to entail a long, hard fight.

349. "Grand Jury Investigations: Ten Simple Rules," *AV* 3 (August 1990):72.
As authorities begin to investigate animal rights movement, activists are increasingly at risk to be called to testify before a grand jury. Ten tips for handling such an occurrence.

350. Hentoff, Nat. "Lawyers for Animals," *WP* 28 April 1990: A23:1.
Animal Protection Committee of the American Bar Association (ABA) Young Lawyers Division offered a resolution at ABA meeting that would encourage courts to treat animals as more than property. The resolution failed, but more and more lawyers are speaking up for animals. The Animal Legal Defense Fund, made up of 320 volunteer lawyers, "stands ready to appear in any court, in any jurisdiction, to promote animal justice and defend animals' rights."

351. Holden, Constance. "Congress and Animal Rights," *Science* 247 (February 2, 1990):530.
Congress has two new caucuses—the Animal Welfare Caucus, which supports use of animals in agriculture and medical research, and Congressional Friends of Animals, which defends animals.

352. Holton, A. Camille. "The Standing of Animal Protection Organizations Under the Animal Welfare Act," *Journal of*

*Contemporary Health, Law and Politics* 4 (Spring 1988): 469–78.

The ruling on *International Primate Protection vs. Institute for Behavioral Research, Inc.*, prevented animal welfare organizations from obtaining standing to enforce Animal Welfare Act. Organizations may now seek to change legislation to address the problem.

353.  Kuntz, Phil. "Animal Rights Activists Find Themselves on Defensive," *Congressional Quarterly Weekly Report* 48 (July 21, 1990):2300–2.

Legislation is starting to turn against animal rights movement. Discusses several pieces of legislation passed or pending, with emphasis on a series of proposed bills that would make breaking into a lab and removing or disseminating lab documents a felony.

354.  Leavitt, Emily S., et al. *Animals and Their Legal Rights: A Survey of American Law from 1641 to 1990*, 4th ed. Washington, DC: Animal Welfare Institute, 1990.

Historical overview of laws pertaining to animal welfare in U.S. Looks at treatment of farm animals, laboratory animals, companion animals, and others. Texts of significant laws on animal welfare included.

355.  "More Humane Treatment of Animals," *CSM* 16 August 1984:19.

Two bills proposed in Congress that would regulate the treatment of lab animals and ban steel leghold traps are facing stiff opposition. The growth of animal rights organizations and membership in traditional animal welfare organizations is growing.

356.  Moretti, Daniel S. *Animal Rights and the Law*. New York: Oceana Pubs, 1984.

Compilation of state and federal laws enacted to regulate people's actions toward animals. Includes sections on anticruelty laws, laboratory welfare, trapping, animal fighting, wildlife legislation, food animal slaughtering, and animal transportation.

357. Quade, Vicki. "Animal Rights Law: Barking up a New Tree," *American Bar Association Journal* 68 ( June 1982):663.

358. Regan, Tom. "Foreword: Animal Rights and the Law," *Saint Louis University Law Journal* 31 (September 1987): 513–17.

359. Rikleen, Laureen Stiller. "The Animal Welfare Act: Still a Cruelty to Animals," *Boston College Environmental Affairs Law Review* 7 (1978):129–45.
A look at Animal Welfare Act (AWA), with particular focus on the role of the enforcing agency, the U.S. Department of Agriculture (USDA). Failure of AWA is primarily due to USDA administrative problems and USDA's lack of interest in this particular law.

360. Ross, Kenneth D. "Patient or Property," *AA* 9 (February 1989):14–15.
Animals are classified legally as chattel or property, and when they are maltreated, the courts have traditionally awarded only "market value" or replacement cost to owner as recompense. Yet some courts in Texas, New York, and Hawaii have awarded as much as $3,000 when an animal has been maliciously killed, recognizing owner's anxiety, stress, and mental suffering. Tips included for pet owners on how to protect animals from veterinarian malpractice.

361. Siepp, Catherine. "We Have Rights: Who Speaks for Animals?" *Los Angeles Daily Journal* 95 ( January 11, 1982):6.

362. Sitomer, Curtis J. "Do Animals Have Rights?" *Los Angeles Daily Journal* 102 (February 1, 1989):6.

363. Stevens, Christine. "The Legal Rights of Animals in the United States of America," *Animal Regulation Studies* 2 (December 1979):93–102.

364. Stewart, James B., "Animals Lose a Voice in the Fight for Their Constitutional Rights," *WSJ* 12 December 1983:29.

*Animal Rights Law Reporter* headed up by Brooklyn attorney, Mark Holzer, has folded. A paucity of animal rights decisions is the reason given for the journal's demise.

365. Swanson, Janice C. *Animal Welfare Legislation and Regulations, January 1979–February 1991,* Quick Bibliography Series QB 91–63. Beltsville, MD: Animal Welfare Information Center, National Agricultural Library, March 1991, A17.18/4:91–63.

Approximately 330 citations taken from AGRICOLA database, examining legislation and regulations on care, use, and treatment of animals in the U.S. and other countries. Includes books, magazine articles, government documents, and organizational proceedings.

366. Tischler, Joyce S. "Rights for Non-Human Animals: A Guardianship Model for Dogs and Cats," *San Diego Law Review* 14 (March 1977):484–506.

Proposes guardianship model for animals, which emphasizes rights they have independent of human interests and provides a means by which to protect these rights.

367. United States. Congress. Conference Committees, 1976. *Animal Welfare Act Amendments of 1976: Report to Accompany S1941.* Washington, DC: U.S. Government Printing Office, 1976, 94–2: H.rp.976.

368. United States. Congress. House. *Animal Welfare Act.* Hearing before the Subcommittee on Administrative Law and Governmental Relations of the Committee on the Judiciary House of Representatives, 100th Cong., 2nd Sess., on HR1770, September 16, 1988. Washington, DC: U.S. Government Printing Office, 1989, Y4.J89/1:100/76.

Hearing held on HR 1770, which would allow an individual or organization to commence civil action on behalf of any animal protected by the Animal Welfare Act.

369. United States. Congress. House. *Animal Welfare Act Amendments of 1975.* Hearing before the Subcommittee on

Livestock and Grains of the Committee on Agriculture,
94th Cong., 1st Sess., on HR5808 and Related Bills,
September 9–10, 1975. Washington, DC: U.S. Government Printing Office, 1975, Y4.Ag8/1:An5/9.

Hearing on the proposed HR5808 and other bills that
would give protection to animals in transport, strengthen
enforcement of Animal Welfare Act regulations, and improve conditions for laboratory animals.

370. United States. Congress. House. *Commission on Humane
Treatment of Animals.* Hearing before the Subcommittee on
Livestock and Grains of the Committee on Agriculture,
94th Cong., 2nd Sess., on HR1112, September 30, 1976.
Washington, DC: U.S. Government Printing Office, 1976,
Y4.Ag8/1:An5/10.

371. "Vivisectors vs. the Right to Know," *AA* 9 (May 1989):23.
New York Supreme Court dismissed a 1984 libel suit
brought against editor of the *Journal of Medical Primology,*
Dr. Jan Moor-Jankowski, who ran a letter from
International Primate Protection League revealing
Immuno Corp. planned to use chimpanzees in hepatitis
research in Africa. Moor-Jankowski was backed up by
American Civil Liberties Union and several animal pro-
tection groups but not by publisher of the journal.

372. Winters, Mary A. "Cetacean Rights Under Human
Laws," *San Diego Law Review* 21 (July/August 1984):
911–40.

373. Wise, Stephen. "Legal Advice for Avoiding Lawsuits," *AA*
10 (July/August 1990):24–5+.
Animal rights activists and organizations are increasingly being sued for defamation by furriers, factory farmers, and biomedical researchers. Discusses protection of
free speech under First Amendment and definition of slander and libel and gives suggestions for avoiding lawsuits.

374. Zak, Steven. "Why Prosecutors Shouldn't Let Animal

Abusers off the Hook," *Los Angeles Daily Journal* 20 September 1990:6.

Laws exist in America to protect animals, but enforcement is spotty and prosecutions rare. Courts should take another look. When animal abuse is not punished, viciousness is trivialized.

375.   Zelezny, John. "The Crusade for Animal Rights Is Definitely Here to Stay," *Los Angeles Daily Journal* 96 (December 7, 1983):4.

# IV FACTORY FARMING AND VEGETARIANISM

Millions of cows, their calves, chickens, pigs, lambs, and other animals are bred, raised, and slaughtered each year for meat and by-products. Many of these factory-farmed animals spend their lives in overcrowded pens or cages under severe restriction of movement that disallows even the most basic instinctual behaviors. Transport to the slaughterhouse and standard slaughtering procedures are often brutal.

Regulationists wish to see legislation that would eliminate the worst abuses of factory farming. Appropriate housing, the opportunity for an animal to live a more or less "natural" life, and the institution of humane slaughtering methods are all targets of an agenda for reform.

Abolitionists condemn the abuses of the factory farm, believing the killing of animals for food is a violation of an animal's basic right to its own life. They believe humane slaughter is a contradiction in terms and promote vegetarianism as part of an ethical life-style. In addition to these arguments, activists also point to the negative impact livestock production has on the environment and to research documenting the unhealthy consequences of an animal-centered diet high in saturated fats and low in fiber.

Animal rights activities include the investigation and exposure of factory-farming practices, an educational campaign focusing on the advantages of a vegetarian diet, and legal initiatives to better the lives of animals raised for food.

## General

376.    Adams, Carol J. *The Sexual Politics of Meat: A Feminist-Vegetarian Critical Theory.* New York: Continuum, 1990.

Vegetarianism and feminism are contrasted with meat eating and societal male dominance. Meat eating is usually identified with men and often stands as a symbol of men's virility. Vegetables on the other hand are women's food and feminine, representing passivity. Attitudes toward meat as well as the practice of securing it have their counterpart in oppression of women. Many early feminists were vegetarians, and literature is filled with meat-eating and vegetarian symbols relating to female characters; yet both these factors are often ignored or downplayed by biographers and literary critics.

377. Amato, Paul R., and Sonia A. Partridge. *The New Vegetarians.* New York: Plenum, 1989.
     Many contemporary vegetarians say they adopted a meatless diet for ethical reasons and out of concern for factory-farm animals.

378. "Animal Rights Group Here to Stay," *National Provisioner* 202 (April 30, 1990):12+.
     Meat industry hears at national conference that animal rights movement will continue to yield influence. Meat and poultry processors must respond by information programs, legislative initiatives, and facility design that considers animal welfare.

379. "Animal Welfare Movement Not Temporary Fanatics," *Feedstuffs* 57 (February 11, 1985):3–4.

380. Bartlett, Kim. "Of Men and Meat: A Conversation with Carol Adams," *AA* 10 (October 1990):12–4+.
     Carol Adams, author of *The Sexual Politics of Meat,* discusses male dominance and patriarchal societies as reflected in the custom of meat eating.

381. Bebee, Charles N. *Farm Animal Welfare, 1979–1987.* Quick Bibliography Series QB 87–69. Beltsville, MD: Special Services Branch, National Agricultural Library, 1987, A17.18/4:87–69.

More than 250 citations drawn from AGRICOLA database, assessing behavioral needs, housing conditions, health, and husbandry practices of farm animals covering journal articles, books, government, and organizational publications.

382. Berry, Rynn J. *The Vegetarians*. Brookline: MA: Autumn Press, 1979.

383. Blaz, Michael. "Getting Serious About Animal Rights," *Humanist* 43 (July/August 1983):30.
     A contradiction exists when people become indignant over the mistreatment of some animals while eating others. Yet vegetarianism requires a radical change in behavior that many are unwilling to make. Suggests those who find it hard to go all the way become semivegetarians by cutting consumption of animals raised in highly degrading environments or by eating animal flesh only on special holidays. We can easily survive without murdering animals, a compelling moral argument for not doing so.

384. Brown, Larry. "Should Fish Be Exempt from Humane Consideration," *AA* 8 (September/October 1988):38–39.
     Fifty-nine million people in America see fishing as a sport and justify it as necessary for food. Yet a fish yanked from water can take hours to die, suffocating slowly as its need for water-born oxygen goes unmet.

385. Callen, Paulette. "Childhood Memory," *AV* 2 (February 1989):36–37.
     The author's childhood recollection of a visit to a pig slaughterhouse; the smell of blood and raw flesh; the sight of struggling; terrorized pigs; the sound of their screaming.

386. Clifton, Merritt. "Death Before Slaughter," *AA* 9 (February 1989):24.
     About 11.4 percent of all factory-farm animals never live long enough to make it to slaughter: 36 million laying hens, 18 million turkeys, and 24 million pigs die from heat,

stress, and disease. More than 5.2 billion animals are slaughtered, and the deaths of 667 million are listed as from "other" causes.

387.  Clifton, Merritt. "The Myth of the Good Shepherd," *AA* 3 (May 1990):24–8+.

A hard look at the sheep industry and the abuse inherent in the practice of breeding and raising sheep and lambs for wool and meat. The concept of the "Good Shepherd" is called into question.

388.  Clifton, Merritt. "World Veggies, Farm Animals, and Gandhi's Birthday," *AA* 9 (January 1989):29.

Members of the Farm Animal Reform Movement held a sit-in at the offices of the U.S. Department of Agriculture in support of a proposal to establish a federal Farm Animal Welfare Advisory Commission. The sit-in was in conjunction with World Farm Animals Day, World Vegetarian Day, and Gandhi's birthday. Other activities to commemorate these special days included memorial services at the United Nations building, vegetarian banquets in Raleigh, North Carolina, a funeral procession at the Denver Livestock Exchange Building, and demonstrations outside the Meat Board in Chicago.

389.  Coats, David. *Old MacDonald's Factory-Farm: The Myth of the Traditional Farm and the Shocking Truth About Animal Suffering in Modern Agribusiness.* New York: Crossroads/Continuum, 1989.

Children's books idealize animal life on the farm, with many having pictures of Old MacDonald tending kindly to his cows as they contentedly chew on their cud. Today's factory farms are a far cry from that romantic picture. High-volume, high-tech factory farming has rendered such traditional scenes outdated and inaccurate. Details the abusive practices and cruelty to animals raised in this new environment.

390.  "Danger: Animal Lovers," *Progressive* 45 (October 1981): 10–11.

Discusses the steps agribusiness can take to make life more humane for livestock.

391. Dean, Tom. "A Call for an Eggless Easter," *Christian Century* 107 (April 11, 1990):358–59.
Condemns the unnatural and harsh living conditions under which factory-farm chickens live and urges readers to send a message to the poultry industry by having Easter eggless hunts.

392. "Delaware Activists Raid a Henhouse," *NYT* 15 June 1986:A34.
Farm Freedom Fighters liberated twenty-five hens from Sydel's egg farm to draw attention to farm animal oppression.

393. Eftink, B. "All Animal Rights Activists Are Not the Same," *Successful Farming* 85 (January 1987):B1.

394. Feder, Barnaby J. "Pressuring Perdue," *NYT Magazine* 26 November 1989:32.
Henry Spira, 62-year-old animal rights activist, has launched a public relations attack against Frank Perdue and the inhumane way he raises chickens. It's no picnic for humans who work there either. Looks at other animal rights organizations, their tactics, and issues and places Spira as a moderate among more radical voices in the movement. He operates as a lone wolf with some financial backing from the Humane Society and the American Society for the Prevention of Cruelty to Animals.

395. Foster, Catherine. "Behind the Veal Protest That Hit Burger King," *CSM* 7 December 1982:7.
Burger King removes veal sandwich from its menu but denies that the animal rights boycott and protests influenced its decision.

396. Foster, Catherine. "Why Animal Rights Groups Target the Veal Sandwich," *CSM* 20 May 1982:1.
A coalition of fifty animal rights groups are boycotting

Burger King in the U.S., Canada, and New Zealand in an effort to have the restaurant remove veal from its menu.

397.   Fox, Michael W. *Agricide: The Hidden Crisis That Affects Us All.* New York: Schocken Books, 1986.
       Not only is factory farming cruel to animals bred and raised for food, but it also destroys our environment, wastes our resources, and pollutes our land and water.

398.   Fox, Michael W. *Farm Animals: Husbandry, Behavior, and Veterinary Practice.* Baltimore: University Park Press, 1984.
       Outlines behavioral and health problems produced in livestock by factory-farming methods. Suggests ways to improve living conditions for farm animals for both humane and practical reasons.

399.   Fox, Michael W. "Intensive Factory-Farming and the Question of Animal Rights," *Animal Regulation Studies* 2 (1980):175–90.

400.   Frank, Jonny. "Factory Farming: An Imminent Clash Between Animal Rights Activists and Agribusiness," *Boston College Environmental Affairs Law Review* 7 (1979):423–61.
       Offers strategies of reform in factory farming for animal interest groups. Describes abusive conditions of factory farming, surveys and critiques federal and state legislation and the lack of protection it affords farm animals, and looks at foreign laws as possible models for reform.

401.   Free, Ann Cottrell. "A Snarling Carnivorous Column," *WP* 25 June 1983:A17.
       Accuses the *Washington Post* of media ambivalence on animal issues and chastises it for its recent frivolous and cutesy article on meat eating. Many religions and humanists consider vegetarianism, as well as other animal welfare issues, worthy of serious discussion.

402.   Freese, Betsy. "Production," *Successful Farming (Iowa Edition)* 88 (May 1990):25.
       Admits there are some abuses to farm animals. Lists

four production changes that farmers could make to become more humane. Standard defense by agriculturalists
that if animals were abused, they wouldn't grow so darn
well isn't good enough anymore.

403.   Grandin, Temple. "Calf-Handling Needs Improvement,"
       *Meat and Poultry* 36 (July 1990):88.
       Dairy industry's record of handling newborn calves is
       not good. Survey done by Humane Society indicated calf-
       throwing and dragging as high as 25 percent at livestock
       auctions. Such blatant cruelty could be overcome by better
       management and better-trained employees.

404.   Handley, Virginia. "The Slave Market," *AV* 2 (February
       1989):50–52.
       Injury and pain to animals during transportation and
       unloading at feedlots and slaughterhouses are common oc-
       currences. Milk cows who cannot get off the truck on their
       own are tied to a post and the truck driven out from under
       them. Animals kept overweight and inactive during most of
       their short life are unable to navigate the maze of chutes
       and ramps, so are kicked, prodded, and clubbed toward the
       slaughterer. Those that are injured, or "downers" as they
       are called, are left to die without food, water, or veterinary
       help. The meat industry loses a billion dollars a year from
       these types of deaths, illnesses, and injuries but can absorb
       the cost due to the great volume of animals slaughtered.

405.   Hibbert, Bob. "Animal Rights or Animal Welfare?" *Meat
       Processing* 29 (June 1990):20.
       Meat industry must take the positions that while animals
       should be treated humanely, they do *not* have rights, and
       that it is legitimate to use them for human needs such as
       food, clothing, and scientific research. Animal rights car-
       ried to its logical extreme would be the end of the meat in-
       dustry.

406.   Hillinger, Charles, and Mark A. Stein. "Animal Activists
       Blamed in Wide Ranch Sabotage," *LAT* 19 November
       1989:A1.

FBI warns Nevada ranchers to be on lookout for animal rights activists and militant vegetarians who may be attacking remote ranches in attempt to undermine sheep and beef-growing industries.

407.  Holden, Constance. "Rights for Farm Animals," *Science* 223 (March 2, 1984):914.
       The Humane Society of the United States will try to promote more humane treatment of livestock. Veterinarian Michael Fox, a longtime advocate for reform on the farm, wants to forge an alliance among small farmers, independent producers, and public who care about food, animals, and the environment. A congressional bill introduced by Rep. James Howard would create a commission to investigate animal husbandry practices.

408.  "How to Cope with Animal Welfare: Be Positive," *Farm Journal* 105 (October 1981):23.

409.  James, Carollyn. "Keeping 'Em Down on the Farm," *Science* 5 (September 1984):77–78.
       The Humane Society of the United States (HSUS) and its scientific director, Michael Fox, are launching a public campaign during National Meat Week to improve living conditions of livestock and to eliminate stress, cruelty, and disease inherent in factory-farming methods. HSUS is asking the American meat eater to "be a vegetarian or conscientious omnivore."

410.  Knight, Jerry. "Force Feeding Moral Issues onto Corporate Agendas," *WP* 11 March 1985:WB1.
       Animal rights activist Peter Lovenheim has filed a lawsuit that would force Iroquois Brands Co. to include a resolution in its proxy statement calling for an investigation into treatment of French geese raised for pâté.

411.  Kopperud, Steve. "Media Campaign Attacks Veal Production," *Feedstuffs* 53 (December 21, 1981):1–2.

412.  Linneman, Judith Ann. "The Structure and Correlates of

Iowans' Attitude About Farm Animal Welfare Issue: A LISREL Approach." Ph.D. dissertation, Iowa State University, 1985.

Animal rights movement is growing in U.S. and Western Europe, but sociologists have yet to study it. Linneman attempts to characterize status of farm animal welfare issue in Iowa, using a linear structural relationship model to show demographics of those who support animal welfare legislation and those who do not.

413. "Livestock Producers Told to Heed Animal Welfarists Before Government Acts," *Feedstuffs* 53 (April 13, 1981): 6–7.

414. Logsdon, Gene. "Maybe the Animal Rights Movement Is Good for Us," *Farm Journal* 113 (January 1989):26-D.

Most animal rights activists pose less of a threat to farming industry than do no-till chemical companies and large-scale livestock farming interests, which are pushing out small farmers. Animal rights activists have a good point when they say it is possible and profitable to produce chemically free, healthful, and delicious food while also treating animals humanely.

415. Macauley, David. "From Craft to Commodity: Leather and the Leather Industry," *AA* 8 (September/October 1988):14–21.

History of leather making and its gradual evolution from a family trade and means of survival to a $1.5-billion industry that requires the death of millions of animals each year. Leather is now an article of status and an accessory to fashion, but animals are the losers.

416. Macauley, Dave. "From the Forest to the Factory: Turkeys and the Turkey Industry," *AA* 7 (November 1987):36–38.

How the majestic wild turkey became the diseased and deformed domestic one raised on today's factory farms.

417. Mason, Jim. "And the Cow Jumped Over the Moon," *AV* 2 (February 1989):42–49.

Documents difference between raising livestock on the family farm and raising them on the factory farm. With each new technological advance, billions of pigs, cows, chickens, and turkeys are housed in smaller and more crowded conditions. Many factory-farm animals are kept indoors and in darkness, chained perpetually to their crate or stall. They are fed antibiotics and hormones and squeezed to their biological limits to produce meat, milk, and eggs. Livestock are looked at as machines and are treated accordingly.

418.   Mason, Jim. "Down on the Factory Pharmacy," *AA* 10 (July/August 1990):47–49.
       Fifteen million pounds of antibiotics are used in animal production each year to stave off the disease endemic to animal populations kept indoors in the overcrowded, dirty conditions of the factory farm. Drugs offer agribusiness a tool to keep intensive farming profitable when otherwise it would be a disaster.

419.   Mason, Jim. "Indiana: The Chicken Feed State, or How Our Food Choices Affect Wildlife," *AV* 3 (August 1990):76.
       Asking the butcher to wrap your meat in paper instead of styrofoam is being environmentally penny-wise and pound-foolish. One has to stop eating the meat to end the waste of energy, croplands, labor, and other resources that go into meat production and steal habitat from our planet's wildlife.

420.   Mason, Jim. "Indoctrination down on the Farm," *AV* 9 (October 1990):50.
       Activist remembers how as a child growing up on a farm he resisted the teaching that animals felt nothing and were on earth to serve humans' needs.

421.   Mason, Jim, and Peter Singer. *Animal Factories.* New York: Crown, 1980.
       A detailed look at how pigs, cows, chickens, and veal calves are bred and raised on America's factory farms.

Explains why treatment of animals as "machines" is inefficient, wasteful, and costly. Sees farmer and consumer as much victims of agribusiness as animals. Asserts vegetarianism to be the ultimate solution to eliminating factory farming and its abuses but is willing to entertain a transition stage during which farmers return to traditional and more humane ways of raising livestock.

422. Mason, Jim, and Peter Singer. *Animal Factories,* rev. ed. New York: Harmony Books, 1990.
First published in 1980, this revised edition documents how factory farming not only brutalizes animals but also threatens the existence of small, family-run farms and damages our environment.

423. Mayes, Dorothy. "20,000 March to Stop Animal Agriculture," *National Hog Farmer* 35 (July 15, 1990):28+.
Overview of animal rights march in Washington in June 1990 from the hog farmer's perspective. Activists are being heard in Congress and they have allies there, but others in medical and congressional communities are fighting back.

424. McCarthy, Coleman. "The Great American Meatout," *WP* 28 March 1987:A21.
March 20 is set aside by animal protection advocates to promote the idea of vegetarianism for health and moral reasons. Quotes philosopher Tom Regan as saying the "struggle for animal rights is also a struggle with self. What we are trying to do is transform the moral zombie that society would like us to be into the morally advanced beings we are capable of becoming." McCarthy cites achievements of the animal rights movement.

425. McCarthy, Coleman. "Slaughterhouses: Butchery for Animals, High Danger for Those Who Kill and Hack," *LAT* 12 April 1988:II,7.
Slaughterhouse employees have highest injury and illness rate of all industries as well as the highest annual

turnover rate: 60–100 percent. Urges all to stop eating meat for sake of the worker and the animals.

426.   McGuire, Richard. "Agriculture and Animal Rights," *Vital Speeches* 55 (October 1, 1989):766–68.
       Commissioner of agriculture and markets of the state of New York thinks the decision to use animals as food is one that all of society, not a minority of people, must make. Debate is necessary. Laws already protect farm animals, and it's in best interest of farmer to treat animals well.

427.   "McVeggie Burgers?" *Forbes* 133 (January 2, 1984):16.
       Animal lovers who boycotted veal at Burger King are now agitating for McDonald's to include a veggie burger on its menu.

428.   "Meatout," *AA* 10 (June 1990):35.
       Farm Animals Reform Movement sponsors a vegetarian buffet for members of Congress and their staffs. Across the country, 400 events, from protests to feeding homeless, marked sixth Annual Great American Meatout.

429.   Moran, Victoria. "A Little Fish Now and Then," *AA* 9 (March 1989):49.
       Fish removed from their watery habitat can take up to 7 hours to die from suffocation, and their behavior during that time suggests they are in pain. If that isn't reason enough to stop eating fish, consider depletion in the oceans not only of fish targeted for food but also of other marine animals, such as dolphins and turtles, which also get caught and killed along with the fish.

430.   Muirhead, Sarah. "Agriculture Takes Proactive Stance Toward Animal Rights," *Feedstuffs* 62 (February 19, 1990):18.
       Dr. Hugh Johnson of the American Farm Bureau Federation predicts increased violence, consumer intimidation, and legislative initiatives by animal rights movement. Gives farmers suggestions for preparing to deal with

animal rights activism, including having a clean, well-run operation and improving security.

431. "National Meatless Day Attracts Only Scant Support," *NYT* 21 March 1990:C10.

The Sixth Annual Great American Meatout was marked in cities across the country. Soup kitchens went vegetarian in Pittsburgh, teenage vegetarians passed out leaflets in Philadelphia, and the mayor of Des Moines signed a proclamation recognizing one-day boycott of meat.

432. O'Neill, Molly. "Will Too Many Sentiments Spoil the Cook?" *NYT* 8 August 1990:C1.

Public is becoming more aware of animal rights message about the cruelties involved in raising and eating animals for food. Focuses on boiling lobsters alive and how consumers are beginning to get squeamish about such practices. Notes decrease in veal sales by 15 percent last year as educational campaign showed brutal conditions under which calves are raised. New sensitivity to animal's plight, plus environmental impact and health implications of eating animals, is starting to tweak the public's conscience.

433. Pardue, Leslie. "Hundreds March for Farm Animals," *AA* 8 (September/October 1988):26.

Six hundred people protest inhumane conditions suffered by farm animals at Lancaster Stockyards in Pennsylvania. Protesters, including North American Vegetarian Society, Farm Sanctuary, Trans-Species Unlimited, and Associated Humane Societies, want stockyards to accept basic standards of providing food, water, adequate shelter, and humane euthanasia for downed animals.

434. Robbins, John. "Brave New Chicken," *AA* 9 (June 1989): 12–8+.

Today's culture looks at nature and animals as things to dominate and exploit. An in-depth examination of practices in raising chickens on the factory farm, which frustrates and perverts all the fowl's natural urges and in process produces food unhealthy for humans to consume.

435.   Robbins, John. "The Ground Beneath Our Feet," *AV* 2 (February 1989):59–65.

Makes the connection between the environment and our addiction to meat. Eighty-five percent of soil erosion is due to production of crops fed to livestock. Huge amounts of fertilizer pollute our rivers and water supply and destroy ozone layer. Crops fed directly to humans would make us able to feed more people more healthily and with less damage to the land. It would also save forests here and abroad from being cut down to make room for more cattle grazing.

436.   Robbins, John. "The Joy and Tragedy of Pigs," *AA* 9 (January 1989):12–21.

Discusses undeserved reputation pigs have. They are intelligent, clean, friendly, and good-natured, with a higher IQ than dogs. The only thing disgusting about pigs is our attitude toward them. We use them in cruel experiments and for food, raise them in abominable conditions. Pork producers are in it for profit, and anything cutting into that profit, even something as simple as providing straw to relieve the discomfort of concrete or slatted floors, is not on the agenda.

437.   Schuster, Lynda. "Livestock Lib: Protest Grows on Way Many Farmers Confine Pigs, Hens, Veal Calves: Animal Rightists Seek to Ban Tight Pens, Neck Chains, and Cutting," *WSJ* 18 December 1981:1+.

Article documents change in farming practices from yesteryear to today. Livestock that once ranged freely now are confined and chained, unable to move or turn around. Farmers say a return to traditional practices would make food prices skyrocket. Animal rights activists say they will fight to improve conditions for farm animals and call for a national boycott if necessary.

438. Smith, Rod. "Animal Front Nearly Ready to Raid Farms, Labs," *Feedstuffs* 57 (October 7, 1985):1–2.

439. Smith, Rod. "Animal Rights Advocates, Farmers Must Work Together, Runner Says," *Feedstuffs* 57 (October 14, 1985):29–30.

440. Smith, Rod. "Gross Cruelty Reported at Some Livestock Operations," *Feedstuffs* 53 (June 22, 1981):15–16.

441. Steinmetz, Johanna. "Humane Society Raises Unappetizing Questions About Pâté," *WP* 11 May 1983:A7.
      The Humane Society introduced stockholders' resolution at Iroquois Brand Limited asking the company to stop importing liver pâté from France. Geese are restrained in metal brace with their necks stretched and are force-fed with funnel inserted 10 to 12″ down their throats. An elastic band around the neck prevents regurgitation. The resolution was voted down.

442. Swan, Christopher. "Factory-Farming: Machines with Feeling," *CSM* 8 November 1979:B1+.
      Animals on factory farms are treated like machines, but they are sentient, feeling creatures that can and do suffer when treated abusively.

443. Swinehart; C. "Association Keeps Eyes on Animal Rightists," *National Provisioner* 203 (July 23, 1990):19.
      Suggestions to meat industry for dealing with the animal rights movement include assessing industry's vulnerability and responding to charges with honest and verifiable facts.

444. Thomas, H. S. "Viewpoint: The Animal Rights Issue Is a Reality We Should Not Ignore," *Successful Farming* 83 (June 1985):H14.

445. "Veal Production: Separating Myth and Reality," *Meat Processing* 29 (February 1990):68+.
      Scenes of anemic veal calves languishing in wooden

crates do not reflect reality. Most animals are well treated. One meat-processing company says more buying stations in several states would improve calf treatment at auction or at least reduce amount of time calves are treated badly.

446.  Willman, Michelle L. "The Animal Rights Movement Is Here to Stay," *National Provisioner* 203 (November 5, 1990):8–9.
      In order to fight animal rights movement effectively, meat industry from cattlemen to processors needs to know who the activists are and what they are telling the public.

447.  Wolinsky, Leo C. "Animal Rights Group Says It 'Liberated' 127 Turkeys," *LAT* 25 November 1986:I,3.
      Animal Liberation Front raided two ranches near Sacramento, releasing turkeys destined for Thanksgiving table.

## Philosophy, Ethics, and Religion

448.  Auxter, Thomas. "The Right Not to Be Eaten," *Inquiry* 22 (Summer 1979):221–30.

449.  Berman, Louis A. *Vegetarianism and the Jewish Tradition.* New York: KTAV Books, 1982.

450.  Clooney, Francis X. "Vegetarianism and Religion," *America* 140 (February 24, 1979):133–34.
      Vegetarians are no longer considered oddballs in our society. Reviews reasons for vegetarianism: health, economic, global hunger, ethical. Concludes vegetarianism may be a prudent and religious choice for some Christians.

451.  Devine, Philip E. "The Moral Basis of Vegetarianism," *Philosophy* 53 (October 1978):481–505.
      Examination of the moral and ethical arguments for and against vegetarianism.

452.  Diamond, Cora. "Eating Meat and Eating People," *Philosophy* 53 (October 1978):465–79.

Animal rights discussions often compare treatment of animals with that of humans, saying if it is wrong to kill humans, it must be wrong to kill animals. Instead they should explore issue of why it is wrong to eat humans. One reason is that we have a relationship with humans and don't regard each other as something to eat. The relationship defines the behavior. Philosophers like Tom Regan and Peter Singer are approaching the problem of proper treatment of animals wrongly when they talk about rights and moral status of animals.

453.  Dombrowski, Daniel A. *Philosophy of Vegetarianism*. Amherst, MA: University of Massachusetts Press, 1984.

Historical look at tradition of vegetarianism as an ethical issue, with particular focus on early Greek philosophers.

454.  Dombrowski, Daniel A. "Vegetarianism and the Argument from Marginal Cases in Porphyry," *Journal of the History of Ideas* 45 (January/March 1984):141–43.

Many philosophers of antiquity were vegetarians motivated by reasons of health, belief in transmigration, or concern for animals. Brief look at Porphyry, who argued humans could not claim privileged status against being eaten on basis of rationality, autonomy, or as users of language, since there are many marginal cases within human species, such as infants and the mentally enfeebled, who lack these characteristics.

455.  Dyer, Judith. "Philosophical Aspects of Diet, Ethics, Philosophy, Religion, Animal Rights," in *Vegetarianism: An Annotated Bibliography*, Judith Dyer, comp. Metuchen, NJ: Scarecrow, 1982, pp. 111–23.

Contains 132 citations of books and magazine and journal articles about the philosophical and moral bases of vegetarianism.

456.  Frey, R. G. *Rights, Killing, and Suffering: Moral Vegetarianism and Applied Ethics*. Oxford, England: Blackwell, 1983.

457. Isen, Susan. "Beyond Abolition: Ethical Exchange with Animals in Agriculture," *Between the Species* 1 (Fall 1985):17–24.

458. Kalechofsky, Roberta. *Haggadah for the Liberated Lamb.* Marblehead, MA: Micah Pubs., 1985.

459. Kapleau, Philip. *To Cherish All Life: A Buddhist Case for Becoming a Vegetarian.* San Francisco: Harper & Row, 1982.
    Founder and director of the Zen Center in Rochester, New York, examines the breeding, raising, and slaughter of food animals from a Buddhist perspective. Although some Buddhists eat animal flesh, Kapleau believes interpretation of Buddhist precept of harmlessness to living beings excludes eating animals. Includes a section on how to be a healthy vegetarian and hazards of consuming meat.

460. Narveson, Jan. "Animal Rights," *Canadian Journal of Philosophy* 7 (March 1977):161–78.
    A human's interest in eating meat is not trivial but can give great pleasure, just as does Beethoven's music. Major interests of lesser beings (animals) are not necessarily more important than minor interests of greater beings (humans). The amount of pleasure people get in eating meat exceeds discomfort or pain endured by animals raised for food.

461. Regan, Tom. "But for the Sake of Some Little Mouthful of Flesh," *AV* 2 (February 1989):26–9+.
    Most people love animals. At the same time they eat them. How is it possible to eat what one loves? The answers are varied: habit, ignorance, prejudice. Religion and philosophy, too, play their part. Religion says animals lack a soul, philosophy à la Descartes that they lack consciousness. Yet animals are some body, not some thing, and their death ends a biographical as well as a biological life.

462. Regan, Tom. "The Moral Basis of Vegetarianism," *Canadian Journal of Philosophy* 5 (October 1975):181–214.

463. Regan, Tom. "Utilitarianism and Vegetarianism Again," *Ethics and Animals* 2 (March 1981):2–7.

464. Regan, Tom. "Utilitarianism, Vegetarianism, and Animal Rights," *Philosophy and Public Affairs* 9 (Summer 1980): 305–24.

465. Richards, Stewart. "Forethoughts for Carnivores," *Philosophy* 56 (January 1981):73–88.
     Asks the meat eater three questions: is it morally preferable to kill than not to kill, to eat animals that have suffered cruelly throughout their lives as part of meat production system, and to eat flesh raised on plant protein that could be fed to starving millions? If answer is no to these questions, then perhaps one's moral judgment is being impaired by custom, convenience, or ignorance.

466. Rosen, Steven. *Food for the Spirit: Vegetarianism and the World Religions.* New York: Bala Books, 1987.

467. Schwartz, Richard H. *Judaism and Vegetarianism.* Marblehead, MA: Micah Publications, 1988.

468. Singer, Peter. "Absence of Malice," *AV* 2 (February 1989):8–9.
     Prominent animal rights philosopher is irritated at the way arguments for meat eating keep returning even after being refuted, especially the one that contends that because animals eat other animals, we should too.

469. Singer, Peter. "Utilitarianism and Vegetarianism," *Philosophy and Public Affairs* 9 (Summer 1980):325–37.

470. Sumner, L. W. "The Carnivore Strikes Back," *Dialogue* 23 (December 1984):661–68.
     Disagrees with R. G. Frey's arguments of Multiplicity (becoming a vegetarian will not affect the market or treatment of animals) and Catastrophe (if people stop eating meat, it would result in disastrous economic consequences). Although both Sumner and Frey use utilitarian

arguments, the former finds support for moral vegetarianism, and the latter doesn't.

## Law and Legislation

471.  Aoki, Elizabeth N. "Bill on More Humane Treatment of
      Veal Calves Gains," *LAT* 6 April 1988:I,13.
      A California bill requiring humane treatment of veal
      calves was approved by Senate Judiciary Committee and
      now goes to Senate Appropriations Committee. Hearings
      were often heated, as animal rights groups and members
      of veal and dairy industries clashed.

472.  Aoki, Elizabeth N. "Senate Panel Delays Vote on Bill to
      Protect Veal Calves," *LAT* 23 March 1988:I,19.
      California assemblyman Tom Bates has asked the vote
      on his bill, which would eliminate some of the cruelty in
      raising veal calves, be delayed, citing a full agenda and ab-
      sence of key members as his reasons. His bill is meeting
      stiff opposition from California state agriculture depart-
      ment and California Farm Bureau.

473.  Bennett, Richard E., and Richard F. McCarthy. "Statutory
      Protection for Farm Animals," *Pace Environmental Law
      Review* 3,2 (1986):229–55.
      Examines effectiveness of present state and federal leg-
      islation as it pertains to protection of animals used in agri-
      culture. Focuses on existing statutes, applicable regula-
      tions, and pertinent case law.

474.  "Cow Branding Issue Halts U.S. Plan on Milk Surplus,"
      *WSJ* 17 April 1986:45.
      U.S. District Judge Telesca blocks U.S. Agriculture de-
      partment from requiring dairy cows be branded on the
      face with a hot iron.

475.  House, Charles. "Committee OKs Farm Protection Bill,"
      *Feedstuffs* 62 (October 29, 1990):5.
      House Agriculture Committee approves legislation that

will protect farm and farm research facilities from theft, vandalism, and breaking and entering by animal rights activists.

476. "Humane Society Sues USDA over Branding," *WP* 10 April 1986:A22.

Humane society sues agriculture department for its policy of face branding of dairy cows, alleging it violates established public policy, which favors humane treatment of animals.

477. Richburg, Keith B. "Agriculture Inspectors Scored for Neglecting Animal Welfare," *WP* 9 November 1984:A25.

Agriculture department, charged with enforcing Animal Welfare Act of 1967, isn't fulfilling that responsibility, say animal rights groups.

478. Ross, Elizabeth. "Referendum Would Toughen Massachusetts Farm Rules," *CSM* 1 November 1988:3+.

A Massachusetts referendum sponsored by the Coalition to End Animal Suffering would mandate larger stalls for veal calves, ban the destruction of male chicks by inhumane methods, and impose humane procedures for castrating and dehorning animals. Animal rights activists say every segment of society that uses animals has established some guidelines for animal protection, no matter how minimal. The livestock industry is the one exception.

479. Schneider, Keith. "U.S. Judge Forbids Branding of Cows: Hot Iron Method Endorsed by Administration Is Called Unnecessarily Cruel," *NYT* 17 April 1986:B9.

The Humane Society of Rochester brings a suit against the U.S. Department of Agriculture (USDA) for requiring face branding of 1.55 million livestock. Judge says USDA should have considered alternatives, because face branding obviously constitutes cruelty to animals.

480. Sinclair, Ward. "Protests Fail to Head Off Cow-Branding," *WP* 15 March 1986:A6.

Despite protests of animal rights advocates, agriculture department plans to require dairy cows be face branded as a means of identification. Advocates maintain there are other, less painful and less dangerous ways, such as indelible tattooing.

481.    Sommer, Mark. "Farm Animal Abuse Goes to the Ballot," *AA* 9 (February 1989):26–27.
        Farm animals are the largest group of animals killed each year but are also the most overlooked by animal protection groups and federal regulation standards against cruelty. The Humane Farming Initiative, which would have given greater protection to farm animals in Massachusetts, however, was defeated by the electorate by more than 2:1.

482.    Tischler, Joyce S. "Humane Slaughter: Contradiction in Terms," *AV* 2 (February 1989):80–81.
        Current federal and state laws relating to care, transportation, and slaughter of farm animals offer minimum protection.

483.    United States. Congress. House. *Veal Calf Protection Act.* Joint hearing before Subcommittee on Livestock, Dairy and Poultry and the Subcommittee on Department Operations, Research, and Foreign Agriculture, 101st Cong., 1st Sess., on HR84, June 6, 1989. Washington, DC: U.S. Government Printing Office, 1989, Y4.Ag8/1:101–18.
        Hearing on a bill that would prohibit confining calves in small crates, feeding them a diet deficient in iron, and isolating them from contact with other members of their species.

484.    Wise, Stuart M. "Of Farm Animals and Justice," *Pace Environmental Law Review* 3 (1986):191–227.
        Use of farm animals is fundamentally unregulated at either state or federal level, and animals are treated as nothing more than raw materials. The law allows no outlet for remedy by those who are concerned. In addition, the government does not provide consumer with appropriate or accurate information about the quality of meat.

# V TRAPPING AND FUR INDUSTRY

The animal rights movement is united in its belief that the raising, trapping, and killing of fur-bearing animals for their pelts or
skins cater to the most trivial of human wants. Activists have cam-
paigned vigorously to end the demand for fur coats and other fur
apparel by educating the public to the brutality of the fur industry, by lobbying diligently on state and national levels to abolish
the use of the steel-jaw leghold trap, and by staging large, antifur
demonstrations and rallies in cities across the country.

Of all the animal rights issues, this one enjoys the most unqualified support not only among activists but also among much
of the general public as well.

## General

485. "Anti-Fur Activists Rally in Major Cities," *Women's Wear
     Daily* 155 (February 16, 1988):20.

486. "Anti-Fur Groups Protest in New York," *Women's Wear
     Daily* 153 (June 1, 1987):6.

487. Beck, Melinda, et al. "The Growing Furor over Fur: A
     Brutal Status Symbol," *Newsweek* 112 (December 26,
     1988):52–3.
     Antifur movement is becoming most visible part of the
     animal rights movement. No effect has yet been seen on
     sales in this country, but fur sales in Europe dropped 80
     percent following a similar antifur campaign.

488. Belkin, Lisa. "For Thriving Furriers, Protesters Pose
     Threat," *NYT* 17 December 1985:D1.

Animal rights activists protest across country this weekend with aim of educating public to the suffering fur represents. Fur industry fears power of animal rights appeal, even though its sales reached $1.6 billion this year. Industry is focusing its counterattack on role fur-trapping plays in controlling population of wild animals.

489. Berkman, Meredith. "The Fur Is Flying," *Savvy* 10 (August 1989):18.

The fashion world is in disarray over controversy on fur coats and other such apparel. Some designers are continuing to use animal pelts, but others are signing on to the animal rights antifur campaign.

490. Bradshaw, Patricia. "Fur-tive Behavior," *NYT* 21 December 1989:A31.

Animal rights activists should "grandmother" the fur coat, allowing older women to go unharassed. As fur is seen more and more as suitable for old women, young women will abandon it. Animal rights movement is an urban phenomenon, because in the country, people recognize animals as the nuisances they are. Author wears her fur coat in the country, where people are more sensible about animals.

491. Brown, Elizabeth A. "Furor over Fur Coats Heats Up," *CSM* 17 January 1990:12.

Discusses tactics and arguments of animal rights activists in ending the fur trade. Looks at declining fur sales and financial losses of furriers since 1987.

492. Butler, J. George. "Jaws of Hell: Cruelties of the Leghold Trap," *Christian Century* 92 (July 9–16, 1975):662–65.

Brief history of invention and use of leghold trap, especially in its connection with the Oneida, New York, community and its members' belief in Christian perfectionism. Efforts to ban trap in federal lands is opposed by U.S. Department of the Interior Fish and Wildlife agencies, but many countries and some U.S. states have outlawed them for the great suffering they cause.

493. "Charges Are Dismissed Against 70 Protesters," *Women's Wear Daily* 153 (March 31, 1987):10.

494. Clifton, Merritt. "Antifur Demonstration Began Early This Season," *AA* 9 (January 1989):23.
    Retail fur industry is spending $9 million this year to fight antifur activism, but demonstrations continue in U.S. and Canada.

495. Clifton, Merritt. "How Trapping Affects the Forest," *AA* 9 (November 1989):43–5+.
    Despite trappers' claims to the contrary, trapping has an adverse ecological impact on a forest, which goes far beyond the death of a single animal or even a whole species.

496. Clifton, Merritt. "Knocking Fur to the Canvas," *AA* 10 (September 1990):32–34.
    Antifur movement is making great gains. The last of twenty-two fur salons on upper Broadway closed on July 25. The same is happening in other cities, but fur industry keeps insisting all is well. Animal advocates must keep up the pressure.

497. Clifton, Merritt. "A Profile of the American Trapper," *AA* 8 (November 1987):30–34.
    The typical animal trapper is a male, Caucasian, non-farming rural resident of the Midwest with a high school education.

498. Clifton, Merritt. "Trapbusting for Fun and Exercise," 7 (November 1987):46–47.
    Knowing state regulations and the trapper's techniques and habits can help the animal advocate who wants to deactivate traps set to catch animals.

499. Clifton, Merritt. "TSU's Fur-Free Friday Draws Thousands," *AA* 9 (February 1989):25.
    Two thousand antifur demonstrators marched down Fifth Avenue on November 25 on Fur-Free Friday, led by

television game-show personality Bob Barker. Groups picketed fur stores in fifty other cities as well.

500.  de Kok, Wim. "Prisoners of Vanity," *AV* 2,6 (1989):20–23.
      Fur farming is as cruel as trapping wild animals, for whereas wild animals are in agony for only a few weeks, specially bred minks, chinchillas, raccoons, polecats, beavers, lynxes, and martens languish in small, wire-mesh cages for as long as seven months. Frustrated by not being able to engage in behavior natural to their species, they pace constantly and often indulge in self-mutilation.

501.  Denton, Herbert H. "Cultures Clash Over Game Hunts in Arctic: Canada's Eskimos Battling Array of Animal Rights Groups," *WP* 7 December 1987:A27.
      Eskimos and animal rights activists clash over hunting of wild animals who roam the tundra of the Arctic region. Eskimos remember the "Save the Baby Harp" campaign, which wiped out international markets for seal fur and destroyed marginal, local economies. John Sperry, Anglican bishop of the Arctic, says animal rights movement will be guilty of genocide if it brings an end to fur industry.

502.  Foltz, Kim. "Fur Industry Assails Critics in National Campaign," *NYT* 4 December 1989:D11.
      Fur industry fights back with $2-million public relations campaign against antifur activism. Goal is to convince consumers fur is a freedom-of-choice issue, and next things animal rights will try to ban are leather, wool, and meat. Furriers are worried protest will have same effect in U.S. as in Germany, where animal rights movement destroyed one of the largest fur businesses in the world.

503.  "Fourteen Protesting Fur Sales Arrested Inside Macy's," *NYT* 16 December 1985:B3.
      Activists from Trans-Species Unlimited held a sit-in at Macy's in New York and in stores in Sacramento and Philadelphia as part of nationwide campaign against fur industry.

504. Frankel, Glenn. "Fur Flies from Harrod's: Flat Sales Kill Famed London Salon," *WP* 15 February 1990:B1.

Harrod's, Britain's best-known department store, closed its world-famous fur salon due to slumping sales. Animal rights activists call it a triumph, but fur industry blames demise on economic reasons.

505. "Fur Executives Distressed Over Hike in Violent Acts," *Women's Wear Daily* 153 (May 5, 1987):12.

506. "Fur Industry Seeking Friends," *AA* 10 (October 1990):28–29.

Fur industry founds a group called Putting People First to fight animal rights activism. Group will include furriers, trappers, biomedical researchers, factory farmers, hunters, and fishermen.

507. "Fur Takes a Hiding," *AA* 9 (May 1989):20.

Reports indicate sale of fur fell in 1988 for second straight year. Fur industry and antifur movement each have their own supporters. On furriers' side are celebrity Loni Anderson, ex-ball player Rusty Staub, and trapper John Wisket. On animal rights side are actor River Phoenix, singers Belinda Carlisle and Jane Weidlin, and fashion designer Bill Blass.

508. "The Furriers Fight Back: Attacked, the Fur Industry Shows Its Own Claws," *Newsweek* 114 (December 18, 1989):82.

Fur sales are flat, with some furriers going out of business. The fur industry is spending $2 million on public relations to counter antifur campaign.

509. Gibson, Robert W. "Activists Aim to Skin the Fur Industry: Animal Rights Assaults," *LAT* 30 April 1989:I,1.

Animal advocates in Holland have reduced fur shops from 400 to 32, and the country is being called first "fur-free" society. American activists hope to have equal success in dismantling fur industry in this country. They have been

consulting with top Netherlands animal rights activists and
using some Netherlands' public awareness materials.

510.    Glover, Mark. "And All in the Name of Fashion," *AV* 2,6
(1989):18–20.
An indictment of the steel-jawed leghold trap, which inflicts severe and immediate injury on the trapped animal
held prisoner by it for hours, days, and sometimes weeks
before being suffocated, shot, or beaten to death by the
trapper. An inessential activity based only on the dictum
that it is fashionable to wear fur.

511.    Gornery, Greg. "Trappers Convention Draws 200
Protesters," *AA* 7 (November 1987):18–19.
Demonstrators from five states and eight animal rights
organizations protested at National Trappers Association
Convention in Mansfield, Ohio.

512.    Hirsch, James. "Animal Rights Groups Step Up Attack on
Furriers," *NYT* 27 November 1988:I,50.
Animal rights groups are mounting antifur campaign in
New York—the fur capital—trying to make fur wearing as
unfashionable as cigarette smoking. Furriers and associated trade groups say activists have vandalized their stores
and harassed customers. Animal rights leaders say their
aim is to embarrass and stigmatize fur wearers, not to injure them.

513.    Hochswender, Woody. "As Image of Furs Suffers, So Do
Revenues," *NYT* 14 March 1989:A1.
Fur industry has fallen upon hard times as sales fall and
flatten. Furriers, who are quoting the Bible to justify their use
of animal skins, say animal rights protest not the only threat
to the industry. Foreign competition has also taken its toll,
some designers like Blass and Herrera have stopped using
fur, and fur is becoming deglamorized and unfashionable.
Fur district in New York has shrunk from 800 manufacturers
in 1979 to 300 today. Discusses economic and marketing
changes as furriers try to cope with changing times.

514. Kasindorf, Jeanie. "The Fur Flies: The Cold War Over Animal Rights," *New York Magazine* 23 (January 15, 1990):26–33.

    Looks at reasons behind antifur campaign and escalating battle between animal rights advocates and the fur industry. Identifies animal rights movers and shakers, their activities, tactics, and strategies, as well as consideration of counterattack by fur industry.

515. LaGanga, Maria. "Thousands Demonstrate Against Sales of Furs," *LAT* 25 November 1989:D2.

    Antifur activists marched in ninety-one cities in fourth annual fur-free Friday after Thanksgiving.

516. LaGanga, Maria L. "Furriers: Protests Have Hurt Sales for Some Retailers: Others Report Growth," *LAT* 3 December 1989:D1.

    Furriers say although sales dollars are flat, number of units sold is up. Furriers also disagree with animal rights people about the state of health of fur business. Some stores are closing, but many are enjoying increases in sales.

517. Lawson, Carol. "As Women Pull Out Their Furs, Some Wonder Whether They're Asking for Trouble," *NYT* 19 November 1989:I,50.

    Thanksgiving is usually the time women bring their furs out of storage, but some are hesitating this year, fearful of being harassed by antifur activists, and some because they are having second thoughts about morality of wearing fur. Others, however, feel it is a freedom-of-choice issue and plan to wear their furs at times and places when harassment will be unlikely.

518. Mann, Judy. "Pelting Illogical Activism," *WP* 2 December 1988:D3.

    Minks are nasty little animals who have no redeeming value other than their pelts. Mann chastises animal rights activists for championing these animals but says nothing about the millions of food animals killed each year. In any case, why make such a fuss about cruelty to minks when there are homeless people, high illiteracy, and increasing school-dropout rates?

519. Martin, Douglas. "Clubbing of Whitecoat Harp Seal Pups Appears to Be at an End in Canada," *NYT* 10 February 1985:18.
Sealers and opponents to sealing agree commercial clubbing of white-coated harp seal pups in Canada is probably ended for all time. Worldwide protest and legislation reduced demand for pelts from 200,000 in late '70s to 24,000 in 1984.

520. Mason, Jim. "From the Desk of Jim Mason," *AV* 3 (March/April 1990):71.
Fur industry's new public relations campaign attempts to align furriers with other groups targeted by animal rights movement for their abuse of animals.

521. McCarthy, Coleman. "Trapping the Fur Industry," *WP* 8 April 1989:A19.
Characterizes protesters who harass fur customers and wearers with spray paint and screaming as "crackpot wing"of animal rights movement. Traditional methods of educating public about fur industry are more effective in bringing down demand for furs.

522. McDonough, Yona Zeldis. "Sisters Under the Skin," *NYT* 2 April 1988:23.
McDonough defends owning and wearing a fur coat. Chastises female animal rights activists for their rudeness and brutish tactics in accosting women wearing fur coats.

523. "Miss USA Fake Fur Incites Boycott of CBS," *Women's Wear Daily* 153 (February 19, 1987):14.

524. Moran, Victoria. "When the Fur Wearer Isn't the Furbearer," *AA* 9 (September 1989):50–51.
Comments from five animal rights activists on how they confront fur wearers and why.

525. Oakes, John B. "The Fur Coat Trap," *NYT* 29 December 1986:A21.

    Calls for ban of steel leghold traps, citing cruelty and animal suffering as reasons. Opposition to ban comes from National Rifle Association, fur industry, trapper organizations, and U.S. Department of the Interior.

526. Oakes, John B. "Trapped," *NYT* 13 February 1979:A19.

    Steel leghold trap by which the vast majority of fur animals are caught represents torture and suffering. Animals thrash wildly, some biting off their paw in order to escape, but most after hours of struggle lie inert and exhausted to wait sometimes for as much as three days for trapper to come and kill them.

527. "Parsons Named Head of 'Fur Is for Life,' " *Women's Wear Daily* 152 (October 28, 1986):16.

528. "Pride in Fur Is Promoted by Alaskans," *NYT* 20 March 1990:A20.

    Alaskan natives are fighting back against antifur campaign. Will include special labels indicating fur garment was made by traditional methods, with the hope of inspiring consumer pride in supporting Native Alaskan life-style.

529. "Protest at Macy's Leads to 65 Arrests," *Women's Wear Daily* 153 (February 17, 1987):24.

530. "Protesters Picket New Haven Show," *Women's Wear Daily* 154 (September 8, 1987):49.

531. "Protests Make Small Impact on Holiday Business for Stores," *Women's Wear Daily* 152 (December 4, 1986):16.

532. Reed, J. D., Scott Brown, and Andrea Sachs. "The Furor Over Wearing Furs," *Time* 134 (December 18, 1989):72.

    Until now, a fur coat was a status symbol, but a better understanding of how fur is obtained and condemnation of fur by celebrities and others have started to change minds.

533. Regan, Tom. "On the Secret Life of the Fur Trade: Vacant Vault," *AV* 2,6 (1989):24–32.

     Fur Information Council of America is launching a new public relations effort to fight antifur movement. Council advises fur industry to avoid debating animal rights advocates in a public forum, to withhold advertising dollars from media that gives time to antifur messages, to keep the story off television and out of the press, to paint animal rights activists as terrorists comparable to the IRA and Libyans. Nevertheless, fur sales continue to decline.

534. Richter, Paul. "Furrier Seeks Chapter 11 Bankruptcy Protection," *LAT* 30 December 1989:D2.

     Antonovich, Inc., files for bankruptcy, and Fur Vault, Inc., is up for sale. Animal rights advocates celebrate, but fur industry blames its problems on overexpansion rather than antifur protests.

535. "Rights Group Holds Anti-Fur Protest," *Women's Wear Daily* 154 (November 30, 1987):10.

536. Rosen, Yereth. "Native Alaskans Defend Tradition," *CSM* 12 April 1990:6.

     Native Alaskans say basis of their economy is fur, and the antifur movement threatens their culture. They are fighting back and have created the 500-member Yukon Flats Fur Cooperative, which will market Alaskan furs sewn in traditional Alaskan fashion.

537. Solomon, Jolie. "Long Shot Ad Campaign: Making Furriers an Animal's Best Friend," *WSJ* 7 October 1986:35.

     Furriers, fearing animal rights activities will hurt sales, try to change their image with ad campaign slogans of "Fur Is for Life" and "An Industry in Harmony with Nature."

538. Stange, Mary Zeiss. "When 'Faux' Replaces Fox," *LAT* 20 December 1989:B7.

     Animal rights argument that real people wear fake fur is

illogical. If one feels compassion for furred creatures, why would one want to wear a coat that mimics a jaguar or tiger. Animal rights folks also use real furs as props in anti-fur protests in a way that does not convey respect for animals.

539. Trachtenberg, Jeffrey A. "Fur Industry Braces for a Rough Season: Activism Grows But Sellers Hold Some Optimism," *WSJ* 6 November 1989:B1.
    Furriers deny decline in fur sales is due to animal rights antifur campaign and say warm weather and overproduction are the reasons. Some in fur trade say the downward trend will reverse and sales will reach a record high in the coming year.

540. Trebay, Guy. "Fur Flies," *Village Voice* 34 (February 7, 1989):15.
    Animal rights groups step up activities in attacking the fur industry and harassing people who wear furs.

541. Yen, Marianne. "Animal Rights Groups Harass Fur Wearers," *WP* 11 March 1989:A3.
    New York is capital of $2-billion fur industry and focus of animal rights antifur protests.

## Law and Legislation

542. "Anti-Trapping Bill Expected in N.Y.," *Women's Wear Daily* 150 (November 14, 1985):22.

543. Baughman, Michael. "The Authors Sees a Vote for Trapping as One for Needless Pain and Death," *Sports Illustrated* 53 (November 3, 1980):93.
    Oregon-Ballot Measure 5 would prohibit use and sale of leghold, snare, and body-grip traps for fur taking.

544. Bishop, Katherine. "California Supports Opponents of Animal Traps," *NYT* 27 October 1987:A28.

Opponents of steel-jawed leghold traps welcome news from the California attorney general's office that any county may ban these traps without being preempted by state law. Animal rights activists are now planning to move county by county for such ordinances.

545.   "Fur Democratized," *WSJ* 16 February 1990:A12.
Editorial about Aspen's electorate's voting down 2:1 the proposal to ban fur sales.

546.   Harris, Ron. "The Fur Is Flying in Trend-setting Aspen Over a Measure to Ban the Sale of Animal Skins," *LAT* 25 December 1989:A41.
In a few months, residents of Aspen, Colorado, will cast a vote for or against ban on sale of fur in their city. A summer poll shows antifur group trailing by 36–47 percent

547.   Harris, Scott. "Aspen Voters Reject Ban on Clothing Made of Animal Pelts," *LAT* 14 February 1990:A3.
Aspen County voters defeated proposed ban on sale of animal furs by 2:1. Fur backers said it was a matter of freedom of choice, while Mayor Bill Stirling; his wife, Katherine Thalberg, head of Aspen Society for Animal Rights; and Peter Singer, activist/philosopher, said banning furs expands human ethical horizons.

548.   Johnson, Dirk. "Some View Battle in Snow Country as Turning Point in War Over Fur," *NYT* 12 February 1990:A18.
Issue debated by mainstream America now comes to a vote in Aspen, Colorado. Should the selling of fur be banned?

549.   "Law to Ban Leghold Traps Sought by Wildlife Groups," *NYT* 29 March 1980:25+.
Wildlife and animal welfare groups step up efforts to have leghold traps banned. Comments from trappers, wildlife conservationists, game officials, and animal rights groups.

550. "N.J. Assembly to Vote on Ban of Steel Leg Traps," *Women's Wear Daily* 147 (January 5, 1984):8.

551. Passamano, Russell J. "Animal Protection—Trapping Regulations—N.J. Stat. Ann. 23:4–11 (West 1984)," *Seton Hall Legislative Journal* 8 (1984):382–85.
    Provisions of New Jersey law that prohibits manufacture, possession, sale, and use of steel-jaw leghold traps.

552. Reid, T. R. "Animal-Rights Referendum Sets Fur Flying in Aspen," *WP* 13 February 1990:A3.
    Proposed referendum to ban sale of fur in Aspen, Colorado, is part of new political battle between the rich and not-so-rich.

553. Shiflett, Dave. "The Fur Flies in Aspen," *WSJ* 8 February 1990:A16.
    Aspen's mayor Bill Sterling campaigns for a ban on fur sales in the city.

554. "Suffolk County Vetoes Steel Jaw Trap Ban," *Women's Wear Daily* 152 (December 16, 1986):10.

555. United States. Congress. House. *Painful Trapping Devices.* Hearing before the Subcommittee on Fisheries and Wildlife Conservation and the Environment of the Committee on Merchant Marine and Fisheries, 94th Cong., 1st Sess., on HR66, November 17, 18, 1975. Washington, DC: U.S. Government Printing Office, 1976. Y4.M53: 94–118.

# VI COMPANION ANIMALS

Many in the animal rights movement consider as companions or friends the dogs and cats who share our homes. Overpopulation of these animals by indiscriminate breeding or human indifference, however, has produced a crisis today in animal shelters and pounds, where millions of stray, abandoned, or surrendered animals are euthanized each year while others end up as experimental subjects in research laboratories.

Confronting the problem of the overpopulation of companion animals has been associated primarily with traditional animal welfare organizations, but in the past few years, animal rights advocates have taken a harder look at the problem and tried to find ways to eliminate the slaughter of so many animals. Educational campaigns, support for low-cost neutering and spaying clinics, and legal initiatives to restrict the indiscriminate breeding of dogs and cats are the main focus of their activities. They have also worked to stop animal research labs from obtaining such animals, believing that "pets" don't belong in the laboratory and that the practice of releasing shelter animals to research laboratories undermines the public trust in shelters as safe havens for abandoned animals.

556.  Anchel, Marjorie. "Shelter Animals Make Poor Research Subjects (letter)," *NYT* 21 March 1987:26.
      President of Scientists Group for Reform of Animal Experimentation says pound animals are unsuitable for scientific research because of their unknown genetic and medical background. In addition, using such animals invalidates shelters as places where people can leave their animals and know they will be provided for.

557.  "Animal Research and People Sense," *LAT* 8 July 1983:II,6.
      Editorial maintains research using shelter and pound

animals is all right, because animals would only be put to death anyway. Opposes Roberti bill, which would ban selling or buying of pound animals by research institutions in California.

558. "Animals and Research," *LAT* 29 May 1984:II,4.

Editorial maintains Roberti bill to ban sale of shelter animals to research appeals to the heartstrings, not the mind. Supports instead Filante bill, which would establish a balance between heart and mind by protecting pets as well as research that saves human lives.

559. "Behind the Pet Store Window," *AV* 3 (March/April 1990):33.

Pet stores encourage and support puppy mills, an industry that produces litters of unhealthy animals deprived of adequate shelter, cleanliness, sufficient food, water, and veterinary care.

560. "A Christmas Cat Sparks a Street fight," *Newsweek* 108 (December 8, 1986):68.

Animal welfare groups protest Neiman-Marcus's marketing of specially bred cats at $1400 each as advertised in its Christmas catalog. Activists say the company is marketing animals as impulse purchases without addressing the needs of the animals.

561. Christopher, Kristen. "Battle Over Rights of Animals Heats Up: Outcry Stirred by Military Tests Is Only a Part of Nationwide Fight," *LAT* 7 August 1983:I,5.

Under pressure from animal rights groups, defense department canceled its wound experiments on dogs, but battle over animal experimentation using shelter animals is just beginning to heat up. Activists say it's morally wrong and scientifically invalid, because researchers cannot know a pound dog's genetic background and past diseases, nor the vaccinations and medications an animal may have received. Many researchers prefer pound animals to those specially bred, however, because they are cheaper.

562. Cocroft, Anne. "Use of Shelter Dogs in Surgical Training Urged in Loudoun," *WP* 12 March 1984:B1+.

     Animal rights activists protest proposal to allow animal shelters in Loudoun County, Virginia, to give their animals to nearby community college for veterinary surgical training program.

563. DeBakey, Michael E. "Medicine Needs These Animals," *WP* 4 June 1987:A23.

     Famous heart surgeon says much medical progress has been made through animal research and many more future discoveries are possible. Argues pound animals that can be had cheaply would allow researchers to continue their work and that costly purpose-bred animals would close many labs down.

564. Dorschner, John. "See Spot Die," *AV* 3 (March/April 1990):35–38.

     Between 12 and 20 million unwanted pets are euthanized each year at pounds and shelters. Documents grim reality behind these statistics.

565. Dunayer, Eric. "Overpopulation: Do Veterinarians Care?" *AV* 3 (March/April 1990):40.

     Officer in the Association of Veterinarians for Animals Rights says veterinarians contribute to overpopulation of cats and dogs not only because of their apathy to the problem, but also because of their active opposition to low-cost spay/neuter clinics.

566. Dunayer, Joan and Eric. "The Customized Companion Dog," *AA* 10 (November 1990):12–14.

     American Kennel Club and purebred-dog breeders are responsible for breeding inherited defects into dogs for trivial goal of meeting artificial physical standards. Epilepsy, the tendency to develop malignant tumors, hip dysplasia, deformed skulls, and other contrived features that cause suffering and early death are result of selective breeding.

567. Duvin, Edward S. "Benign Neglect," *AV* 3 (March/April 1990):17+.

Animal shelters rationalize euthanization of millions of dogs and cats each year, thus encouraging the public's lack of concern over the tragedy of surplus companion animals. Suggests more aggressive strategy by shelters to involve community in solving overpopulation problem. Calls for a stronger commitment among activists to address this problem in the same way they have done with other animal rights issues.

568. Duvin, Edward S. "In the Name of Mercy," *AV* 3,1 (1990):10–12.

Calls for overhaul of nation's animal shelters. There should be a national umbrella association to gather necessary statistics about shelters, coordinate media campaigns, and most of all find ways to stop euthanizing millions of unwanted animals.

569. Earl, Christopher. "Massachusetts Bans Strays," *Nature* 307 (January 5, 1984):5.

Massachusetts legislature, responding to overwhelming public support, bans selling of dogs and cats by pounds and animal shelters for research purposes. Researchers say this will greatly increase the cost of research, because they will be forced to buy purpose-bred animals; animal advocates say pound animals are not viable research subjects, because their genetic and physical backgrounds are variable and unknown.

570. Engel, Margaret. "Do House Pets Belong in Research Labs?" *Glamour* 85 (September 1987):252.

571. Fogelson, Gail. "Aggressive Behavior in Pit Bulls: Learned or Inborn? Are These Dogs Victims Themselves?" *AA* 9 (January 1989):50–1+.

Are pit bulls genetically aggressive or merely responding to training? Negative publicity may account for false perception of the breed's personality traits. Of the 1–3 million dog bites reported to public agencies each year, only a small fraction can be attributed to pit bulls, and those by ones that were trained and used for dogfighting.

572.   Fox, Jeffrey L. "Animal Rights Bill Defeated in California," *Science* 224 (June 29, 1984):1414.
       Examines recent successes for biomedical community. A California bill was defeated that would have banned the use of pound animals in research, and in Maryland, animal anticruelty laws were amended to be more accommodating to researchers who use lab animals.

573.   Fox, Jeffrey L. "Massachusetts Forbids Use of Impounded Pets in Labs," *Science* 223 (January 13, 1984):151.
       A new law will prevent Massachusetts researchers from obtaining animals from pounds. The state's biomedical research community reluctantly joined animal welfare groups in supporting legislation, fearful worse restrictions would be imposed otherwise.

574.   Francione, Gary. "The Paradigm of Property," *AV* 3 (March/April 1990):68.
       In the eyes of the law, animals are merely property. If a companion animal dies from a veterinarian's negligence, the loss is valued only at the animal's market value, with the veterinarians escaping all claims of liability.

575.   Goldman, Ari L. "Bill Would End Research Using Unclaimed Pets: Senate Debates Treatment of Animals Before Vote," *NYT* 8 May 1979:B3.
       New York State senate repealed a law forcing animal shelters to give their dogs and cats to scientific research institutions.

576.   Greanville, David Patrice. "Holocaust at the Animal Shelter," *AA* 10 (January/February 1990):44–46.
       Activists and the public need to find ways to prevent euthanasia of millions of animals at shelters each year.

577.   Grunow, Steve. "A Reason for Surrender," *AV* 3 (March/April 1990):19–21.

Personal essay by the director of humane education at Santa Clara's Humane Society, listing superficial and often heartless reasons given by those who surrender their dogs and cats to shelters and eventual death.

578. Herbert, W. "State Law Halts Pet Research Projects," *Science News* 125 (January 14, 1984):21.
Massachusetts bans selling of pound animals to research. Both animal rights activists and researchers support law as a compromise.

579. Herrington, Alice. "An Almost Totally Nonfunctional ASPCA (letter)," *NYT* 27 March 1982:22.
Herrington claims American Society for the Prevention of Cruelty to Animals (ASPCA) has $12 million and isn't using it on animal control. Says the city should seize ASPCA assets and take on responsibility of animal control.

580. "In the Name of Mercy: The *Animals Voice* Magazine Takes a Stand," *AV* 3 (December 1990):52–53.
*AV* editor supports Ed Duvin's call for open discussion of euthanization of millions of animals in shelters each year and challenges animal rights organizations and individuals to find creative solutions to problem instead of ignoring it.

581. Kelling, Vanessa. "This Is One Hell of a Job and We Couldn't Do It Without You," *AV* 3 (December 1990): 20–21.
Peninsula Humane Society in San Mateo, California, wants a law passed that would put a moratorium on breeding dogs and cats as a way of decreasing overwhelming number of unwanted animals killed in shelters each year.

582. Kullberg, John F. "Animal Shelter Animals Make Poor Research Subjects (letter)," *NYT* 21 March 1987:26.
President of American Society for the Prevention of Cruelty to Animals says shelters violate public trust when they are forced to sell dogs and cats to biomedical research.

583. Loop, Michael S. "Painful Choices in Pet Protection vs. Research," *WSJ* 3 June 1988:18.

Assistant professor of physiological optics at University of Alabama says implementation of Pet Protection Act, which would ban sale or use of shelter animals to research labs, will raise cost of research. Since most experiments don't involve pain, euthanization of animals whether in an animal shelter or in a lab is a distinction without a difference.

584. Mason, Jim. "For the Pleasure of Their Company," *AV* 3 (March/April 1990):25–27.

Explores psychological reasons behind pet keeping, saying this practice is often a reflection of our conflict both to love and to control nature at the same time.

585. "Massachusetts Outlawing Laboratory Use of Pets," *NYT* 27 December 1983:A21.

Massachusetts state legislature passes a law banning sale of pound dogs and cats to research institutions and forbids import of pound animals from other states. The bill passed in response to pressure from animal rights groups and was not opposed by researchers for fear a more stringent law would be passed in referendum by the public.

586. McCarthy, Coleman. "Shoot Dogs? Or Just Ban Them?" *WP* 20 August 1983:A15.

While much fuss is made about the eighty dogs scheduled to be shot by the Pentagon in wound experiments, nothing is said about the 5 million dogs gassed and drugged each year at animal shelters or about irresponsible owners who let their dogs roam, spreading waste and filth.

587. McDonald, Kim. "Massachusetts Law May Cut Use of Dogs in Research," *Chron H Ed* 27 (January 18, 1984):1.

Harvard, Tufts, Boston University, the University of Massachusetts, and Massachusetts Institute of Technology worry new ban on use of pound animals will raise cost of research so much that some scientists will be unable to continue their research.

588. McGinnis, Terri. "Sticking up for Pets," *Family Health* 11 (September 1979):15.
   The idea man and animals share the earth and humans should have respect and reverence for animal life is starting to attract followers. Some scientists and animal welfare people are working together on ethics and animal rights issues. Suggests ways to become more involved on a personal level.

589. Mrazek, Robert J. "Animals and Research," *LAT* 8 August 1987:II,2.
   Congressional Representative Robert J. Mrazek defends his bill, which would outlaw sale of pound animals to research. Denies such action would raise cost of research and says eleven states and four foreign countries already have such a law. The World Health Organization and the Council of Europe also recommend against use of pound animals in research.

590. Mrazek, Robert J. "The Least We Owe to Animals That Are Sent to Shelters," *WP* 25 June 1987:A17.
   Author of a bill that would prevent sale of pound animals to research takes issue with Dr. Michael DeBakey's opposition. Bill is not intended to end animal research but to reassure those who voluntarily surrender a pet to the shelter that their pet will be either adopted or euthanized humanely. To undermine this trust could lead to serious animal control problems in a community.

591. Newman, Edward. "Animal Research, People Sense," *LAT* 20 July 1983:II,4.
   President of California Humane Council favors Roberti bill, which would prohibit sale of shelter animals to research. It is supported by 677 doctors, the Los Angeles City Council, the Animal Regulation Department, and the Los Angeles Animal Control Directors Association, as well as 102 humane groups.

592. "Picking Up the Pieces at the Animals Farm Home," *AA* 8 (September/October 1988):23+.
     Animals Farm Home, operated by Justin McCarthy in Ellenville, New York, and once portrayed positively by media as a haven for stray animals, is now hit with twenty-five counts of animal cruelty, as local society for the prevention of cruelty to animals discovers emaciated dogs, goats suffering from arthritis and urinary tract disease, and horses with laminitis. Many animals who could not be saved were euthanized.

593. Roberti, David. "Research on Pound Animals," *LAT* 6 September 1983:II,4.
     California senate president pro tem David Roberti defends his bill to ban sale of shelter animals to animal researchers and takes the *Los Angeles Times* to task for inaccuracy and lack of sound reasoning in its editorial. His bill, far from being bizarre and radical, is already law in several other states and countries.

594. Sahagun, Louis. "San Bernardino to Vote on Sale of Pound Dogs," *LAT* 21 May 1986:I,27.
     San Bernardino voters will have opportunity to decide if shelter animals may be sold to research centers for experiments. Animal groups and scientists are both watching this closely for its national ramifications.

595. "San Diego Council Unit Supports Sale of Stray Animals for Research," *LAT* 8 July 1988:I,31.

596. "Science Under Attack," *WSJ* 16 June 1987:30.
     Editorial says animal rights groups are trying to make it illegal for researchers to buy and use animals from shelters in their experiments. Scientists such as Dr. Michael DeBakey are worried this ban on a cheap source of animals will price many important research projects out of existence. Although animal rights activists have artificial populist appeal, the public should be more informed about purposes of modern scientific endeavor.

597.   "Seeking Silence," *AA* 10 (September 1990):36.
       Kansas passes law making it illegal to take pictures in-
       side animal facility without owner's permission. Some see
       this as a response to exposé of puppy mills in that state,
       which received national news coverage.

598.   Silas, Faye A. "The Dogs Win: Mass. Curbs Medical
       Research," *American Bar Association Journal* 70 (April
       1984):37.
       New Massachusetts law prohibits research facilities from
       buying animals from state pounds and importing them
       from other states.

599.   Sun, Marjorie. "California Universities Block Animal
       Rights Bill," *Science* 221 (September 2, 1983):934.
       California bill introduced by senate president pro tem
       David Roberti, which would have banned sale of pound
       animals to research, was pulled for fear it wouldn't pass.
       Stanford and University of California celebrate their vic-
       tory, believing that their public relations appeal that in-
       cluded testimony from movie stars and medical patients
       won the day.

600.   "The Torture Is Legislative," *LAT* 25 August 1983:II,6.
       Senate president pro tem David Roberti withdrew his
       proposed bill that would have banned the sale of shelter
       animals to research institutions. The bill lost support when
       Assemblyman William Filante introduced a bill that would
       ban only sale of animals that could be identified as pets.

601.   Trull, Frankie L. "There's No Rescue in Bill to Save Pound
       Animals," *LAT* 3 May 1987:V,5.
       Argues pound animals should be used in research. No
       one wants them and they would only die anyway. Forcing
       researchers to use purpose-bred dogs and cats would cost
       $70 million or more a year.

602.   United States. Congress. House. *Pet Theft Act of 1988.*
       Hearing before the Subcommittee on Department
       Operations, Research, and Foreign Agriculture of the

Committee of Agriculture, 100th Cong., 2nd Sess., on S2353, September 28, 1988. Washington, DC: U.S. Government Printing Office, 1989, Y4.Ag8/1:100–109.

603.  Vetri, Kristi. "Animal Research and Shelter Animals: An Historical Analysis of the Pound Animal Controversy," *St. Louis University Law Review* 31 (September 1987):551–75.

604.  White, Kenneth. "Broken Contracts," *AV* 3 (March/April 1990):46–48.

Ten to 18 million dogs and cats are euthanized in American shelters and pounds each year. Explains reasons why this happens and how the community can end this tragedy.

605.  White, Kenneth. "Earth Day, from Another Perspective," *AV* 3 (August 1990):75.

April 22, 1990: While 125,000 people attended Earth Day activities in San Francisco, 13 cats and 4 dogs were euthanized at local animal shelter. Our new sensitivity to the environment should include a new awareness of our responsibility to the suffering and death of so many abandoned animals in our pounds and shelters each year.

606.  White, MacDonald. "Better Off at the Pound (letter)," *WP* 27 June 1987:A25.

President of United Action for Animals cites a $244,000 study that electroshocked the tails and paws of kittens and a $641,000 study that pawshocked dogs. While Dr. Michael DeBakey defends medical advances using pound animals, he doesn't mention the millions of taxpayer dollars wasted on experiments like these.

# VII WILDLIFE

Animal rights advocates differ in degree from environmentalists in their approach to wildlife, for they think an individual animal is as important as the species to which it belongs. As a result, although they may support and be active in campaigns to protect endangered species and preserve wildlife habitat, they are also interested in protecting individual wild animals whether living freely in a natural habitat or in captivity. Most animal rights advocates condemn hunting, believing that sport frivolously destroys animal life, reduces biological diversity, and requires poor land management practices in order to create a surplus of game animals.

Activities to protect wildlife have included education campaigns, legislative and legal initiatives, protests, and demonstrations.

## General

607. Amory, Cleveland. *Man Kind? Our Incredible War on Wildlife.* New York: Harper & Row, 1974.

Ground-breaking book exposing the senseless and costly slaughter of our wildlife by hunters, ranchers, and the federal government.

608. Booth, William. "Chimps and Research: Endangered?" *Science* 241 (August 12, 1988):777–78.

U.S. Fish and Wildlife Service was petitioned by Humane Society of U.S., Jane Goodall Institute, and World Wildlife Fund to reclassify chimpanzees from threatened to endangered. National Institutes of Health opposes the move, saying such a reclassification would affect supply of chimps used in biomedical research.

609.    Clifton, Merritt. "Driftnets: Scourge of the Seas," *AA* 9 (October 1989):7–8+.

    Driftnets kill countless seabirds, seals, sea lions, dolphins, turtles, and even whales each year as Japanese, Taiwanese, and South Korean fishermen try to meet increasing demand for fish.

610.    Clifton, Merritt. "The Wily Coyote," *AA* 7 (May 1990):49–51.

    State and federal wildlife agencies massacre over 150,000 coyotes a year. The cost to the taxpayer is ten times more than the cost of livestock losses allegedly due to coyote predation.

611.    Dommer, Luke. "The Killing Machine," *AV* 2 (August 1989):59–61.

    After *Jaws*, war was waged on the great white shark even though the number of humans killed by them is infinitesimal compared to the number of accidents and murders humans commit against one another. On the other side of the ledger, humans kill anywhere from 8 to 50 billion animals a year for food, scientific experiments, sport hunting, and so on. As we continue to damage the environment and the creatures in it, we destroy the very foundation of our own existence.

612.    Dommer, Luke. "Wildlife Refuges—Or Killing Fields," *AA* 9 (October 1989):17–18.

    National wildlife refuges established to protect and preserve wildlife have become killing grounds for hunters. Their influence on land management has produced more game species at expense of nongame ones, including predators. Urges support of Refuge Wildlife Protection Act.

613.    Grant, Gordon. "Five Hundred and Fifty Goats Saved," *LAT* 29 July 1985:II,3.

    Defense Secretary Caspar Weinberger allowed Fund for Animals under Cleveland Amory's direction to rescue 1,300 goats living on San Clemente Islands. U.S. Navy, which owns the islands, was planning to shoot the goats.

614. Greanville, David Patrice. "Roadkills—The Orphan Issue," *AA* 10 (June 1990):47–49.

    Up to a million animals are killed or maimed by motor vehicles each year. This issue has had minimal response from animal defense organizations and needs greater attention.

615. "Helping Hands," *AA* 10 (January/February 1990):36.

    Congressional initiative made to ensure capuchin monkeys used in Helping Hands program for handicapped are treated properly.

616. " 'Helping Hands' Is a Cruel Hoax, Trainer Tells Congress," *AA* 9 (November 1989):34–35.

    Zoologist Alison Paska, who has worked in the program of turning capuchin monkeys into aides for paraplegics called the program cruel and costly. The monkeys' teeth are pulled, their behavior is modified by electric shock, and they are separated from their own kind. Unreliable and untrustworthy as a human's companion or helpmate, only eight monkeys have been placed so far, at a cost of almost $1 million.

617. "IDA Victory," *AA* 10 (December 1990):44.

    In Defense of Animals wins an injunction against the U.S. Navy's plan to poison squirrels at several weapons stations in California.

618. "Interest Grows in Contraception as a Means of Wildlife Management," *NYT* 10 April 1988:A43.

    Animal rights activists would like to see wildlife overpopulation managed by contraceptive methods rather than by hunting. Contraceptive methods were discussed at two-day conference sponsored by Humane Society of the United States.

619. Kirkpatrick, Jay D. "Animals on the Pill—Pipe Dreams or Promise," *AA* 9 (March 1989):36–7+.

    Examination of myths and realities of contraception for

wild animals. Research during the past twenty years has shown some success in controlling populations of feral cats, deer, goats, and wild horses, but federal agencies that deal with wildlife have not shown much interest in contraceptive research despite its potential for controlling wildlife in nonlethal ways.

620.  Mason, Jim. "A Trip to the World's Largest Exotic Animal Auction," *AA* 9 (June 1989):46–48.
      Author goes undercover to see the exotic animal trade first-hand at the annual auction at Cape Girardeau, Missouri. Wild animals of every kind, including lion cubs, monkeys, ostriches, and giraffes, are sold to hunting ranches, collectors, petting zoos, and drive-through safari parks. When the author brought his experience to the attention of animal rights/welfare groups, all were too busy or involved with something else to help. There is a need to organize a group to fight exotic-animal trade.

621.  Mulvaney, Kieran. "Ahab's Revenge," *AV* 3 (October 1990):32–46.
      History and legislation dealing with whaling industry and the fate of whales and dolphins slaughtered toward extinction.

622.  Pacelle, Wayne. "Seabert: From Hunt Target to Hunt Saboteur," *AA* 7 (November 1987):10–1+.
      Television programming that promotes compassion and respect for animals and nature is hard to find, but "Seabert," an animated cartoon whose main character is a harp seal, does so. Opposition by the fur industry and others to end the program is mounting.

623.  "Protecting the Rights of Wild Horses," *NYT* 26 July 1987:A34.
      In violation of the Wild and Free Roaming Horse and Burro Act of 1971, Bureau of Land Management released thousands of horses to adopters who planned to slaughter them for profit.

624. Satchell, Michael. "The Final Roundup for America's Wild Horses," *U.S. News & World Report* 107 (March 2, 1987):68.

    Twenty thousand wild mustangs have been rounded up and will be held until Interior Secretary Hodel decides what to do with them. Animal rights activists say Bureau of Land Management is bending to pressure of ranchers who want more land for beef grazing.

625. Schmidt, William E. "U.S. Weighs Fate of Unwanted Wild Horses," *NYT* 27 December 1987:A1.

626. Solomon, Wendy E. "Interest Grows in Contraception as a Means of Wildlife Management," *NYT* 10 April 1988:A43.

    Humane Society of the United States will hold a conference in East Windsor, New Jersey, to discuss contraceptive methods to alleviate overpopulation in some groups of wildlife such as deer. Hunters and game commissioners believe hunting is best method of managing wildlife populations, pointing also to revenues generated by hunting license fees and firearms taxation.

627. Taylor, Ronald B. "Adopted Mustangs Are Slaughtered, Critics Say," *LAT* 1 February 1988:I,3.

    Ranchers find loophole in law that allows them to adopt wild mustangs and then sell them to meat packers for $250 a head. Animal welfarists are trying to stop Bureau of Land Management from releasing horses to ranchers.

628. Taylor, Ronald B. "U.S. Agency Halts Mass Adoption of Wild Horses," *LAT* 16 April 1988:I,31.

    Bureau of Land Management has suspended mass adoption program of wild horses, saying it has found other ways to cope with overpopulation. Animal rights activists have accused the agency of knowing horses adopted by ranchers on fee-free basis have been pastured for a year and then sold for slaughter in violation of the Wild Horse and Burro Act of 1971.

629.  "To Save the Wild Chimps," *Science News* 135 (March 11, 1989):155.
      Chimps' reclassification from threatened to endangered species will prevent importation of wild chimps but will not help those purposely bred for biomedical research.

630.  Trimmingham, Scott. "Killing Cetaceans," *AV* 3 (August 1990):38–39.
      Loopholes in international moratorium on whale hunting passed in 1985 have allowed the killing of whales to continue.

631.  "Two Thousand Horses Starve in Failure of Plan to Sell Meat," *NYT* 29 January 1984:A23.
      Ranchers' scheme to make huge profits buying wild horses and selling them for horsemeat in Europe backfires.

632.  "U.S. Plan to Use Eagles in Poison Test Is Protested," *NYT* 14 October 1989:7.
      Agriculture department is testing compound 1080, a highly toxic poison banned since 1972, in an experiment using injured golden eagles. Researchers want to find a compound that will kill coyotes but not injure eagles, who might also feed on the poisoned lures. Animal rights advocates are strongly protesting the experiment.

633.  "Using Chimpanzees for AIDS Study: Conservationists Worry Research Will Endanger Wild Chimps," *CSM* 12 July 1988:3+.
      Jane Goodall Institute, World Wildlife Fund, and Humane Society have filed a petition that would reclassify chimpanzees from threatened to endangered. Only about 200,000 are left in Africa, yet biomedical research continues to obtain many of its chimps from the wild to study medical problems, including AIDS. For every one chimp captured and exported successfully, five to ten die.

634.  Webster, Bayard. "Is Banding of Birds for Research Often Unnecessarily Cruel," *NYT* 27 July 1982:C1+.

More than 40 million birds have been banded in the past ten years for U.S. Fish and Wildlife Service. Many birdwatchers and some scientists feel banding can be harmful to birds' health or life, since many banders are often inexperienced and injure the birds. Only 6.5 percent of all birds banded are recovered, and the information gained from those birds can just as easily be gathered by observation.

635.    Woldenberg, Susan. "Walls of Death," *AV* 3 (August 1990):36–37.
        Driftnets, in addition to killing targeted fish like tuna, also take the lives of 100,000 sea mammals and a million seabirds each year.

## Hunting

636.    Begley, Sharon, and Tad Brooks. "A Firing Squad for Buffalo," *Newsweek* 113 (March 6, 1989):51.
        National Park Service allows hunters to shoot buffalo that wander outside Yellowstone National Park, but because the animals are so docile, the result is more like a firing squad than a hunt. The kill rate is 100 percent.

637.    "Carnage in the Woods Endangers All Species," *AA* 9 (April 1988):29.
        Game wardens and innocent home owners are in danger as hunters take to the woods.

638.    Causey, A. S. "On the Morality of Hunting," *Environmental Ethics* 11 (Winter 1989):327–43.
        Violent death is part of nature, and man's desire to participate in it by hunting can be both natural and culturally valuable.

639.    Clifton, Merritt. "Bear-ly There," *AA* 9 (September 1989):12–4+.
        Predicts extinction of several species of bears as loss of habitat, overhunting, and accelerated poaching bite into

their numbers. Bear hunting occurs legally in twenty-nine states, with about 24,000 bears killed each year. Fire, wildlife agents, police, and ranchers also take their toll on bear population.

640. Clifton, Merritt. "Killing the Female: The Psychology of the Hunt," *AA* (September 1990):26–30+.
Examines five stages hunters go through before entering last stage of enjoying nature without killing. Forecasters say hunting population will continue to decrease as present population ages and new hunters fail to materialize in sufficient numbers to offset them.

641. Dolan, Maura. "Drawing a Bead on Hunting," *LAT* 28 August 1989:I,1.
Animal rights advocates have focused on preserving wildlife in California, supporting several laws and regulations to restrict hunting. They are currently seeking a ban on mountain lion hunting, and they criticize the California Department of Fish and Game for issuing permits to hunt this and other species without having adequately studied size of animal population and effect hunting will have on it. Fish and Game has a pro-hunting bias, they say, not a preservationist one.

642. Dommer, Luke A. "A Hunter's Delusions," *AV* 2 (April 1989):82–3+.

643. Dommer, Luke A. "Killing for Fun," *AV* 2,6 (1989):38–43.
Hunting in America not only is crippling our environment, but also is totally unnecessary. It costs $25 per pound of venison, while 50 percent of all animals killed are wasted because they are not dressed or handled properly. Hunting is often nonselective, removing genetically perfect animals and leaving the weak to live, thus perpetuating an inferior species. At the same time, it reduces predator population and nongame animals, further upsetting ecological balance. Over 200,000 million animals are killed, crippled, or maimed each year by 7 percent of the American population.

644. Dommer, Luke A. "Legacy of a Killer," *AV* 2 (February 1989):90–1.

    The first prehistoric creature to walk erect and kill anything that didn't bear its own likeness, the *Australopithecus africanus,* is still with us today. Aided by government agencies like the Bureau of Land Mismanagement and the Environmental Procrastination Agency, 17 million hunters slaughter 150 million wild animals each year, leaving many more wounded and dying. Should we continue to follow the example of *Australopithecus africanus,* or instead realize that all things in creation have an intrinsic value and have something to contribute to the ecosystem?

645. "Earth," *Omni* 7 (October 1984):20–21.

    From a small band of diehards, anti-hunters have grown to thousands who harass hunters and scare away potential game. "Tips for Hunt Saboteurs" lists fourteen ways to annoy hunters, including use of blaring radios and filling hunting equipment with manure.

646. Favre, David S., and Gretchen Olsen. *Surplus Population: A Fallacious Basis for Sport Hunting.* Clarks Summit, PA: Society for Animal Rights, 1982.

    Examines the nature of "surplus" population, an argument often proposed by hunters as justification for sport hunting. Concludes argument is misleading and inaccurate. The annual cycle of animal population does not mandate nor require existence of sport hunting. Hunting is a moral issue, not one of science or wildlife management.

647. Francione, Gary. "Hunting Hunters," *AV* 2,6 (1989):48.

    Hunter harassment statutes supported by National Rifle Association have been passed in over twenty-five states. In Connecticut, Francelle Dorman was arrested while peacefully attempting to dissuade hunters from their activities. Dorman filed a suit in federal court, which eventually led to overturning the law as unconstitutional.

648. Greanville, David Patrice. "Trapping Unwitting Sources," *AA* 7 (November 1987):40–41.

Dissection of content of magazines catering to hunters.

649.  Hentoff, Nat. "Canada Geese, Beware," *WP* 21 May 1988:A27.
      Francelle Dorman was arrested in Niantic, Connecticut, allegedly in violation of the Hunter Harassment Act. The case was dropped, because the arresting officer didn't have probable cause. Dorman asked U.S. District Court to declare the act a violation of her First and Fourteenth Amendment rights. Judge agreed, but hunters plan to appeal.

650.  Lewis, Jennifer. "Our National Wildlife Refuges: Sanctuaries or Shooting Galleries?" *AA* 8 (November 1987):22–23.
      Of the 439 national wildlife refuges in this country set aside primarily for wildlife protection, 250 allow hunting and 90 trapping. Legislation is pending that would return refuges to inviolate sanctuaries for animals.

651.  McCarthy, Coleman. "Bring 'Em Back Dead, Texas Style," *WP* 14 January 1989:A23.
      George Bush's kinder and gentler America doesn't extend to the quail he hunts at Lazy F Ranch. Hunting preserves where exotic animals are stocked so hunters can shoot them are on the increase. Some lions are so tame from contact with humans that hunters have to throw stones to make them run away.

652.  McCarthy, Coleman. "Courage of Her Convictions," *WP* 11 August 1990:A21.
      Biographical sketch of Heidi Prescott, national outreach director of Fund for Animals, who spent fifteen days in a Maryland jail for rustling leaves and speaking to hunters in violation of the Hunter Harassment Act.

653.  McFarland, Cole. "A Killing on the African Plains of Texas," *AV* 3 (August 1990):17–21.
      Author visits Y.O. Ranch in Texas, one of 10,000 exotic game ranches in the United States, where animals, some

endangered, are bought or bred for hunters to kill for fun
or profit.

654.   Newmann, Holly. "Animal Lovers Look Suspiciously at
       Their Tax Forms in New Jersey," *WSJ* 22 February
       1982:25.
           Alice Herrington, president of the Friends of Animals,
       believes the money that taxpayers check off for
       Endangered and Non-Game Species of Wildlife Conser-
       vation Fund on their tax form will be used for benefit of
       hunters. Division of Fish, Game, and Wildlife will bolster
       certain animal populations so New Jersey can reclassify
       them from endangered species to game animals.

655.   Norman, Michael. "Our Towns: The Anti-Hunters Take
       to the Connecticut Woods," *NYT* 6 December 1984:B2.
           The Animal Rights Front patrols Connecticut forests
       and attempts to disrupt hunting season. One of the ac-
       tivists discusses philosophical basis behind his activities.

656.   Pacelle, Wayne. "Federal Court Affirms Unconstitutional-
       ity of Hunter Harassment Statute," *AA* 9 (April 1989):30.
           State appeals decision Connecticut hunter harassment
       law is unconstitutional and loses again in Second Circuit
       Court of Appeals.

657.   Pacelle, Wayne. "Game Commission Arms Florida
       Youths," *AA* 9 (January 1989):24–25.
           Governor Martinez supports youth deer hunts spon-
       sored by the Florida Game and Fresh Water commission
       despite animal rights protests. This event is an effort to
       boost dwindling number of hunters as the sport continues
       to decline in that state.

658.   Pacelle, Wayne. "When the Non-Hunting Majority
       Speaks, Government Agencies Don't Listen," *AA* 10 (Jan-
       uary/February 1990):19+.
           Government wildlife agencies, rather than protecting
       wildlife and biological diversity, function as agencies to

propagate game species for hunters, who make up only 7 percent of the population.

659.  "Poll Backing Hunting Was Bogus," *AA* 10 (September 1990):39.
      Poll saying 90 percent of people oppose hunter harassment by animal activists was repudiated by Gallup organization as being flawed and unscientific.

660.  Rabe, Marsha. "From Hot Dogs to Deer Hunts: A Vegetarian's Thanksgiving," *AA* 123 (November 1987): 28–29.
      Account of ethical vegetarian's participation on Thanksgiving day to protect deer from hunters by entering Yale University forest property and scaring deer away.

661.  Regenstein, Lewis. "The End of the Game," *AV* 2,6 (1989):44–45.
      Although big game hunting has fallen somewhat into disrepute, it still takes a toll on endangered species. Department of the Interior encourages this sort of hunting by downgrading status of endangered species to threatened, so American hunters will be able to bring back their trophies of leopards and other exotic animals killed abroad.

662.  "Roar of the Lion Echoes in Land of the Longhorn," *NYT* 2 May 1988:A16.
      Lions stocked on Texas safari ranches for hunters to shoot have created a million-dollar industry. Many of the lions are tame, defanged, and declawed. Animal rights activists want legislation to ban these ranches.

663.  Satchell, Michael. "American Hunter Under Fire," *U.S. News & World Report* 108 (February 5, 1990).
      Public debate over morality of hunting increases as animal rights activists put on the pressure.

664.  "Save Raccoons—Boycott Ralston Purina and Royal Canine," *AA* 10 (June 1990):37.

Calls for boycott of dog food companies, which sponsor raccoon hunting with dogs and awards prizes up to $10,000.

665. Stoller, Kenneth P. "Trained to Kill," *AV* 2,6 (1989):52.

National Rifle Association spent $83 million last year to encourage training of children in handling and firing guns, but as children learn it is all right to kill rabbits, squirrels, deer, and other animals, they also learn a disrespect for life. An extreme example is the case of a 9-year-old boy exposed to guns and hunting, who loaded a lever-action Marlin one day and shot his 7-year-old neighbor from his bedroom window.

666. Weintraub, Daniel M. "Plan to Restore Lion Hunts Stirs Emotional Struggle," *LAT* 5 April 1987:I,1.

Mountain Lion Coalition goes toe-to-toe with hunters in California over whether Fish and Game commission should lift ban on hunting mountain lions. Public opinion is running 8:1 against the hunt.

# VIII CIRCUSES, ZOOS, RODEOS, DOG AND HORSE RACING, PIGEON SHOOTS, AQUATIC THEME PARKS, AND OTHER RECREATIONAL USE OF ANIMALS

The use of animals for entertainment or in recreational activities is pervasive in American society. Zoos, aquatic theme parks, circuses and carnivals, rodeos, horse and dog racing, dog and cock fights, and animals trained to perform in movies, television, and nightclub acts represent the major areas of concern for animal rights activists. In such environments, animals often suffer physical injury or severe stress from living in unnatural and sometimes unhealthy settings and from being forced to perform or behave in ways uncharacteristic to their species. Pigeon shoots and rabbit and prairie dog drives result in the slaughter of thousands of animals, and leave many others wounded or maimed.

Animal rights advocates' attempts to bring these issues to the public's attention have not met with a great deal of success except for a few notable exceptions such as the well-publicized protest at the annual Hegins Pigeon Shoot in Hegins, Pennsylvania.

667.  "AHA Pickets 'Gate,' " *Variety* 302 (April 29, 1981):3.
       American Humane Association is planning to picket the movie "Heaven's Gate" for maltreatment of pack mules, trip-wiring of horses, and staging of an actual cockfight.

668.  Anderson, Christopher. "Court Loss May Hurt Activists," *Nature* 346 (August 16, 1990):597.
       In a defamation and invasion of privacy lawsuit, People for the Ethical Treatment of Animals and Performing Animal Welfare Society were told to pay $4.1 million for distributing videotapes of Bobby Berosini's striking of

orangutans he uses in his Las Vegas club act. Organizations will appeal case, but fear the ruling will have a devastating effect on investigation of animal abuse.

669. Barnes, Donald J. "Pigeon Shooting: A Game the Whole Family Can Play," *AV* 2,6 (1989):53–54.
   Describes annual Labor Day pigeon shoot in Hegins, Pennsylvania, and the demonstrations and protests against it. Muses over the fact that some animal advocates find slaughtering pigeons and hunting wild animals repulsive but do not experience the same queasiness about killing and eating other kinds of animals. Animal rights advocates should be more consistent in their views. In the twentieth century, there is no justification for subjecting any animal to pain, suffering, and death.

670. Batten, Peter. *Living Trophies*. New York: Crowell Pub., 1976.
   An exposé of the abuse of zoo animals and an examination of the system that perpetuates an environment of neglect in American zoos.

671. "Birdshooters, Police Attack Activists at Hegins," *AA* 10 (September 1990):40–41.
   The 57th Annual Hegins Pigeon Shoot at Hegins, Pennsylvania ended in violence as one activist was hit by a car and another had his shoulder fractured in three places.

672. Brownlee, Shannon. "First It Was 'Save the Whales,' Now It's 'Free the Dolphins,'" *Discover* 7 (December 1986): 70–72.
   Animal rights activists say it's wrong and cruel to keep dolphins, whales, sea lions, and other intelligent marine mammals in captivity for the amusement of humans. Mortality rates are much higher than in the wild, and the animal's life in a tank is monotonous and inappropriate, causing lethargy, ill health, and even neuroticism. Aquarium curators, dolphin trainers, veterinarians, and scientists, who make a livelihood of working with captive marine animals, counterattack, saying marine species

often thrive in captive conditions, as evidenced by their excellent breeding record.

673. Clifton, Merritt. "Pulling for Horses," *AA* 10 (March 1990):36.
The status of the carriage trade in American and Canadian cities and the reform regulations, passed or pending, that would offer carriage horses more protection.

674. "Demonstrators Protest Pigeon Shoot," *NYT* 8 September 1987:C9.
Animal rights groups protest for second year against annual Labor Day pigeon shoot in Hegins, Pennsylvania. Two hundred activists marched to the capitol in Harrisburg.

675. Derby, Pat. "The Cruelest Show on Earth," *AV* 2,5 (1989):24+.
Circus life for animals is grim, often involving severe confinement, physical punishment, and food deprivation, but it is difficult for animal rights activist to get message across to the public because of history, tradition, and publicity surrounding the circus.

676. Dines, Sheila. "Stop the Labor Day Pigeon Slaughter (letter)," *NYT* 16 September 1986:A26.
Participant in the animal rights protest at the Labor Day pigeon shoot in Hegins, Pennsylvania says activists were physically threatened by supporters of the shoot.

677. Doherty, Shawn. "A Unicorn—or a Goat?" *Newsweek* 105 (22 April 1985):32.
Animal rights activists protest against Ringling Brothers and Barnum and Bailey Circus for exhibiting a "unicorn," a goat whose horns were fused in a surgical procedure. American Society for the Prevention of Cruelty to Animals Director John Kullberg asks: If humans are mutilating animals for cheap circus thrills, then what's to stop them from "playing around with eye sockets and making a Cyclops?"

678. Engelmayer, Paul A. "Infiltrating Dogfight and Cockfight Rings Takes Guile and Guts: Humane Society Investigator Paves the Way for Raids," *WSJ* 2 March 1984:1.

  Robert Baker, an ex-stockbroker, works for the Humane Society as an infiltrator of secret and illegal cockfighting and dogfighting rings, relaying information to law enforcement agents for raids. In the South and the West where this bloody sport is part of a long-standing tradition, Baker's job can be a dangerous one.

679. "Federal Zoo Inspections Criticized as Inadequate," *NYT* 23 July 1984:A6.

  The General Accounting Office, an investigative arm of Congress, says the Agriculture department, which is responsible for enforcing Animal Welfare Act, has overlooked inhumane treatment of animals at zoos for years.

680. Fox, Michael W. "The Captive Panther," *AA* 8 (September/October 1988):40–41.

  Vice president of Humane Society of the United States remembers visit to Parisian zoo as a youngster. He noticed an emaciated panther, which, in pacing so monotonously against a tree stump, has rubbed one side raw. The author felt himself entering the panther's consciousness and understanding what it was like to live in a body with no purpose or spirit.

681. Fritsch, Jane. "Animal Activists Vandalize Zookeeper's Home," *LAT* 15 October 1988:I,26.

  Animal Liberation Front (ALF) vandalizes cars and homes of three zookeepers who participated in chaining and beating a San Diego Wild Animal Park elephant with axe handles during several sessions over two days. ALF said it was motivated by fact that no charges of animal cruelty have yet been pressed against those responsible for the beating.

682. Fritsch, Jane. "Elephant Beating Was Abuse, Society Reports," *LAT* 2 June 1988:I,26.

  Humane Society of the United States says the beating of

the elephant, Dunda, at San Diego Wild Animal Park was a case of animal abuse. Agriculture department is investigating.

683. Fritsch, Jane. "Keepers Struck Elephant More Than a Hundred Times, Trainer Says," *LAT* 26 May 1988:I,3.

Keepers at San Diego Wild Animal Park struck the elephant, Dunda, on the head more than 100 times with an axe handle over the course of two days. Officials at park say it was necessary to discipline the animal, but senior elephant trainer at San Diego Zoo says Dunda had not been given a chance to adjust to her new environment at the park and was terrified.

684. Fritsch, Jane. "USDA Aide Will Urge Citation in Animal Beating," *LAT* 21 July 1988:I,30.

Agriculture department recommends the Zoological Society be cited formally for violating federal anticruelty regulation in connection with the beating of the elephant, Dunda, at San Diego Wild Animal Park.

685. Fritsch, Jane. "Zoo Official Says Wild Animal Park Trainers Injured Aggressive Elephant," *LAT* 25 May 1988:I,3.

Various groups are investigating charges that the elephant, Dunda, was abused after being transferred to San Diego Wild Animal Park. Officials at the park say they were merely disciplining the aggressive elephant, but former trainers of the animal said the beating was excessive and brutal.

686. Gruson, Lindsay. "Pigeon Shoot: A Barrage of Charges," *NYT* 2 September 1986:A14.

Trans-Species Unlimited led a coalition of animal rights groups in protesting annual Labor Day pigeon shoot at Hegins, Pennsylvania. Activists maintain the shoot is cruel; promoters say it's entertaining and a good way to raise money for community projects.

687. Hanauer, Gary. "The Killing Tanks," *AV* 3 (October 1990):22–25.

Sea World, aquatic theme park, is under the gun from animal rightists and environmentalists for neglect and mistreatment of its marine mammals.

688. "Hegins Convictions," *AA* 10 (December 1990):43.
Animal rights protesters, after being physically injured at the annual Hegins Pigeon Shoot, were arrested and convicted of disorderly conduct.

689. Henry, Neil. "Cockfighting: Cruelty or a Sport Honored Through History?" *WP* 5 March 1983:A1+.
History of cockfighting and Humane Society's effort to have it banned in Maryland, one of the seven remaining states where it's still legal.

690. Herrington, Alice. "The Cruel Rodeos (letter)," *NYT Magazine* (November 1, 1981):27.
President of the Friends of Animals says rodeos are not a touch of the Old West and a bit of Early Americana but "highly profitable, commercialized cruelty to animals."

691. Herrington, Alice. "Let's Do Away with Central Park Zoo," *NYT* 21 November 1981:27.
President of Friends of Animals attacks zoos for their practice of keeping animals in small cages and improper environments. Calls for transfer of Central Park Zoo animals to more suitable habitat.

692. Hewitt, Bill, and Linda Marx. "Flipper's Ex-Trainer Wants His Favorite Mammals Free to Swim with the Fishes," *People Weekly* 32 (September 4, 1989):40–41.
Ric O'Barry, former trainer of the dolphin Flipper, condemns swim parks, where dolphins are kept captive in tanks to swim with paying patrons. Such practice is both dangerous and abusive for the dolphins.

693. Jordan, Debra. "Living Trophies," *AV* 2,5 (1989):22–26.
Zoos are more interested in promoting human recreation and their commercial image than they are the welfare of animals they claim to protect.

694.  Kullberg, John F. "Stop the Labor Day Pigeon Slaughter (letter)," *NYT* 16 September 1986:A26.
    President of the American Society for the Prevention of Cruelty to Animals tells of a suit pending in Schuylkill County Court that would prevent future pigeon shoots there.

695.  Lorch, Donatella. "Horse-Carriage Drivers Call New Law's Reins Too Tight," *NYT* 3 December 1989:I,58.
    New York City law bans horse carriage drivers from streets outside Central Park and restricts the hours horses must work. Animal rights advocates supported the bill as a means to protect carriage horses, but the New York Horse and Carriage Association will appeal to state supreme court. Drivers interviewed say they love their horses but will have to sell them for dog meat if law remains in place.

696.  Maggitti, Phil. "They Shoot Up Horses, Don't They?" *AA* 10 (September 1990):18–24.
    Abuse of horses in racing is widespread. One of the biggest unaddressed problems is use of powerful drugs to keep horses running when injured or to make them run faster. When their racing days are over, most horses end up sold to a slaughterhouse.

697.  Maggitti, Phil. "Where the Unicorn Is King: A Look at the Circus," *AA* 9 (November 1989):22–8.
    Chronicles abuses against circus animals, which include depriving wild animals of their proper environment, forcing them to perform acts unnatural to their species, neglect, and physical abuse.

698.  McCarthy, Coleman. "Exploiting the Old Gray Mares," *WP* 15 July 1989:A21.
    Discusses abuse of carriage horses in New York City and the weak legislative efforts to eliminate it.

699.  McFarland, Cole. "Death in the Afternoon," *AV* 2,6 (1989):37.
    Bullfighting is no sport. Picadors repeatedly lacerate a bull's shoulder muscles so he is unable to raise his head.

Banderilleros follow, thrusting two lances apiece into the bull's shoulders and crippling his defenses even more. By the time the matador enters the ring, he is facing an exhausted animal. Most spectators are tourists, and 90 percent of them will never return to see another bullfight, but because there is a constant flow of new tourists, bullfighting remains a thriving business in Mexico and Spain.

700. McFarland, Cole. "In Cold Blood," *AV* 2,6 (1989):46–47.
Fish have no allies or advocates for their protection, and even animal rights people have somewhat ignored the issue. Yet over a billion fish are taken in sport each year that according to many marine scientists, are anatomically able to feel the kind of pain humans feel when undergoing dentistry without anesthetic.

701. McFarland, Cole. "Tranquil Seas, Deadly Waters," *AV* 2 (February 1989):19–21.
Describes the Alabama Deep Sea Fishing Rodeo held annually by the Mobile Jaycees in the Gulf of Mexico. Sponsors promote the event as a "family affair," but some onlookers see it as the senseless slaughter of 100,000 fish ranging from sharks to dolphin.

702. Meade, Bill. "Cockfighting: Cruelty, Not Courage," *AA* 9 (February 1989):44–46.
Cockfighting is on the increase in the U.S., even though forty-four states and the District of Columbia prohibit it. Arguments for and against cockfighting, plus a model anticruelty bill that would eliminate this blood sport once and for all.

703. Mills, Eric. "The Cruel, Wild West Continues," *AV* 2,5 (1989):34–37.
Animal rights activists dispute those who say rodeos are re-creations of the Old West, instead calling it institutionalized animal cruelty with spurs, bucking straps, pain, and fear as the predominant features for the animals forced to participate.

704. Mills, Eric. "Rodeo: American Tragedy or Legalized Cruelty?" *AA* 10 (March 1990):25+.

    Looks at treatment of rodeo animals inside and outside the arena. Notes that although rodeos earn millions for their sponsors, no money is spent on veterinary care for the animals before, during, or after the event.

705. Mulvaney, Kieran. "Oceans Apart: Turning Sentience into a Sideshow," *AV* 2,5 (1989):30–33.

    Founder of Whale and Dolphin Conservation Society condemns capture, confinement, and display of dolphins and whales at Seaworld and other aquatic theme parks. Animals suffer from these unnatural environments, with mortality rates far exceeding those in the wild. As long as such ventures are profitable, however, exploitation of marine mammals will continue.

706. O'Barry, Richard, with Keith Coulbourn. "Dolphins in Captivity: Wasted Lives, Wasted Minds," *AA* 9 (March 1989):12–6+.

    Trainer of the dolphin Flipper has second thoughts about justness of keeping dolphins in captivity under environmentally inappropriate conditions. He discusses dolphins' intelligence, their mode of communication, and his relationship with specific dolphins he has known.

707. Perry, Nancy. "Racing for Their Lives," *AV* 2,5 (1989):20.

    Greyhound racing is the sixth largest spectator sport in America, but that statistic doesn't tell the story about how these gentle animals are treated and trained or the large percentage of them that will be killed or sold to research laboratories because they are not winners on the track.

708. "Ride 'Em Cowboy, Gently," *Newsweek* 77 (28 June 1971):83.

    Rodeos are under attack by environmentalists and animal rights groups for cruelty and inhumane treatment of animals. Discusses steer busting and use of electric prods and flank straps on rodeo horses to make them buck.

709. "Ripples of Controversy After a Chimp Drowns," *NYT* 16 October 1990:A22.

Detroit zoo and its director are under attack by animal rights activists after a chimp drowned in the outmoded moat surrounding the chimpanzee enclosure. A similar incident had almost claimed the life of another chimp earlier. Activists are also protesting the killing of hundreds of surplus animals at the zoo.

710. Salisbury, David F. "Exotic Birds: Report Cites Dangers of Imports," *CSM* 10 March 1981:3.

*The Bird Business*, a study conducted by Greta Nilson of Animal Welfare Institute, concludes the import of exotic birds to the U.S. has a negative impact upon bird population of export country as well as on America's native bird populations and farmers' crops and poultry.

711. Schmidt, William E. "Protests Fail to Stop Diving Mules," *NYT* 5 October 1985:6.

Animal rights activists protest mule-diving exhibition at Alabama State Fair in Birmingham, claiming that plunging from a 30-foot-high platform into 6 feet of water is not a natural act for a mule. Animal cruelty officer says he finds nothing cruel about it.

712. Schneider, Keith. "Tennessee's Walking Horses Draw New Cheers and Charges of Cruelty," *NYT* 27 August 1986:A8.

Discusses practice of "soring" to exaggerate Tennessee walking horse's natural gait. American Horse Protection Association protests practice while American Horse Shows Association refuses to recognize the breed.

713. Smith, Lucinda, Leah Feldon, and Eleanor Hoover. "Speaking up for Abused Animals, Bob Barker Is Hit with a Lawsuit," *People* 32 (September 18, 1989):75–76.

Game show host and animal rights activist Bob Barker accuses American Humane Association (AHA), which monitors the treatment of animals on movie sets, of not doing the job and specifically cites the filming of "Project X," which involved chimpanzee characters. AHA denies the charge and slaps Barker and United Activists for Animal Rights with a libel suit for $10 million.

714.  Swan, Christopher. "Not Guilty—But Sentenced to Life," *CSM* 3 April 1979:B18.
      Pattycake, a gorilla at Central Park Zoo, is good example of victimization of animals living in captivity. Isolated from others of her kind and confined to a barren, tile-walled enclosure, she has nothing but tedium and boredom to keep her company.

715.  Wells, Ken. "Boy, These Guys Sure Know How to Take the Fun Out of Rodeos," *WSJ* 20 April 1988:25.
      Animal rights group protests steer dressing, greased pig chasing, and chicken scrambling planned for rodeo in Hayward, California, as being even more frivolously cruel than the usual rodeo events. Sponsors agree to drop the events.

716.  Zawistowski, Stephen. "In the Pits," *AV* 2,6 (1989):50–51.
      Historical overview of pitting animals, usually dogs, against one another in fights to the death.

# IX ANIMAL EXPERIMENTATION

Estimates of the number of animals used in biomedical research, product safety testing, and educational settings in the United States range widely from 17 to 70 million a year. Animal rights advocates believe much of such vivisection is unnecessary, inflicts great pain and suffering on animals, and yields misleading or erroneous data. Regulationists aim at reducing substantially the number of animals used, replacing animals with alternative methods of testing whenever possible, and eliminating animal experiments altogether in research that is trivial or duplicative. Abolitionists would like to see a halt to all animal experimentation.

Of all the issues that animal rights activists have brought to the public's attention, none is more controversial nor has generated more literature than animal experimentation. It has provoked a strongly negative reaction from a wide array of opponents, including the biomedical industry, medical and veterinary schools, and some government agencies. In the past few years, those groups have orchestrated an aggressive public relations and legislative campaign to counteract the increasing exposure of the animal rights movement's position on animal experimentation.

## General

717. Adler, Jerry, and Mary Hager. "Emptying the Cages: Does the Animal Kingdom Need a Bill of Rights," *Newsweek* 21 (May 23, 1988):59–60.

   Animal rights movement is one of the fastest-growing causes in America. It is attempting to overthrow principles that have governed relations among species since Adam, with the use of animals in research as one of its primary areas of focus.

718.  Ali, Cairo Fatima. *Animal Rights and Animal Research.* Ph.D. dissertation, Ohio State University, 1987.
      Looks at animal rights movement's impact on national policy concerning psychological and biomedical research. Assessment of movement's ideology, tactics, and funding sources.

719.  Anderson, Christopher. "Animal Research: Conspiracy Can't Be Proved," *Nature* 344 (April 12, 1990):577.
      Animal rights activists are unable to uncover any evidence that researcher Adrian Morris has been paid by federal agencies to act as lead man in an attack against animal rights movement.

720.  Balzar, John. "State Drops Plan to Have Prisons Run 'Puppy Farm,'" *LAT* 1 November 1984:I,25.
      Governor Dukmejian of California has dropped a plan to have inmates at state prisons raise puppies for laboratory research. Negative public response caused the change of heart.

721.  Barinaga, Marcia. "Animal Rights Activists Raise a Storm in California," *Nature* 333 (June 2, 1988):386.
      Animal rights activists unsuccessfully attempt to prevent California legislature from funding new $12.5-million animal research center at University of California at Berkeley.

722.  Barker, Bob. "Animal Research (letter)," *LAT* 17 February 1988:II,6.
      Bob Barker, television game show host, and others attack Betty Ann Kevles's recent essay that promotes use of animals in experimentation. Barker says even Dr. Charles Mayo, founder of Mayo Clinic, thought animal experimentation barbaric and useless.

723.  Barnard, Neal. "The Nazi Experiments," *AA* 10 (April 1990):8–9.
      Contrary to opposition's claims, animal experimentation flourished under the Nazis. During Nazi regime, German law and regulations covering animal experimentation were very similar to those we have in this country today.

724. Barnes, Deborah M. "Tight Money Squeezes Out Animal Models," *Science* 232 (April 18, 1986):309–11.

     Scientists say animal models bred to replicate certain aspects of human disease are being "terminated" for lack of funding. Some feel pressure from animal rights groups will exacerbate problem.

725. Barnes, Donald J. "Abusing Animals in Research Is Itself a Disease," *WP: A Weekly Journal of Medicine, Health, Fitness, and Psychology* 21 May 1986:WH6.

     Psychologist who once experimented on nonhuman primates for a living says immorality of imposing pain and suffering upon sentient beings in vain hope of relieving human suffering is itself a disease.

726. Barnes, Donald J. "Animal Rights (letter)," *WP* 30 April 1984:A10.

     Director of the National Anti-Vivisection Society says animal rights supporters are reverse of being antiscience. It is medical science that is stuck in rut of tradition by persisting in trying to make medical progress through animal experimentation and ignoring other more effective approaches such as preventive medicine.

727. Barnes, Fred. "Animal Rights Groups," *Vogue* 179 (September 1989):542.

     Emergence of a new political force, the animal rights movement, was marked on Capitol Hill by a reception for members of Congress and their staff. Sponsored by People for the Ethical Treatment of Animals, which supports an end to research with animals, the reception elicited worry from scientists such as Dr. DeBakey, the heart surgeon, and Dr. Fauci, head of AIDS research at National Institutes of Health.

728. Beardsley, Tim. "Animal Passions: A Study of Laboratory-Animal Use Founders in Acrimony," *Scientific American* 257 (October 1987):30.

     A report on animal experimentation sponsored by National Academies of Sciences and Engineering is cause of dissension and disagreement. Animal rights activists refuse to sign it, because it was unbalanced, containing serious omissions, while some animal experimenters wrote a minority report on the plight of the scientific investigator.

729.  Beene, Richard. "UC Cuts Use of Animals in Experiments," *LAT* 30 April 1988:I,35.

University of California report says use of experimental animals has dropped from 600,000 in 1982–83 to 469,394 in 1986–87. Percentage of large-animal experimentation remains at 2–3 percent. Animal rights advocates criticize report, saying it was same old nonsense.

730.  Begley, Sharon, with Mary Hager and Susan Katz. "Liberation in the Labs: Animal Rights Groups are Gaining Clout and Respect," *Newsweek* 104 (August 27, 1984):66–67.

Animal rights groups are gaining influence as they become increasingly vocal and organized in effort to protect lab animals. Focuses on Draize and LD-50 tests and their alternatives.

731.  Blum, Deborah. "Animal Rights in the Lab: More Scientists Acknowledge Concerns, But Weigh Priorities," *Los Angeles Daily Journal* 13 December 1984:4.

Some scientists, researchers, and laboratory veterinarians admit animal rights movement has made many experimenters shape up and take better care of their animals. Addresses issue of why researchers took so long to react and why they didn't instigate changes themselves without outside pressure.

732.  Boffey, Philip M. "The Rights of Animals and Requirements of Science," *NYT* 11 August 1985:E8.

Animal rights groups are on the offensive. Break-ins at two animal labs garnered activists' documentation of animal mistreatment. Subsequent sit-ins have resulted in rescinded National Institutes of Health grants and introduction of a number of congressional bills designed to protect laboratory animals.

733. "Breakthroughs Don't Require Torture (letter)," *WSJ* 19
     May 1989:A15.
     Letters from Stephen Zawistowski, American Society
     for the Prevention of Cruelty to Animals, Suzanne E. Roy,
     Physicians' Committee for Responsible Medicine; and
     Stephen Kaufman, Medical Research Modernization
     Committee, criticizing an anti-animal-rights editorial in
     *Wall Street Journal,* April 24, A14.

734. Bresnick, Peter Haskell. "Behind the Laboratory Door,"
     *Progressive* 54 (March 1990):20.
     Activities by animal rights advocates range from rescu-
     ing lab animals and peaceful demonstration to promoting
     stronger legislation and regulations to protect lab animals.

735. Briggs, Anna C. "Animals Can't Write to Ann Landers (let-
     ter)," *WP* 8 October 1983:A17.
     President of the National Humane Education Society
     claims much of the animal experimentation Ann Landers
     defends is senseless. Alternatives are already available for
     many tests, and others can be developed.

736. Budiansky, Stephen. "Winning Through Intimidation,"
     *U.S. News & World Report* 103 (August 31, 1987), 48–49.
     Extremists are out to stop animal experimentation
     through militant action and new federal regulations.
     Pressure is taking a toll by limiting animal research and
     frightening researchers.

737. Budkie, Michael A. "Researching Your Local Research
     Facility," *AA* 10 (October 1990):16–18.
     How to learn about type of animal experimentation
     being conducted at local research facilities. Includes dis-
     cussion of Freedom of Information Act, reference sources
     available in libraries, and U.S. government publications.

738. Burgos, Javier. "Animal Rights: The Suicide of a
     Movement," *AA* 9 (January 1989):39+.
     Director of Students United Protesting Painful Research
     Experiments on Sentient Subjects says the animal rights

movement is losing battle against vivisection by using idiotic slogan "animal rights," by capitulating to biomedical industry that some animal experimentation has helped humans, and by hewing to ethical and philosophical arguments against vivisection instead of exposing scientific fraud inherent in vivisection.

739.    Cave, George P., and Dana Stuchell. "The Path to Anti-Vivisection," *AA* 9 (January 1989):39+.

Directors of Trans-Species Unltd. believe issue of vivisection is one in which the animal rights movement has had its least success in communicating its position to the public. At present there are two voices: factual abolitionists, who base their position on the argument that vivisection has never benefited humans, and ethical abolitionists who call for abolition based on ethical arguments. Latter group questions tactics of the first for defending extreme and absurd opinions that sabotage the animal rights movement's credibility and subvert attention from many cases in which animal experimentation really is scientifically useless.

740.    Charlton, Linda. "A Plan to Ship Caged Chimps to Texas by Truck Protested," *NYT* 24 July 1979:B4.

Animal welfare groups protest plan to ship chimpanzees from New York to San Antonio on a 40-hour trip in small cages. Dr. Moor-Jankowski, head of the New York School of Medicine, said the chimps were being asked to go too long without food and water, and he questioned the method of ground transportation.

741.    Chui, Glennda. "Activists Beset UC, Stanford Labs," *Science* 239 (March 11, 1988):1229–32.

Neighborhood activists, environmentalists, and animal rightists join to protest against plans for new research labs at three California universities. Some think labs housing radio isotopes and recombinant organisms are dangerous to neighborhoods, but scientists say this is just the latest tactic of the animal rights movement. President Kennedy of Stanford University says public is uninformed about scientific matters and are bamboozled by these foolish issues.

742.  Citron, Alan. "Foes of Vivisection March on UCLA," *LAT*
      30 April 1984:II,2.
      Two thousand people, led by television game-show per-
      sonality Bob Barker, observed World Day for Laboratory
      Animals by marching to University of California Medical
      Center, where animal research is done. Researchers an-
      swered demonstrators by insisting certain kinds of research
      cannot be done without live animals.

743.  Clingerman, Karen J. *Welfare of Experimental Animals,
      January 1985–March 1991.* Quick Bibliography Series QB
      91–83. Beltsville, MD: Animal Welfare Information
      Center, National Agricultural Library, April 1991,
      A 17.18/4:91–83.
      Contains 581 citations drawn from AGRICOLA data-
      base, representing a wide variety of materials on labora-
      tory animal welfare from both animal rights and biomed-
      ical viewpoints.

744.  Clingerman, Karen J., and Jean A. Larson. *Welfare of
      Experimental Animals, January 1979–August 1989.* Quick
      Bibliography Series QB 90–10. Beltsville, MD: Animal
      Welfare Information Center, National Agricultural Library,
      1989, A 17.18/4:90–10.
      Contains 394 citations from AGRICOLA database for
      and against animal experimentation as well as technical in-
      formation on housing and care of lab animals. Covers books,
      journals, society publications, and government documents.

745.  Cohen, Murray J. "The Grand Illusion," *AV* 2 (June
      1989):8–9.
      Why do 80 percent of Americans think animal experimen-
      tation is necessary? A look at how children adopt a number of
      false assumptions early in life that later lead to unquestioning
      acceptance of using animals for human purposes.

746.  Cowen, Robert C. "Research Critics: Their Points Are
      Valid, Their Underlying Goals Aren't," *CSM* 26 July
      1984:19.
      Animal rights activists are raising valid issues but should

not try to eliminate abuse of some laboratory animals by banning use of all animals in research and thus restricting scientists' pursuit of knowledge.

747.  Cowley, Geoffrey, et al. "Of Pain and Progress: A Growing Social Movement Raises a Thorny Ethical Question: Do the Practical Benefits of Animal Experimentation Outweigh the Moral Costs," *Newsweek* 112 (December 26, 1988):50+.

A look at increasing popularity of animal rights movement, its issues, activities, and philosophy, with a special focus on animal experimentation.

748.  Curtis, Patricia. "New Debate Over Experimenting with Animals," *NYT Magazine* (December 31, 1978):18–23.

Most scientists believe animal experimentation is necessary, but some want to raise level of awareness of importance of animal care and be a link with animal humane organizations. Describes kinds of animal testing, some specifically designed to make animals writhe with pain, which critics see as nonuseful for studying human disease. Such tests yield unreliable data, because the stress from crowded conditions, callous treatment, pain, and fear affect an animal's metabolism and physiological responses.

749.  DeSilver, Drew. "Lab Warning: Vegetarian Applicants May Be Activists in Disguise," *Vegetarian Times* 140 (April 1989):8.

Biomedical laboratories are being warned not to hire vegetarians for fear they could be undercover animal rights activists bent on mischief.

750.  Devenport, L. D., and J. A. Devenport. "The Laboratory Animal Dilemma: A Solution in Our Backyards," *Psychological Science* 1 (July 1990):215–16.

Domestic pets studied in their own backyards can provide an ethical, cost-effective, and scientifically acceptable source for behavioral studies.

751.  Dewsbury, D. A. "Early Interaction Between Animal Psychologists and Animal Activists and the Founding of

the APA Committee on Precautions in Animal Experimentation," *American Psychologist* 45 (March 1990):315–27.

Historical overview of confrontation between animal rights activists and animal behaviorists of the late nineteenth century, which led to formation of an American Psychological Association committee to handle the problem. Contemporary battle between two groups is unprecedented with respect to scope and extent of media coverage and is broader, encompassing factory farming and hunting in addition to animal experimentation, but arguments and counterarguments are pretty much the same.

752. Dodds, W. Jean, and F. Barbara Orlans, eds. *Scientific Perspectives on Animal Welfare: A Symposium.* New York: Academic Press, 1982.

753. "Double Talk on Animals: NIH Seems More Ready to Risk Its Reputation Than to Meet Serious Critics on Animal Care," *Nature* 309 (May 3, 1984):2.

National Institutes of Health (NIH) is launching a public relations campaign to win public support for animal experimentation. Instead, it should be considering proposals like those suggested by Senator Robert Dole to eliminate persistent abuses in animal experimentation. NIH should face up to these issues instead of playing a public relations game.

754. Eckholm, Erik. "Fight Over Animal Experiments Gains Intensity on Many Fronts," *NYT* 7 May 1985:C1+.

In effort to head off criticism, biomedical industry is supporting animal welfare legislation, which one animal rights activist calls "window dressing." Researchers are also launching a public relations campaign, appealing to majority of Americans who support animal research. Animal rights activists believe they are part of a social reform movement in the tradition of those who fought for abolition of slavery and child labor.

755. Ellis, Gary B. "Necessary Fuss," *Bioscience* 36 (June 1986):356.

Scientist from Office of Technology Assessment says

new legislation and regulations on animal experimentation have benefited scientists, animal welfare advocates, and laboratory animals. Yet three trends are on a collision course: public's desire for medical progress, public's anxiety over safety of products, and animal welfarists' criticisms of the use of laboratory animals.

756.  "The Evidence," *AV* 3 (November/December 1990):8–15.
      A pictorial of laboratory animal abuse.

757.  Feeney, Dennis M. "Human Rights and Animal Welfare," *American Psychologist* 42 (June 1987):593–99.
      A paraplegic explains why alleviation of human suffering should take precedence over animal welfare and pain. Disabled persons should be consulted more about the issue of animal experimentation and their side of the story told. Condemns animal rights people, their philosophy, and activities.

758.  Feral, Priscilla. "Harbinger of Things to Come," *AV* 2 (June 1989):55.
      President of Friends of Animals warns against covert surveillance of animal rights groups and cites planting of microphone in her organization's telephone lines as well as possible setup of pipe bomb scheme by U.S. Surgical.

759.  Festing, Sally. "Animal Experiments: The Long Debate," *New Scientist* 121 (January 28, 1989):51–54.
      Debate over animal experimentation is hundreds of years old. The eighteenth century in particular had its antivivisection champions such as Samuel Johnson and Alexander Pope. Reform in nineteenth century is rooted in the eighteenth.

760.  Fields, Cheryl M. "Psychologists Emphasize Their Commitment to Humane Use of Animals in Research," *Chron H Ed* 29 (September 5, 1984):5+.
      Animal rights activists picketed American Psychological Association's annual meeting to protest behavioral research on animals. Psychologists discussed ways to minimize num-

ber of animals used in the future, defined research that had
provided benefits for humans, and revised guidelines for
use of animals. Animal advocates argue 80–90 percent of
research on animals is irrelevant to humans.

761. Fields, Cheryl M. "Radical Animal Rights Groups Pose a
Danger to Future Research, Psychologists Are Told," *Chron
H Ed* 27 (September 7, 1983):5–6.
Edward Taub of Silver Spring monkeys notoriety
warned American Psychological Association not to under-
estimate political and economic power of animal rights
groups that want to stop use of animals in scientific research. Animal rights activists protested outside the convention hall.

762. Fox, Jeffrey L. "Chimps in Research: Responding to a
Growing Nationwide Shortage, Federal Agencies Are
Developing a Controversial Plan to Manage Chimpanzees," *Bioscience* 35 (February 1985):75–76.
Biomedical researchers propose establishing a breeding
colony of chimpanzees to provide a ready source of chimps
for research. Animal rights advocates protest idea.

763. Fox, Michael W. "Animal Research: Right or Wrong?"
*McCall's* 112 (September 1985):158.
Scientific director of the Humane Society of the United
States says he is not opposed to all animal experiments, but
only those that are needlessly repetitive and cruel or involve drug and alcohol addiction or the testing of military
weapons and car safety.

764. Francione, Gary L. "The Importance of Access to Animal
Care Committees: A Primer for Activists," *AA* 10
(September 1990):45–47.
Professor of law at Rutgers University Law School explores purpose and effectiveness of animal care and use
committees. Although the committees have little control or
authority over animal experiments, they are crucial for
providing information about specific experiments, which
can be shared with the public.

765.  Francione, Gary L. "Xenografts and Animal Rights," *Transplantation Proceedings* 22,3 (1990):1044–46.
      How does the possibility of saving human life by way of the transplantation of an animal's organ affect the moral issue of using animals for human purposes? Trying to balance interests of humans and animals will result in using animals for transplants, but if idea of animal rights prevails, xenografts will be judged immoral.

766.  Frazier, Claude A. "Lessons from a Cat," *AA* 10 (May 1990):44–45.
      Personal essay by a physician who changed his mind about using animals in research because of a cat named Sweet Thing.

767.  Friedman, Ruth, comp. *Animal Experimentation and Animal Rights*. Phoenix, AZ: Oryx Press, 1987.
      Bibliography of primarily journal articles and books on the pros and cons of animal experimentation.

768.  Gallistel, C. R. "Bell, Magendie, and the Proposals to Restrict the Use of Animals in Neurobehavioral Research," *American Psychologist* 36 (April 1981):357–60.
      Argues against Research Modernization Act, saying it would devastate behavioral neurobiology. Bases this position on an experiment done by François Magendie in 1822 and his discovery that "dorsal and ventral roots are the sensory and motor roots." He used puppies for this intensely painful experiment. If he'd applied for permission from today's Humane Vivisection Committee, he probably would have been refused.

769.  Gallup, Gordon G., and Susan D. Suarez. "On the Use of Animals in Psychological Research," *Psychological Record* 30 (Spring 1980):211–18.

770.  Gluckstein, Fritz P. *Laboratory Animal Welfare*, Specialized Bibliography Series 1984–1. Bethesda, MD: Reference Services Division, National Library of Medicine, 1984, HE20.3614/6:1984–1.

Bibliography about historical, ethical, and philosophical aspects of animal experimentation from journal articles and monographs.

771. Gluckstein, Fritz P. *Laboratory Animal Welfare, Supplement I,* Specialized Bibliography Series 1985–1. Bethesda, MD: References Services Division, National Library of Medicine, 1985, HE20.3614/6:1985–1.

772. Gluckstein, Fritz P. *Laboratory Animal Welfare, Supplement II,* Specialized Bibliography Series 1986–1. Bethesda, MD: References Services Division, National Library of Medicine, 1986. HE20.3614/6:1986–1.

773. Gluckstein, Fritz P. *Laboratory Animal Welfare, Supplement III,* Specialized Bibliography Series 1987–1. Bethesda, MD: References Services Division, National Library of Medicine, 1987, HE20.3614/6:1987–1.

774. Goodall, Jane. "A Plea for the Chimps," *NYT Magazine* (May 17, 1987):108+.
    Leading chimpanzee expert finds laboratory conditions for chimps horrible. Deprived of social contact and kept isolated in small, bare cages, chimps show behavior of despair and depression. Suggests improvements that would make their lives better, including larger cages, an opportunity for them to interact with one another, and environmental enrichment such as addition of climbing apparatus.

775. Goodman, Walter. "Of Mice, Monkeys, and Men," *Newsweek* 100 (August 9, 1982):61.
    Is animal experimentation in interest of humanity as researchers say, or unnecessary and cruel as animal rights advocates claim?

776. Greenberg, Daniel S. "The Threat to Science Is Self-Inflicted," *LAT* 19 June 1984:II,5.
    Describes Galileo syndrome as a sensory disorder that causes scientists whenever criticized to feel kinship to the persecuted, seventeenth century Galileo. Points to contro-

versy over animal research as a good example, in which scientific community has branded all animal welfarists, even those with modest agendas, as a threat to science.

777. Gwynne, Peter, and Sharon Begley. "Animals in the Lab," *Newsweek* 91 (March 27, 1978):84–85.
Looks at specific and general examples of use of animals in medical research and testing. Discusses animal rights movement's efforts to regulate or abolish animal experimentation and research community's response.

778. Harrison, Barbara Grizzuti. "The Private Eye: What's Wrong with Animal Rights?" *Mademoiselle* 95 (July 1989):76.
Animal rights position on animal experimentation is extreme, and if the position were accepted, would exclude beneficial medical progress.

779. Hatch, Orin G. "Biomedical Research," *American Psychologist* 42 (June 1987):591–22.
Reviews positions on two sides of animal experimentation issue. Discusses Office of Technology Assessment's report that studied alternatives. Although there are some alternatives now available that federal agencies are willing to accept, some animal experimentation will always be necessary.

780. Hazlett, Thomas. "Animal Rights, Animal Crackers," *WSJ* 7 August 1985:16.
Attacks arguments and activities of animal rights activists. If society had followed animal rights antivivisectionist thought to its logical conclusion, animal rights people wouldn't be around today to protest, having died of smallpox, diphtheria, and the black plague.

781. Henig, Robin Marantz. "Animal Experimentation: The Battle Lines Soften," *Bioscience* 29 (March 1979):145–48.
Scientists are beginning to accept fact that sloppy care of laboratory animals affects quality of experiments and data collection. While National Society for Medical Research continues to resist suggestions for increased use

of alternatives or changes modifying use of vertebrates in high school classrooms and science fairs, other researchers such as those from newly founded Scientists Center for Animal Welfare welcome idea of a new discipline centered on applied science of animal welfare.

782. Heston, Charlton. "Promise of Animal Research Is Too Great to Abandon," *WP: Weekly Journal of Medicine, Health, Fitness, and Psychology,* 9 July 1986:WH6.
    Movie star Heston lists ways in which animal experimentation has improved human health. He thanks all laboratory animals from mice to monkeys for his own good health and that of his family and his pets. He also offers thankful prayers for animal researchers who labor and sacrifice to add quality to our lives.

783. Hettinger, Edwin C. "The Responsible Use of Animals in Biomedical Research," *Between the Species* 5 (Summer 1989):123–31.

784. Hoff, Christine. "Immoral and Moral Uses of Animals," *New England Journal of Medicine* 302 (January 10, 1980): 115–18.
    Differences between humans and animals allow former to use latter in experiments. Normal human lives are of far greater worth than animal lives, yet animals should not be used in painful experimentation unless substantial benefits are expected to result. Unfortunately, too many experiments do not contribute to medical science.

785. Holden, Constance. "A Pivotal Year for Lab Animal Welfare," *Science* 232 (April 11, 1986):147–50.
    The past year has been pivotal for animal welfare organizations and difficult for scientists. Animal Welfare Act was amended and Public Health Service established new guidelines for treatment of lab animals. National Institutes of Health moved to suspend funds in several institutions after Animal Liberation Front raids. Available alternatives were used more often and development of others encouraged by federal agencies and animal welfarists. Animal

rights influenced the termination of several research projects.

786. Iglehart, John K. "Of Mice and Medicine: Balancing Scientific Needs and Animal Welfare," *WP: Weekly Journal of Medicine, Health, Fitness, and Psychology* 11 September 1985:12–15.

Videos of University of Pennsylvania baboon experiments led Health and Human Services Secretary Margaret Heckler to suspend funding of project and triggered a debate over obligation humans have toward animals. Most researchers claim animal experimentation is central to quest for new knowledge and believe human life has priority over animal life. Animal rights groups disagree, saying animals suffer just as humans do. Confrontation between the two groups is mounting as each tries to influence policymakers, the press, and the television medium.

787. Iglehart, John K. "The Use of Animals in Research," *New England Journal of Medicine* 313 (August 8, 1985)L 395–400.

Question of animals in research has once again captured attention of public and legislators. Discusses lab break-ins, status of current and past legislation and of regulations about lab animals, and efforts by medical community to defend itself.

788. Jamieson, Dale. "Experimenting on Animals: A Reconsideration," *Between the Species* 1 (Summer 1985):4–11.

789. Johnson, Lisa M., and Edward K. Morris. "Public Information on Research with Nonhumans," *American Psychologist* 42 (January 1987):103–4.

In public relations battle, animal rights advocates are winning because they disseminate their side of the story better than researchers do. Authors sent out requests for information about animal experimentation to animal rights organizations and to research organizations. Animal rights people responded 90 percent of the time, the researchers only 10 percent.

790. Kagan, Connie. "Animal Experiments Foster False Hopes (letter)," *NYT* 23 July 1984:A18.

Head of the Animal Political Action Committee says biomedical industry breeds, sells, and consumes animals, so it has a financial investment in insisting on animal use even though alternatives are available.

791. Kalechofsky, Roberta. "Pro Vivisection Propaganda and the Nazi Lie," *AA* 9 (July/August 1989):54.

German Nazi experiments on humans were a continuation of the same experiments first tried on animals. Some experiments, like the typhus ones carried out at Buchenwald and Auschwitz, were done simultaneously on both humans and animals.

792. Kelly, Jeffrey A. "Psychological Research and the Rights of Animals: Disagreement with Miller," *American Psychologist* 41 (July 1986):839–41.

Author conducted a survey of 4,425 cited references in selected psychological journals and found only 2 percent referred to animal studies. If animal experiments are so important to clinical researchers and practitioners as animal experimenters claim, why are they cited so rarely?

793. Kennedy, Donald. "The Anti-Scientific Method," *WSJ* 29 October 1987:32.

President of Stanford University says animal rights groups, like student activists of the '60s, maintain deniability by having a variety of types in the movement. They repudiate actions of militant extremists and still approve of what they do. A key issue in winning the public's support for animal research is to educate the people so they won't be bamboozled so easily.

794. Kevles, Betty Ann. "Matters of the Heart," *LAT* 5 December 1984:V,1.

Sees both Baby Fae, the infant who was given a baboon's heart, and the baboon whose life and heart were "volunteered" as experimental subjects. The use of Baby

Fae as a guinea pig is ethically and scientifically question-able, but using the baboon is not.

795. Kevles, Betty Ann. "On Use, Abuse of Animals," *LAT* 27 April 1983:V,1+.

Use of animals in experiments presents ethical dilemma for humans, but each case deserves an appropriate re-sponse. Armadillos in England used in study of leprosy seem well treated and might save millions of human lives, but testing safety of cosmetics on rabbits' eyes is cruel and done for a frivolous reason. Concludes best humans can do is to make lab conditions humane for animals and keep searching for alternatives.

796. Kevles, Betty Ann. "To Zealots of Animal Lib, Biomedi-cine Is a Monster," *LAT* 7 February 1988:V,3.

Animal Liberation Front's release of animals used in re-search pulls at public's heartstrings but doesn't confront the fact that many medical advances have been made through use of animals in research. Well-meaning but mis-guided idealists think biomedical community is a monster and don't recognize personal anguish researchers feel as they try to sort out frivolous from necessary experiments.

797. Krauthammer, Charles. "In Defense of Fanatics: It's Not Monkeys That Need Them," *WP* 18 July 1986:A19.

Examines value and moderating effect of extremists in a pluralistic free society. Animal rights advocates have put research labs on their guard and made them safer places for animals. At the same time, while animal rights activists should be given a hearing, they should not be allowed to stop animal experimentation, because medical progress depends upon it.

798. Kuker-Reines, Brandon. *Environmental Experiments on Animals.* Boston: New England Anti-Vivisection Society, 1984.

Descriptive list of experiments conducted on animals under auspices of the U.S. Army research facility at Natick,

Massachusetts. After much suffering endured by animals and hundreds of their deaths, experiments have yet to contribute to either prevention or treatment of heat and cold injuries in humans.

799. Kuker-Reines, Brandon, ed. by Dick Teresi. "Useless Animal Slaughter," *Omni* 3 (March 1981):35.

It's time for a biomedical revolution in which models other than animals are used to find cures for diseases. Billions of animals have been starved, suffocated, shocked, frozen, irradiated, and poisoned, with few results. Animals are far from being the ideal research tool, because they are too different from humans and their diseases inaccurately mimic ours. Some researchers are trying to develop more . accurate models such as test-tube human tumor cells, but it's virtually impossible to get federal financing for non-animal-model research.

800. Landes, Susan Sperling. *Social Determinants of Attitudes Toward Primates and Other Animals.* Ph.D. dissertation, University of California, Berkeley, 1985.

The animal rights activists' position against animal experimentation symbolizes their perceived threat of human technology's manipulation of nature and is a response to anxiety engendered by scientific discovery and technological innovation. They see abolition of animals in research as an important step toward return to balanced relationship between humans and natural world.

801. Langley, Gil, ed. *Animal Experimentation: The Consensus Changes.* New York: Chapman and Hall, 1989.

Ten essays by recognized authorities in their fields address practical and philosophical issues regarding use of animals in biomedical research, testing, and teaching. Purpose is to encourage scientists, whether researchers, doctors, veterinarians, lab animal technicians, or science students, to reconsider their views on animal experimentation.

802. Leccese, Michael. "Of Mice and Monkeys: Animal

Research in Space Is Once Again a Hot Issue," *Space World* 8 (August 1985):16–18.

NASA is experimenting on monkeys and rats on earth and in space in the hope of discovering what causes nausea, rapid aging, and other physical problems in astronauts. Animal rights advocates protest such experiments are irrelevant to humans, a waste of money, and not very good science.

803.  Levey, Gerald S., and Lynn Morrison. "Lab Animals' Use," *NYT* 14 June 1983:A23.

Two professors of medicine maintain animal rights activists are well intentioned but misguided. Lab animals are well taken care of, inspections regular, and government guidelines followed. In any case, human suffering and human lives are more important considerations than animals'. So animal use in research must continue.

804.  Loew, Franklin M. "Using Animals in Research: What's Going on Here?" *Chron H Ed* 31 (September 18, 1985):80.

Antivivisection movement seen from researcher's point of view. It is important animal research continue, but animal rights advocates and the public are paying attention, so it's also important researchers be able to justify their work and demonstrate they take proper care of laboratory animals.

805.  Lopatto, David. "Animal Research: Collateral Issues Concerning Scientific Practice in the Context of Education," *Psychological Record* 36 (Spring 1986):145–54.

Looks at arguments against use of animals in psychology experiments as they relate to method, aim, and practice of science. Animal rights protests cause a researcher to be more conscious about practices and the reasons for them and to be more articulate about such practices.

806.  Mackay-Smith, Anne. "Animal Rights Fight Against Pet Projects Worries Researchers," *WSJ* 30 November 1983:1+.

Animal Liberation Front's break-in at Howard University triggers review of arguments for and against vivisection. The animal rights movement is growing, with 400 groups and 2 million members. Describes animal experimenters' defense against charges of scientific invalidity in the use of animals in research.

807. Magner, Denise K. "Alleged Plot Prompts Extra Security on Some Campuses," *Chron H Ed* 36 (March 7, 1990):A2.

    Based on thirdhand information, police issued advisory of an animal rights plot to murder one veterinary school dean each month. Animal rights groups call the idea absurd and ridiculous, but some college officials are taking extra safety precautions.

808. March, B. E. "Bioethical Problems: Animal Welfare, Animal Rights," *Bioscience* 34 (November 1984):615–20.

    Historical overview of Western treatment of and attitudes toward animals. Addresses question of why there is a surge of concern for animals today on the part of a generation that has lost contact with domestic and wild animals. Includes text of "Universal Declaration of Rights of Animals" and "A Declaration Against Speciesism."

809. "Martha Is Put to Death," *AV* 2 (February 1989):71.

    University of Washington euthanized Martha, an 18-year-old macaque monkey, rather than allow animal rights activists to take her to Primarily Primates, an animal refuge in Texas.

810. McCabe, Jane. "Is a Lab Rat's Fate More Poignant Than a Child's?" *Newsweek* 112 (December 26, 1988):55.

    Mother of a child with cystic fibrosis chastises animal rights activists for caring more about animal than human suffering.

811. McDonald, Kim. "Coalition Against Animal Research Threatens Demonstrations at Universities," *Chron H Ed* 32 (April 16, 1986):6–7.

    Animal rights groups ask 60 university presidents to allow them to photograph animal laboratory conditions at their institutions and to begin discussions on phasing out animal experimentation. The groups also asked for an end to use of strays in experiments and assurance that students who don't wish to participate in dissection or vivisection be protected against reprisals. Universities rejected proposals, calling them a "crude threat" to intimidate academic community.

812.   McDonald, Kim. "More Protests Planned Over Welfare of Lab Animals," *Chron H Ed* 26 (May 4, 1983):3.
       Activists protest at primate research labs at University of California, Davis; Emory University; Harvard University; and University of Wisconsin at Madison.

813.   McDonald, Kim. "Protests Planned Over Use of Animals in Laboratories," *Chron H Ed* 26 (April 13, 1983):3.
       Four hundred animal welfare groups, under leadership of Mobilization for Animals, plan to stage protests at four primate research centers run by National Institutes of Health. Their purpose is to raise public consciousness about need for accountability and standardized procedures in care of research animals. Primate centers are fighting back by public information campaign that emphasizes medical value of animal experimentation.

814.   Medlock, Aaron. "Animal Research Is Not Only Choice," *WP* 2 August 1986:A19.
       Former director of the New England Anti-Vivisection Society refutes pro-vivisection arguments put forth by Charlton Heston. Extending life expectancy has been derived from changes in basic sanitation and sensible living habits, not animal experimentation. We do have choice other than using animals in research.

815.   Miller, Neal E. "The Value of Behavioral Research on Animals," *American Psychologist* 40 (April 1985):423–40.
       Refutes animal rights claim that behavioral research on animals is without value. Cites specific examples to show how animal experimentation has helped both humans and animals.

816.   Mishkin, Barbara. "On Parallel Tracks: Protecting

Human Subjects and Animals," *Hastings Center Report* 15 (October 1985):36–43.

Attorney who helped develop policies for protection of humans participating in research studies compares the attempt to do the same for laboratory animals.

817. "Misplaced Sentimentality," *LAT* 27 April 1989:II,6.

Research on nonhumans is an unfortunate but indispensable part of valid medical science and can't be replaced by tissue cultures and computer simulations. Animal rights advocates are self-absorbed and vulgar, with sentimentality masquerading as compassion.

818. Mitric, Joan McQueeney. "Animal Rights, Human Needs: Scientists and Activists Weigh the Suffering Against the Benefits to Mankind," *WP: Weekly Journal of Medicine, Health, Fitness, and Psychology* 19 February 1986:WH7.

Over 50 representatives of drug and cosmetic companies, universities, medical organizations, and animal welfare groups met to debate animal experimentation at a public, daylong hearing convened by National Academy of Sciences. The 12-member committee hearing the divergent arguments has until late 1987 to draft policy statement and recommendations on use of animals in research.

819. "Mobilizing to Protect Animals," *CSM* 26 April 1983:24.

Mobilization for Animals brings together an international coalition of animal rights groups and others concerned over treatment of laboratory animals.

820. Moll, Lucy. "Animal Research: Who Profits," *Vegetarian Times* 141 (May 1989):39–51+.

Does research using animals better the lives of humans? Some former animal researchers say no. They claim $8 billion spent on animal research could be better used on preventive medicine, but vested interests in biomedical research oppose that approach.

821. Moss, Thomas. "The Modern Politics of Laboratory Animal use," *Bioscience* 34 (November 1984):621–25.

Scientists are starting to realize concern for lab animals is not a minor feature in overall scheme of biomedical progress. Respect for animal life is not any more irrational than respect for human life, and such an attitude on the part of the public is healthy. Rather than reacting negatively, scientists should address public's concern about welfare of lab animals, or scientists will be left out of process of creating legislation on the issue. Discusses Research Modernization Act.

822.    Mouras, Belton P. "Lifting the Curtain on Animal Labs," *USA Today* 116 (March 1988):48–51.

President and founder of Animal Protection Institute chastises animal researchers for responding to public outcry against brutality in their labs by saying it's a public relations problem. Profound need for reform of animal experimentation and institutions supporting it.

823.    Muscatine, Alison. "U.S. Primate Research Center Opens," *WP* 8 June 1984:C1.

One-million-dollar primate center funded by National Institutes of Health opened that will use rhesus monkeys to study stress, anxiety, and depression commonly found in humans. Animal rights organizations did not protest opening.

824.    Newkirk, Ingrid. "A Healthy Respect for Animal Rights (letter)," *WSJ* 2 January 1987:15.

Director of People for the Ethical Treatment of Animals says her organization is not antiscience. Supports all latest research technology, including computer modeling and human cell cloning. At the same time, believes not all research is necessarily good research especially when it comes to animal experiments.

825.    Newman, Alan. "Research Versus Animal Rights: Is There a Middle Ground," *American Scientist* 77 (March/April 1989):135–37.

Discussion of present debate on use of animals in biomedical and product safety testing.

826. "NIH Starts Program in Animal Use Education," *Chemical and Engineering News* 62 (April 16, 1984):10.

National Institutes of Health attempts to win public support for animal experimentation by responding to legitimate concerns of critics.

827. "On Behalf of Medical Science," *LAT* 9 September 1985:II,4.

Editorial supports use of animals in research. After Animal Liberation Front's raid of University of California, Riverside, police should have rounded up animal rights fanatics. At the same time, research facilities should not mistreat their animals, since exposure may endanger their federal grants.

828. Pacelle, Wayne. "Venting Fury at APA," *AA* 7 (November 1987):14.

More than 300 demonstrators protest at annual American Psychological Association convention against use of animals in psychological research.

829. "Poll Finds Support for Animal Tests," *NYT* 29 October 1985:C4.

According to poll conducted by the Media General–Associated Press, 50 percent of the 1,412 people surveyed believed lab animals were treated humanely, and a majority felt it was necessary to use animals in biomedical research.

830. Pratt, Dallas. *Painful Experiments on Animals.* New York: Argus Archives, 1976.

Descriptive list of painful experiments and procedures done on animals.

831. Quigley, Cheryl Ann. "The Torture of Animals Should Torture Our Souls," *LAT* 27 April 1984:II,7.

Looks at World Day for Laboratory Animals and the difficulty of changing status quo on vivisection. Researchers are resistant to idea of employing valid alternatives, because they would have to learn a new methodology and because while doing that, grants would dry up. Also, those who provide lab animals and accessories have enormous financial interest and lobbying power to keep things as they are. Vivisectors need to address ethics of causing intense suffering to animals and to discuss validity of data they collect in animal experiments.

832.  Regan, Tom. "Animals Are Not Our Tasters, We Are Not Their Kings," *AV* 2 (June 1989):22+.
      In days of yore, kings and members of the royal family determined if their food was safe by having a powerless serf taste it first. The idea was to protect those in power, because the killing or injuring of a serf carried no moral importance. Humans have same attitude toward animals, but today as in yesteryear, might still does not make right. Discusses immorality of causing animals to suffer and die for human purposes.

833.  Reinhold, Robert. "Do Two Research Chimps Want to Retire? Ask Them, Some People Say," *NYT* 10 June 1982:A26.
      Nim Chimsky and his brother Ally, two chimps taught sign language, are in danger of being used in hepatitis research in which they would be housed in solitary caging. Several animal protection groups, as well as psychologist who taught the chimps, are trying to negotiate retirement for them at a primate rehabilitation center or refuge.

834.  Ritvo, Harriet. "Plus Ça Change: Antivivisection Then and Now," *Bioscience* 34 (November 1984):626–33.
      Conference held in Boston on "Standards for Research with Animals: Current Issues and Proposed Legislation" triggers comparison of Victorian period's antivivisection movement with today's. Scientists and animal rights advocates hold different views of animal experimentation, which are irreconcilable. Antivivisection will flourish as long as "ordinary sober citizens do not agree with scientists that scientific progress and freedom of investigation override rights and feelings of animals."

835. Rogers, Bonnie. "Have Those Who Stole Dogs Seen Anyone Die of Cancer," *LAT* 21 December 1984:II,7.

Associate director of communications of the City of Hope talks about death of her father from lung cancer and why she believes the misguided people who stole animals used in lung cancer research at the City of Hope are concerned only for a few dogs and not human life.

836. Rollin, Bernard E. *The Unheeded Cry: Animal Consciousness, Animal Pain, and Science.* Oxford, England, and New York: Oxford University Press, 1989.

Do animals possess consciousness? Can they experience pain, anxiety, suffering, happiness? Many scientists answer in the negative. Rollin traces evolution of scientist's approach to animal consciousness from one of common sense in era of Darwin and Romanes to one that denies the obvious under a guise of value-free science today. Such leads to unfortunate moral and scientific consequences.

837. Rollin, Bernard E., and Andrew N. Rowan. "Animal Research—For and Against: A Philosophical, Social and Historical Perspective," *Perspectives in Biology and Medicine* 27 (Autumn 1983):1–17.

Looks at animal experimentation controversy historically and at legislation such as Animal Welfare Act and proposed Research Modernization Act, aimed at giving lab animals increased protection. Recent public concern over the issue is caused by negative perception of science, intellectual revitalization of animal welfare philosophy, growth of militant action, and recognition that alternatives are available. Debate will continue, but things look more hopeful for laboratory animals.

838. Rosenfeld, Albert. "Animal Rights vs. Human Health," *Science 81* 2 ( June 1981):18–19.

Rigorous regulations ensuring humane treatment of animals are already in place and no more are needed. Animal rights movement is a grave threat to important research, because unlike previous movements of similar intent, this one is carefully orchestrated, well financed, and well organized.

839.   Rosner, Fred. "Is Animal Experimentation Being Threatened by Animal Rights Groups," *Journal of the American Medical Association* 254 (October 11, 1985):1942–43.

Animal models have made invaluable contributions to understanding, treatment, and cure of human diseases. Talks about restrictive federal legislation, past and pending, in care of lab animals that would interfere with research.

840.   Rowan, Andrew N. *Of Mice, Models, and Men: A Critical Evaluation of Animal Research*. Albany, New York: State University of New York Press, 1984.

Examination of arguments for and against animal experimentation. Includes history of the debate, analysis of attitudes and assumptions that make reasoned debate difficult, and a consideration of theories on animal pain and suffering. Addresses training of scientists, lack of system to consider ethical issues, and philosophical and practical paradoxes involved in using animals to study humans. Suggests constructive action that would improve conditions for laboratory animals but still allow their use in a research environment.

841.   Rowan, Andrew N. "Why Scientists Should Seek Alternatives to Animal Use," *Technology Review* 89 (May/June 1986):22–23.

Director of the Center for Animals at Tufts University School of Veterinary Medicine believes the public supports animal experimentation in medical research, but not for trivial research or in cruel and unnecessary experiments. The government should fund development of alternatives such as radioimmunoassay and hybridoma technologies, and these methods should be encouraged by funding agencies.

842.   Ruesch, Hans. "Slaughter of the Innocent," *AV* 3 (December 1990):32–46.

Discussion both of the types of useless and pain-provoking experiments being practiced today on laboratory animals and of the enormous sums of money funding these experiments that instead could be spent on human problems. Accompanied by graphic photographs.

843. Salisbury, David F. "Animal Liberation," *Technology Review* 80 (May 1978):8–9+.
Arguments between scientists and animal rights advocates about value of animals and their use in the laboratory.

844. Sapolsky, Harvey M. "The Use of Animals in Research (letter)," *New England Journal of Medicine* 314 (April 10, 1986):994.
Medical community should not blindly defend researchers who fail standards for care of lab animals. Defense of research must be based on solid, scientific grounds.

845. Sapontzis, Steven F. "Some Reflections on Animal Research," *Between the Species* 1 (Winter 1984/85):18–24.

846. "Saving Creatures Great and Small," *U.S. News & World Report* 105 (December 5, 1988):13.

847. Shapiro, Jeremy. "In Defense of Animal Rights (letter)," *WSJ* 25 November 1987:15.
Member of Fielding Institute takes exception to op-ed piece by Donald Kennedy ("Anti-Scientific Method," October 29, 1987). Says scientific ethics have been legitimate issue for debate since invention of atom bomb. The issue of torturing animals in research needs discussion, and to oppose it is to abandon critical rationality and justification for scientific research.

848. Shapiro, Kenneth J. "Animal Rights Versus Humanism: The Charge of Speciesism," *Journal of Humanistic Psychology* 30 (Spring 1990):9–37.
Cofounder of Psychologists for the Ethical Treatment of

Animals explores compatibility of humanistic psychology with emerging animal rights movement and its philosophical tenets. There is potential compatibility and reconciliation between the two through a phenomenological rendering of empathy.

849.  Singer, Peter. "Animal Experimentation: Philosophical Perspectives," in *Encyclopedia of Bioethics, Vol. I.* New York: Free Press, 1978, pp. 79–83.

Overview of the nature and extent of animal experimentation and the legislation that has failed to regulate it effectively. Examines traditional arguments in favor of experimentation and those against it. The latter group represents several factions which differ in philosophical approach but are in accord in desire to see more ethical treatment of animals.

850.  Singer, Peter. "New Attitudes Needed on Animal Testing," *New Scientist* 127 (August 11, 1990):16.

In spite of scientists' protestation that they care about lab animals, many grotesque, painful experiments and inadequate care continue. The scientific community has failed to grapple seriously with issue of the moral status of animals.

851.  Smollar, David. "Research Labs, Zoos for an Uneasy Alliance," *LAT* 23 June 1985:I,3+.

Zoos and the biomedical industry are beginning to interact with one another and will meet for first time in San Diego for joint conference. Animal activists fear zoos will sell surplus animals produced from their overbreeding programs to animal experimenters and research labs, but zoo administrators say they try to place surplus animals in other zoos before selling them to research labs.

852.  Stein, Benjamin J. "It's Not a Cause for Cranks," *WP* 19 March 1983:A17.

Cuts in federal spending should be aimed at $4 billion used in government-funded research using animals. Much of such research is unnecessary and duplicative. Tax dollars can be used better for food stamps and heating-fuel assistance for the elderly and for community development in inner cities. Using available alternatives to animals in testing would also save money, because alternatives are cheaper. Resistance to unnecessary animal experimentation is not a crank cause; it's an issue for all people who deplore the waste of federal money.

853. Stevens, Christine. "Animal Torture in Corporate Dungeons," *Business and Society Review* (Spring 1984):39–43.
     Examines Draize and LD-50 tests, why companies are unwilling to give them up, and the huge profits involved in breeding and selling lab animals. Purposeless animal suffering could be eliminated by passing the Improved Standards for Laboratory Animals Act and funding a federal agency to properly enforce it. Responsible citizens should insist Congress take these steps promptly.

854. Stevens, Christine. "Mistreatment of Laboratory Animals Endangers Biomedical Research," *Nature* 311 (September 27, 1984):295–97.
     Outlines abuses in animal research laboratories and discusses pending congressional legislation proposed by Senator Robert Dole and Representative George Brown, which would remedy some of these abuses. Compares U.S. laws protecting lab animals with British Cruelty to Animals Act and finds the former wanting. Needed reforms include adequate inspections of labs by agriculture department, willingness of researchers to acknowledge and remedy bad lab practices, and provision of analgesics and anesthesia for animals involved in painful experiments.

855. Stevenson, Richard W. "A Campaign for Research on Animals," *NYT* 20 January 1989:D5.
     Art director at Bozell, Jacobs, Kenyon, and Eckhardt in New York volunteered to help Foundation for Biomedical Research by preparing advertisements to counter animal rights appeal. Three ads tie animal experimentation to saving children's lives and extending lives of others, including those of animal rights advocates. People for the

Ethical Treatment of Animals noted that while biomedicine often accuses animal rights advocates of being irrational and emotional, these ads demonstrate it is biomedical researchers who use such tactics.

856.  Sun, Marjorie. "Animal Lovers Might Monitor Labs," *Science* 216 (April 2, 1982):37.
Reagan Administration wants agriculture department to turn over inspection of animal labs to local and state agencies, industry groups, and humane societies. Both animal and research communities protest.

857.  Sun, Marjorie. "Primate Centers Brace for Protests," *Science* 219 (March 4, 1983):1049.
A hundred animal welfare groups, under leadership of Mobilization for Animals, plan to march and protest at primate research centers across the country. Researchers are worried radical elements may cause trouble despite leaders' assurances they plan to march peacefully.

858.  "This Is What You Thought . . . Medical Experiments on Animals," *Glamour* 79 (December 1981):59.
Poll conducted of *Glamour* readers about their attitudes toward animal experimentation.

859.  Torrey, Lee. "The Agony of Primate Research," *Science Digest* 92 (May 1984):70–72.
Primates are closest to humans in sharing psychological and physical characteristics, and for that reason their use in research has caused more controversy than use of other animals. Discusses trapping, shipping, and storage of primates and the high mortality rate of 70 percent that results. Types of experiments done on them include weapons testing, sensory deprivation, drug use, whiplash injuries, car safety testing.

860.  "Torturing Animals," *WP* 28 July 1985:B6.
Research using animals is necessary, but U.S. government should not be subsidizing sadistic experiments. Reports are written regularly about animal abuse in labo-

ratories, and researchers seem slow to accept necessary safeguards. Institutions and handlers need to make a better effort to meet federal guidelines governing treatment of animals.

861. Trizzino, Jeannie. "World Laboratory Animal Liberation Week 1988: A Declaration of War," *AV* 1 (September/October 1988):10–11.

   Summary of activities marking day of protest against animal experimentation in Maryland, Oregon, Texas, California, Missouri, Japan, and England.

862. "UC Berkeley Illustrates How Lab Animal Care Has Changed," *Chemical and Engineering News* 68 (May 7, 1990):14–15.

   University of California, Berkeley, is described as a model of how animal research labs have improved in past ten years.

863. Wade, Nicholas. "NIH Considers Animal Rights," *Science* 199 (January 20, 1978):279.

   Ethics of animal experimentation addressed by National Institutes of Health Deputy Director Thomas E. Malone. Researchers have nothing to fear from public scrutiny.

864. Walton, Susan. "Congress Puts Bioassay to the Test," *Bioscience* 31 (April 1981):287–90.

   Considers pros and cons of using live animals in bioassay (how substances affect living organisms) in terms of economics, ethics, and accuracy. Discusses ramifications of three congressional bills that address issue of studying, promoting, and developing alternatives to animal testing. Suggests chimpanzees should have special consideration and be treated the same as would a human in a research environment.

865. Webster, Bayard. "Should Vivisection Be Abolished," *NYT* 27 September 1983:C1+.

   The most controversial of the animal rights issues is animal experimentation in biomedical laboratories. Animal rights activists argue against needless cruelty and say alternatives are available. Researchers say they have a right to use animals for human benefit. The proper relationship between man and animals is now being discussed by theologians, physicians, businesspeople, and lay people.

866.  "What You Can Do," *AV* 3 (December 1990):58–64.
      Suggestions for what ordinary readers can do to end vivisection, including keeping informed on the issues and writing protest letters against specific experiments.

867.  "World Laboratory Animal Liberation Week," *AA* 10 (July/August 1990):38–39.
      Protests and rallies take place in twenty-three states at government and university animal research facilities to publicize plight of laboratory animals.

868.  "World Week for Lab Animals," *AA* 9 (September 1989):22.
      Hundreds protest in Los Angeles, New York, District of Columbia, Buffalo, Sacramento, and Atlanta against animal experimentation, with eighteen animal rights groups participating.

869.  Worsnop, Richard L. "Animal vs. Human Rights," *Editorial Research Reports* II (July 29, 1983): "Dailies Reminder."
      Pending animal rights issues: Defense Secretary Weinberger's ban on use of dogs in military experiments, and congressional debate over guidelines for care and treatment of lab animals in federally funded projects and facilities.

870.  Worsnop, Richard L. "Animals In Research," *Editorial Research Reports* II (December 4, 1984): "Dailies Reminder."
      Update on year's congressional activities on the use of animals in research: Health Research Extension Act, use of animals in military research by defense department, and bill backed by National Society for Medical Research that would make it a federal crime to break into a federally funded lab.

871. Wortman, Judith. "AIBS Joins Effort to Increase Animal Welfare Funds," *Bioscience* 34 (June 1984):357.
    American Institute of Biological Sciences joins others in supporting adequate funding of Animal and Plant Health Inspection Service to enforce Animal Welfare Act.

872. Zak, Stephen. "Cruelty in Labs," *NYT* 16 May 1983:A19.
    Gruesome, unnecessary animal experiments waste taxpayer money and are examples of callousness as old as human history. It is obvious animals feel pain and show it by their trembling, crying out, and efforts to escape, yet their use in research goes on in spite of available alternatives. Federal law does little to protect the 64 million lab animals used each year in this country.

## Philosophy, Ethics, and Religion

873. "Animal Rights Movement Is Opposed to Humans' Use of Animals," *Chemical and Engineering News* 68 (May 7, 1990):10–11.
    Criticizes position that animals share many of the same rights with humans. Looks at Peter Singer's and Tom Regan's arguments against animal experimentation.

874. Bowd, Alan D. "Ethical Reservations About Psychological Research," *Psychological Record* 30 (Spring 1980):201–10.
    Critical examination both of ethical defense of prevalent research practices that allow use of animals and of institutional factors contributing to attitudes and beliefs psychologists hold toward lab animals.

875. Bowd, Alan D. "Reply to Gallup and Suarez," *Psychological Record* 30 (Summer 1980):423–25.
    Defense of ethical arguments against painful experiments on animals.

876. Burghardt, Gordon M., and Harold A. Herzog Jr. "Beyond Conspecifics: Is Brer Rabbit Our Brother," *Bioscience* 30 (November 1980):763–67.

Lists twenty-six considerations usually involved in determining value, worth, and ethical stance in the use of animals for any purpose. Concludes the best we can do in arriving at our relationship and treatment of animals is to take a culture-bound approach that evaluates various costs and benefits for given types of animal exploitation.

877.  Donnelley, Strachan. "The Heart of the Matter," *Hastings Center Report* 19 ( January/February 1989):26–27.
      Is it ethical to transplant chimpanzee hearts into humans, knowing that there are fewer than 100,000 chimps left in the wild? Yes, if they are used to perfect a technique by which more abundant animals such as pigs and cows could be donors, but not if they are used as a supply source for individuals needing heart transplants. This is based on idea of ethical duty to protect ongoing realm of life as a whole.

878.  Fox, Michael A. "Animal Experimentation: A Philosopher's Changing Views," *Between the Species* 3 (Spring 1987):55–60+.
      Former outspoken apologist for animal experimentation explains why he changed his mind and why he now believes vivisection cannot be justified.

879.  Fox, Michael A. *The Case for Animal Experimentation: An Evolutionary and Ethical Perspective*. Berkeley, CA: University of California Press, 1986.
      Animals are not moral equals of humans and should not be treated as such. Justifies use of animals in research on ethical grounds.

880.  Fox, Michael W. "On the Use of Animals in Research," *American Psychologist* 37 (May 1982):598–99.
      There are ways to enrich human understanding without destroying or causing suffering to animals. C. R. Gallistel's conclusions that researchers can sacrifice certain moral principles to satisfy exclusively human interests is questionable.

881.  Gaylin, Willard. "The Heart of the Matter," *Hastings Center Report* 19 ( January/February 1989):27–28.

Transplantation of chimp hearts to humans presents moral dilemma. In the end, however, author is willing to see the chimp species extinct if such relieved the pain and suffering of children or saved the species homo sapiens.

882. Gendin, Sydney. "The Animal Experiment Controversy," *American Psychologist* 37 (May 1982):595–96.
Maintains C. R. Gallistel misstated provisions of the Research Modernization Act and claimed animal experimentation is needed for continued scientific progress without any supporting arguments. He seems to be unaware of serious literature on moral arguments about animal experimentation, and yet it is axiomatic in scientific and philosophical circles that advances come by responsible reflection and response to those with whom one disagrees.

883. Kelly, Jeffrey A. "Disagreement with Gallistel: The Need for Increased Scrutiny of Animal Research," *American Psychologist* 37 (May 1982):596–98.
Humane treatment of animals is an ethical issue and should be treated as one. Research Modernization Act would ensure that research causing pain to animals be of sufficient scientific merit to justify pain and that it not be replicative nor replaceable by other methods.

884. McCloskey, H. J. "The Moral Case for Experimentation on Animals," *Monist* 70 (January 1987):64–82.
Morality of animal experimentation reflects prima facie duty to maximize balance of good over evil—in this case, the good of alleviating human suffering against the bad of causing animals to suffer. Not all experimentation is equal, however. Suffering to animals should be minimized as much as possible and terminated as soon as possible.

885. "Pro and Con: Use Animal Organs for Human Transplants?" *U.S. News & World Report* 97 (November 12, 1984):58.
Dr. Jack Provonsha, director of the Center for Christian Ethics at Loma Linda University, argues it is justifiable to

kill animals and use their organs for humans, because on an ethical value scale, humans always place above subhumans. Tom Regan, professor of philosophy at North Carolina State University, takes opposite stance, believing animals exist for themselves and not as organ resources for humans.

886.   Regan, Tom, ed. *Animal Sacrifice: Religious Perspectives on the Use of Animals in Science.* Philadelphia: Temple University Press, 1986.

Nine theologians and ethicists from Catholic, Jewish, Muslim, Hindu, Jain, Buddhist, Confucian, and Protestant faiths examine the moral ramifications of using animals in scientific research.

887.   Rodd, Rosemary. *Biology, Ethics, and Animals.* Oxford, England: Clarendon Press, 1990.

Examination of theories and factual discoveries from the life sciences to develop ideas about the moral and biological status of animals. Not intended to be a comprehensive discussion of animal rights but can provide guidelines on how we should go about assessing our behavior toward nonhuman animals.

888.   Rollin, Bernard E. "The Moral Status of Research Animals in Psychology," *American Psychologist* 40 (August 1985):920–26.

Science is not value free, including its commitment to use animals in research. Moral obligation to animals needs to be examined, especially in area of psychology. Rising emphasis on cognitive psychology may see fewer pointless and invasive experiments on animals and more effort toward theory construction.

889.   Rowan, Andrew N., and Jerrold Tannenbaum. "Rethinking the Morality of Animal Research," *Hastings Center Report* 15 (October 1985):32–43.

Examines schools of philosophical thought as they relate to the moral status of animals: ethical skepticism, relativism, absolute dominionism, utilitarianism, anthropocentric consequentialism, reverence for life and humane beneficence. One should approach ethical issue of use of research animals by including a consideration of their suffering, well-being, pleasure, pain, thought and reason, purposiveness, and self-awareness. In addition to these, other areas specific to each animal or species must be considered such as interaction and kinships, and biological nature. Justifies continuing use of animals in research and sets an agenda for future discussion of the topic.

890. Singer, Peter. "To Do or Not To Do," *Hastings Center Report* 17 (December 1989):42–44.

Compares action and morality of two activists who take the law into their own hands—one to save mentally retarded humans from experimentation, the other to save monkeys from the same fate. Addresses morality of these actions vis-à-vis political systems and other avenues of reform.

891. Slicer, Deborah. "Your Daughter or Your Dog: Against the Singer-Regan Approach to Deciding Our Moral Obligations to Animals." **Ph.D.** dissertation, University of Virginia, 1989.

Argues against Tom Regan's and Peter Singer's positions on rights and utilitarianism as they relate to interspecies obligations and especially the morality of the use of animals in research.

## Law and Legislation

892. Anderson, Christopher. "Congress Cracks Down," *Nature* 343 (February 15, 1990):580.

Bills introduced in Congress that would make break-ins or other crimes against animal research labs a federal offense that carries harsh penalties.

893. Anderson, Christopher. "New Laws Divide Lawmakers," *Nature* 344 (March 1, 1990):96.

Congressional bill currently under consideration would make animal laboratory break-ins a federal offense. Justice department opposes the bill on grounds it would transfer power from the states to federal government. Meanwhile, eighty other bills are pending in Congress that oppose or support goals of animal rights and animal welfare.

894.  "Animal Experiments—A Better Way," *CSM* 25 October 1979:24.
       The Research Modernization Act, cosponsored by thirty-one House members, would encourage using alternatives to animal experimentation, developing new testing methods that minimize or eliminate painful experiments, and mandating an end to duplication of animal experiments.

895.  "Animal Politics in Cambridge," *NYT* 27 September 1987:A50.
       City Council of Cambridge, Massachusetts, approves least restrictive of several proposals to regulate animal experimentation within city limits. Animal advocates cease to agitate for a public referendum for fear of antagonizing the council.

896.  "Animal Research Facilities Protection Act Update," *AA* 10 (January/February 1990):35.
       Legislation by Rep. Charles Rose is introduced to counteract the Heflin, Stenholm, Waxman, and Helms bills that would outlaw any unauthorized possession of lab documents, even those showing violations of Animal Welfare Act.

897.  "Animal Welfare," *Scientific American* 256 (February 1987):60.
       Ordinance proposal in Cambridge, Massachusetts, would establish an advisory committee to regulate all animal experiments within city limits, including those at Harvard University and Massachusetts Institute of Technology.

898.  "Animals and Friends: The U.S. Congress Should Avoid Passing Unworkable Animal Rights Legislation," *Nature* 343 (February 15, 1990):578.
       Congress should concentrate on making sure amendments to the Animal Welfare Act don't interfere with scientists' research, instead of focusing on legislation to punish those who break into laboratories.

899. Beardsley, Tim. "Laboratory Animals: U.S. Protection Act Approved," *Nature* 319 (January 2, 1986):7.

Congress passes The Improved Standards for Laboratory Animals Act, which requires a committee made up of at least one disinterested party to justify experiments involving animals and to keep animals' pain and distress at a minimum.

900. Broad, William J. "Legislating an End to Animals in the Lab," *Science* 208 (May 9, 1980):575–76.

The Research Modernization Act, supported by animal rights groups, would create a central clearinghouse at National Institutes of Health to disseminate information on alternatives to animal experiments. Center could cut off funds to any project that used animals when nonanimal alternatives would serve the project better. Researchers feel this would have catastrophic results for them.

901. Brody, Mimi. "Animal Research: A Call for Legislative Reform Requiring Ethical Merit," *Harvard Environmental Law Review* 13 (Summer 1989):423–84.

Existing legal framework fails to require evaluation of research projects using animals, but it should for ethical reasons. Proposes a regulatory scheme that would require justification for each project and a protective scheme to minimize animal pain and suffering for those experiments approved.

902. Brown, George E. "Improving Standards for Laboratory Animals," *Congressional Record* 130 (May 24, 1984): E2453–56.

Introduction of legislation in House of Representatives by Hon. George E. Brown of California would give further protection to laboratory animals.

903. Buyukmihei, Ned. "The Use of Nonhuman Animals in Research," *Law Library Journal* 82 (Spring 1990):351–57.

Veterinarian, who previously used animals in research, questions the ethics and morality of such use, now believing the only reason we do many of the things we do to animals is that we have the power to dominate them. Sees Animal Welfare Act as largely ineffectual in protection of animals.

904.  "Cambridge Eyes Rules on Research Animals," *NYT* 7 December 1986:A89.
       Cambridge, Massachusetts, City Council is considering a proposal sponsored by animal rights groups that would regulate both the use of animals in research and the research itself. Opponents to proposal say they are already regulated enough.

905.  "Cambridge Lab Animal Law a Step Forward," *Vegetarian Times* 146 (October 1989):20.
       Cambridge Committee for Responsible Research gets agreement from the Cambridge, Massachusetts, City Council to pass an ordinance to regulate animal research in thirteen major research institutions including Harvard and Massachusetts Institute of Technology. The ordinance empowers a commission to oversee and enforce lab regulations, and it legislates appointment of animal care committees.

906.  "Cambridge to Supervise Animal Research," *AA* 9 (September 1989):22.
       Cambridge City Council in Massachusetts sets a national precedent by appointing a commissioner who will supervise all animal experimentation done within the city.

907.  Chambers, Tate, and Cathleen Hines. "Recent Developments Concerning the Use of Animals in Medical Research," *Journal of Legal Medicine* 4 (March 1983):109–29.
       Attempts to facilitate compromise between animal rights advocates' legitimate concern for lab animals and researchers' goals of medical progress. Looks at possible statutory solutions proposed by animal rights activists to use alternatives, enforce existing laws, classify animals into groups, and provide animals with legal standing, which would mean they could have human guardians or agents to protect their rights.

908. Chinnici, Madeline. "A Frog's Day in Court," *Discover* 8 (December 1987):42–43.
  Animal rights issues are starting to win recognition from the public and in the courts. Victories for animal advocates include right to attend animal care committee meetings and permission for students to refuse to dissect and for veterinary students to refuse learning surgery by using healthy animals.

909. Clifton, Merritt. "Fight Over the Pet Theft Act," *AA* 9 (February 1989):28.
  Pet Theft Act, opposed by both biomedical industry and some animal rights groups, died in House of Representatives at close of 100th Congress.

910. Cohen, Henry. "The Legality of the Agriculture Department's Exclusion of Rats and Mice from Coverage Under the Animal Welfare Act," *St. Louis University Law Journal* 31 (September 1987):543–49.
  Exclusion of rats and mice from coverage under Animal Welfare Act by agriculture department is inconsistent with language of the act and frustrates Congress's purpose in enacting the law.

911. "Cruelty to Research Animals," *NYT* 31 July 1985:A18.
  Defends use of animals in research but states lab animals should be protected to some degree. Supports passage of bill in Congress that would eliminate major, repeated violations of care standards for lab animals.

912. Dresser, Rebecca. "Assessing Harm and Justification in Animal Research: Federal Policy Opens the Laboratory Door," *Rutgers Law Review* 40 (Spring 1988):723–95.
  Describes new federal provisions for treatment of lab animals. Discusses scientific and philosophical debate over attributing mental states to nonhuman animals and moral significance to an animal's positive or negative experiences. Looks at efforts to define, assess, and alleviate pain and distress in lab animals and to evaluate and promote

their well-being. Analysis of the question about when research is sufficiently meritorious to warrant an animal's pain and/or death.

913.   Dresser, Rebecca. "Research on Animals: Values, Politics, and Regulatory Reform," *South California Law Review* 58 (July 1985):1147–1201.

Investigates problem of regulating research on animals and proposes a model for legal reform that realistically integrates competing ethical claims of researchers' and animals' interests. Surveys historical and contemporary disputes over animal research, nature and scope of animal use today, and current state of laws governing animal research. Examines philosophical arguments about moral status of lab animals. Proposes federal regulations for experiments on humans be a paradigm for regulating animal research.

914.   Dudek, Ronald D. "The Use of Animals in Medical Research and Testing: Does the Tail Wag the Dog?" *Ohio Northwestern University Law Review* 14 (Winter 1987):87–101.

Growing belief in society that lab animals have rights that should protect them from inhumane treatment. Looks at effectiveness of animal rights legislation.

915.   Dukes, Esther F. "The Improved Standards for Laboratory Animals Act: Will It Ensure That the Policy of the Animal Welfare Act Becomes a Reality?" *St. Louis University Law Journal* 31 (September 1987):519–42.

Animal Welfare Act has not protected animals as it should, because agriculture department interprets it narrowly and carries out minimal, unenthusiastic enforcement of it.

916.   Falkin, Larry. "Are State Anti-Cruelty Statutes Sleeping Giants?" *Pace Environmental Law Review* 2,2 (Winter 1985): 255–69.

Examination of state anticruelty laws in light of the Silver Spring Monkeys case (*Taub vs. State of Maryland*). Can they be used to give better protection to laboratory animals?

917. Favre, David. "Laboratory Animal Act: A Legislative Proposal," *Pace Environmental Law Review* 3,2 (1986):123–64.
Proposes a model law to adequately protect animals used in research. The law would accept the concept that animals have individual interests that humans have an ethical duty to recognize.

918. Fields, Cheryl M. "House Committee Approves NIH Bill, Asks for Animal Care Rules," *Chron H Ed* 26 (May 18, 1983):19.
House Committee on Energy and Commerce has approved regulations attached to National Institutes of Health reauthorization of funding for 1986 that would give lab animals more protection and support search for alternatives to animal experimentation.

919. Fields, Cheryl M. "House Panel Approves New Limits on Use of Animals in Research," *Chron H Ed* 26 (March 30, 1983):15–16.
House Subcommittee on Health and Environment approved bill placing new restrictions on use of lab animals as part of reauthorization of National Institutes of Health budget.

920. Fields, Cheryl M. "House Panel Taking Up NIH Bill, Retains Tighter Rules on Use of Research Animals," *Chron H Ed* 26 (May 11, 1983):13–14.
In spite of efforts by scientists and universities, House Energy and Commerce Committee allowed provisions tightening federal standards for use of research animals in funding reauthorization bill of National Institutes of Health to stand.

921. Fox, Jeffrey L. "Bill Proposes Added Review of Animal Research," *Science* 224 (April 6, 1984):36–37.
Discusses Information Dissemination and Research Accountability Act, which calls for all federally funded experiments using animals to be reviewed by panels familiar

with biomedical literature so as to prevent duplication of experiments.

922.  Fox, Jeffrey L. "Lab Animal Welfare Issue Gathers Momentum," *Science* 223 (February 3, 1984):468–69.
      Review of proposed legislation such as the Research Accountability Act, new amendments to the Animal Welfare Act, and NIH reauthorization act, which would give lab animals more protection.

923.  Francione, Gary L. "Access to Animal Care Committees," *Rutgers Law Review* 43 (Fall 1990):1–14.
      Examination of Animal Welfare Act amendment, which requires each research facility to have at least one institutional animal care and use committee (IACUC). Addresses legal maneuvers opponents have used, including defense of academic freedom and academic privilege to oppose IACUCs.

924.  Francione, Gary L. "The Constitutional Status of Restrictions on Experiments Involving Nonhuman Animals: A Comment on Professor Dresser's Analysis," *Rutgers Law Review* 40 (Spring 1988):797–818.
      Critiques Rebecca Dresser's study and her assumption that researchers' First Amendment rights protect their scientific research and inquiry especially as it relates to the use of animals.

925.  Heffernan, Nancy. "Panel Stiffens Law on Lab Animal Thefts," *LAT* 4 June 1985:I,3+.
      Proposed legislation in California would make stealing lab animals a grand theft prosecutable as a felony or misdemeanor.

926.  Hoch, David. "Business Ethics, Law and the Corporate Use of Laboratory Animals," *Akron Law Review* 21 (Fall 1987):201–44.
      In-depth look at Improved Standards for Laboratory

Animals Act of 1985. Does it protect laboratory animals or merely lull public into believing so? Even the animal welfare community is divided on this question.

927. Holden, Constance. "Revised Animal Bill Under Scrutiny," *Science* 216 (June 4, 1982):1084–85.
Bills introduced into the House that would have reduced use of animals in research labs and developed alternatives were vociferously objected to by researchers. One bill was shelved, the other is still pending.

928. Houston, Paul. "Senate Votes Tighter Safeguards for Lab Animals," *LAT* 29 October 1985:I,6.
Acceding to concern of animal welfare groups, Senate approved legislation that will increase the number of animal lab inspections, provide stricter penalties for violators, and require use of painkillers and euthanasia for animals that are used in painful experiments. The legislation will also require scientists to have prior training in animal care, avoid duplication of experiments, and give dogs and primates adequate exercise.

929. Ingiverson, Marshall. "New Victories for Animal Rights as Advocates Gain Political Clout," *CSM* 23 February 1984:6.
Nationwide, seventy-eight bills have been introduced restricting in some way the use of animals in research. Most noticeable one is a pending California bill introduced by Senate president, pro tem David Roberti that would ban research institutions from obtaining shelter animals from inside or outside the state. Democrats support animal welfare bills more often than Republicans, but it's not uncommon to find both parties represented on the same side.

930. Joyce, Christopher. "American City Puts Animal Rights on the Rates," *New Scientist* 126 (June 2, 1990):22.
Cambridge, Massachusetts, establishes precedent by appointing a commissioner of laboratory animals, who will

monitor all experiments using live animals and make unannounced inspections of facilities to make sure Animal Welfare Act provisions are being followed.

931.   Knobelsdorff, Kerry Elizabeth. "Stricter Regulation Sought Over Labs Using Animals in Research: Proposal in Cambridge, Massachusetts, Reflects Goals of National Drive," *CSM* 8 January 1987:7.
    Ordinance under consideration by Cambridge, Massachusetts, City Council would require proper veterinary care for lab animals, including pain monitoring on a regular basis and administration of appropriate pain killers.

932.   Kullberg, John F. "When Animal Experiments Cannot Be Avoided (letter)," *NYT* 31 July 1983:E18.
    Executive director of the American Society for the Prevention of Cruelty to Animals encourages passage of legislation introduced by Senator Dole that would strengthen Animal Welfare Act.

933.   Levy, Claudia. "Rockville Lab Accused of Threatening Inspectors," *WP* 1 December 1988:A34.
    Two inspectors from agriculture department, responsible for enforcing Animal Welfare Act, said they were harassed and threatened by employees of SEMA, a National Institutes of Health contractor, where primates are used in hepatitis and AIDS experimentation. SEMA, an animal rights target because of its high primate mortality rate and caging practices, denies the charge.

934.   Lewis, Patricia Brazeel. "Animal Welfare Hearings Conducted," *Bioscience* 33 (October 1983):541–42.
    American Institute of Biological Sciences and American Physiological Society said they will reluctantly support Senator Bob Dole's Improved Standards for Laboratory Animals Act, which would eliminate unnecessary duplication of experimentation. Association of American Medical Colleges, U.S. Department of Agriculture, and American Farm Bureau Federation continue to oppose it.

935. Lewis, Patricia Brazeel. "Animal Welfare: Jordan Testifies for AIBS," *Bioscience* 32 (January 1982):74.

American Institute of Biological Sciences official testified at congressional hearing on use of live animals in research and testing, which was held after charges of neglect of experimental monkeys kept at a facility in Silver Spring, Maryland.

936. Linck, Peter. "The Law of the Labs," *AV* 2 (June 1989): 92–93.

Summary of the Animal Welfare Act of 1966, its amendments, and the regulations and policies the act and amendments generated in setting standards for laboratory animal care. Looks at state laws in relation to federal ones.

937. Lyall, Sarah. "Suits by Animal Rights Groups are Opening University Research Panels to the Public," *NYT* 22 August 1989:B1.

New York State Supreme Court has ruled animal rights advocates have the right to attend meetings of State University of New York at Stony Brook committee that reviews research using animals. Animal rights groups are becoming more sophisticated, using Freedom of Information Act and local open-meeting laws to obtain information about present or proposed animal experimentation. Researchers fear radical wing of animal rights movement will use the information to stop experiments, harass faculty, or destroy property.

938. Masonis, Robert J. " 'The Improved Standards for Laboratory Animals Act' and the Proposed Regulations: A Glimmer of Hope in the Battle Against Abusive Animal Research," *Boston College Environmental Affairs Law Review* 16 (Fall 1988):149–79.

The Improved Standards Act embodies first major effort to strike a statutory balance between biomedical research and humane treatment of lab animals. Remedies some problems with the early Animal Welfare Act legislation but will still depend upon agriculture department for drafting final regulations.

939. McDonald, Karen L. "Creating a Private Cause of Action Against Abusive Animal Research," *University of Pennsylvania Law Review* 134 (January 1986):399–432.

Proposes animal rights groups be given a cause of action against unjustifiable research under state anticruelty laws.

940. McDonald, Kim. "Agriculture Dept. Is Found Lax in Inspecting Facilities Housing Animals Used in Research," *Chron H Ed* 30 (June 5, 1985):22.

General Accounting Office says agriculture department is lax in inspecting research facilities, zoos, and kennels as mandated by Animal Welfare Act. Lack of money and trained personnel cited as cause.

941. McDonald, Kim. "Scientists Say Animal Protection Bill Could Hinder Laboratory Research," *Chron H Ed* 25 (September 15, 1982):13–14.

Proposed bill would promote development of alternatives to animal experimentation, require all federal grantee institutions to meet rigorous standards of accreditation, have members from outside institution serve on animal care committees, and have Health and Human Services review all research proposals to ensure experiments minimize animals' pain and distress. Scientists oppose the bill, saying such measures would hinder their research.

942. Messett, Marci. "They Asked for Protection and They Got Policy: International Primate's Mutilated Monkeys," *Akron Law Review* 21 (Summer 1987):97–111.

Cites defeat in International Primate Protection League vs. Institute for Behavioral Research, Inc., as example of difficulties animal rights advocates have in litigation. Three legal barriers obstruct success: lack of standing, statutory interpretation, and policy.

943. Metz, Holly. "Suffer the Little Animals: When Does Scientific Research Become Oppression?" *Student Lawyer* 15 (October 1986):12–20.

Focuses on Animal Legal Defense Fund (ALDF), a group of about 200 lawyers and student lawyers, who defend rights of animals and the humans who try to protect them. Discusses changes ALDF would like to see in medical research with animals, examines Animal Welfare Act, agency regulations governing treatment of animals in research, congressional bill that would allow private suits in Animal Welfare Act enforcement, and debate in animal rights movement over whether illegal acts such as break-ins and vandalism of animal labs help or hurt the cause.

944. "New Concern for Lab Animals," *CSM* 10 August 1983:24.
Interest in welfare of laboratory animals is rising as reflected in congressional and state legislation that would better protect animals used in experiments. One law mandates a study to determine how many animals were used in the past five years and how humanely they were treated. The report is due in eighteen months.

945. Pavelock, Lisa A. "Towards Legal Rights for Laboratory Animals?" *Journal of Legislation* 10 (Winter 1983):198–212.

946. "Pending Actions," *AA* 10 (December 1990):44.
Citizens to End Animal Suffering and Exploitation (CEASE) sues New England Aquarium for attempting to give a dolphin to the U.S. Navy. Several animal rights groups are considering filing *qui tam* actions against biomedical researchers for scientific misconduct and misuse of federal funds.

947. "Pet Theft Act: Round Two," *AA* 10 (July/August 1990):40.
Animal rights organizations split in support of Pet Theft Act, which is designed to regulate dealers who procure animals for research. Some activists claim the act has too many loopholes.

948. "Pet Theft Act Passes; Other Bills Dead," *AA* 10 (December 1990):45.
Pet Theft Act will enable agriculture department to shut down facilities violating Animal Welfare Act and will re-

quire animal pounds and shelters to hold dogs and cats five days before selling them for research. Three other bills pending in Congress failed to pass: the Consumer Product Safety Act, the Veal Calf Protection Act, and the Wildlife Refuge Reform Act. A bill still pending passage would make it a federal offense to intimidate people from entering or exiting federally funded facilities.

949.    "Protecting Lab Animals," *CSM* 6 August 1982:24.
        Congressional bill HR6245 would require federally funded laboratories to meet much higher standards in protecting lab animals than currently are in effect. Would also require a layperson be appointed to monitor animals' welfare and would promote development of alternatives.

950.    Ross, Elizabeth. "Cambridge to Vote on Bill to Protect Lab Animals," *CSM* 31 May 1989:7.
        Animal rights groups want city of Cambridge, Massachusetts, home of thirteen medical research facilities, to pass an ordinance that would be most far-reaching measure to protect lab animals in the U.S. It would include provision to oversee animal care and inspect labs, strengthen guidelines for animal care committees, improve housing conditions for animals, and provide social contact for primates.

951.    "Senators Heflin and Helms Sponsor Anti-Animal Rights Bill," *AA* 9 (November 1989):35.
        Two senators introduced Animal Research Facilities Protection Act of 1989, which would make it illegal to publish, copy, or reproduce records from a research facility. This would effectively end exposing abuse of lab animals through documentation kept by the labs themselves.

952.    Shulman, Seth. "Municipal Law on Its Way," *Nature* 338 (April 13, 1989):534.
        Cambridge, Massachusetts, may pass first local ordinance in U.S. that would provide municipal control over the care and treatment of lab animals. Disagreement

among 3-member panel making recommendations on issue still needs resolution.

953. Stevens, Christine. "Animal Rights (letter)," *WP* 30 April 1984:A10.

    Supports amendment to Animal Welfare Act, which would advance good research by eliminating erroneous data and establishing an information service to provide researchers with alternatives to animal research and ways to reduce pain and the number of animals used.

954. Stille, Alexander. "Animal Advocacy: Animal Rights Lawyers Say Their Movement Is an Extension of the Century's Liberation Struggles: Scientists Accuse Them of Hobbling Research," *National Law Journal* 12 (April 16, 1990):1.

955. Subar, Lorin M. "Out from Under the Microscope: A Case for Laboratory Animal Rights," *Detroit College Law Review* (Summer 1987):511–46.

    History of vivisection, pro and con arguments. Reviews *Taub vs. State of Maryland* and *International Primate Protection League vs. Institute for Behavioral Research Inc.*, and Animal Welfare Act Amendments of 1985. Has there been any real progress in protecting lab animals with legislation? The answer is no.

956. Sun, Marjorie. "Animal Welfare and Fetal Research in Bill on NIH," *Science* 220 (April 22, 1983):389.

    Rep. Doug Walgren reintroduced bill that would require finding a way to disseminate to scientists information about alternatives to animal experimentation and would require animal researchers to justify their use of animals in specific experiments.

957. Sun, Marjorie. "Animal Welfare Bills on Legislative Agenda," *Science* 219 (February 25, 1983):939.

    Rep. Doug Walgren and Sen. Robert Dole will likely reintroduce legislation again this year that would encourage or mandate that federal agencies consider alternatives to animal testing.

958.   Sun, Marjorie. "A Push for Animal Welfare Bills," *Science* 221 (August 12, 1983):633.
  Hodgepodge of federal and state legislation protecting lab animals has been introduced in response to lobbying pressure from animal welfare groups. They range from encouraging alternatives to animal experimentation and testing to placing a ban on selling pound animals to research labs.

959.   Thomas, Brenda L. "Antinomy: The Use, Rights, and Regulation of Laboratory Animals," *Pepperdine Law Review* 13 (1986):723–58.
  Antinomy in law and logic means real or apparent inconsistency or conflict between two authorities or propositions. In treatment of laboratory animals, antinomy pits society's desire to be humane and respectful of nonhumans against its maintenance of human superiority and unrestricted use of nonhumans.

960.   United States. Congress. House. *Care of Animals Used for Research, Experimentation, Exhibition, or Held for Sale as Pets.* Hearing before the Subcommittee on Livestock and Grains of the Committee on Agriculture, 91st Cong., 2nd Sess., on HR13957, June 8–9, 1970. Washington, DC: U.S. Government Printing Office, 1970, Y4.Ag8/1:An5/5.

961.   United States. Congress. House. *Humane Care for Animals in Research.* Hearing before the Subcommittee on Health and the Environment of the Committee on Energy and Commerce, 97th Cong., 2nd Sess., on HR6928, December 9, 1982. Washington, DC: U.S. Government Printing Office, 1983, Y4.En2/3:97–189.

962.   United States. Congress. House. *Improved Standards for Laboratory Animals Act and Enforcement of the Animal Welfare Act by the Animal and Plant Health Inspection Service.* Hearing before the Subcommittee on Department Operations,

Research, and Foreign Agriculture of the Committee on Agriculture, 98th Cong., 2nd Sess., on HR5725, September 19, 1984. Washington, DC: U.S. Government Printing Office, 1985, Y4.Ag8/1:98–86.

963. United States. Congress. Senate. *Animal Welfare Improvement Act of 1975.* Hearing before the Subcommittee on the Environment of the Committee of Commerce, 94th Cong., 1st Sess., on S1941, S2070, S2430, November 20, 1975. Washington, DC: U.S. Government Printing Office, 1976, Y4.C73/2:94–55.

964. United States. Congress. Senate. *Consumer Products Safety Testing Act.* Hearing before the Subcommittee on the Consumer of the Committee on Commerce, Science, and Transportation, 101st Cong., 2nd Sess., on S891, November 8, 1989. Washington, DC: U.S. Government Printing Office, 1989, C73/7:S hrg 101–460.

965. United States. Congress. Senate. *Improved Standards for Laboratory Animals.* Hearing before the Committee on Agriculture, Nutrition, and Forestry, United States Senate, 98th Cong., 1st Sess., on S657, July 20, 1983. Washington, DC: U.S. Government Printing Office, 1984, Y4.Ag8/3:S.hrg. 98–470.

966. Weiss, Laura B. "Congress Urged to Require Better Treatment of Animals Used in Scientific Research," *Congressional Quarterly Weekly Report* 40 (November 13, 1982):2855–57.
Humane Care and Development of Substitutes for Animals in Research Act would strengthen existing federal regulations and laws aimed at ensuring proper treatment of laboratory animals and using alternatives when available. Animal welfarists and researchers expect a fight over its passage.

967. Wheeler, David L. "Supporters of Proposal to Curb Animal Research in Cambridge Seek Referendum," *Chron H Ed* 34 (September 30, 1987):A6.

Referendum has been proposed in Cambridge, Massachusetts, which would allow citizens to ban painful experiments on animals, require disclosure of animal experimentation, and permit unannounced inspections of lab animal facilities. Research institutions such as Harvard and Massachusetts Institute of Technology have come out against it but are unsure how the vote will go.

968. Zurvalec, Lori A. "Use of Animals in Medical Research: The Need for Governmental Regulation," *Wayne Law Review* 24 (Spring 1978):1733–51.

Balance is needed in regulation of use of animals in research. Looks at animal rights movement, analyzes applicable law and legislative history, and suggests improvements in treatment of lab animals.

## Agency Rules, Regulations, and Policies

969. Anderson, Christopher. "One Step Forward," *Nature* 346 (1990):782.

Agriculture department released regulations for care of laboratory primates, dogs, and cats, setting off usual debate from researchers, who oppose them, and animal rights activists, who support them.

970. Anderson, Christopher. "Politics Force New United States Rules," *Nature* 345 (June 28, 1990):755.

Agriculture department has agreed to drop proposed regulations that would improve conditions for lab animals, replacing them with ones less restrictive to research community. Some members of Congress and animal rights activists promise to oppose watered-down regulations.

971. Beardsley, Tim. "U.S. Laboratory Animals: NIH Watchdog Committees," *Nature* 315 (May 23, 1985):267.

U.S. Department of Health and Human Services has established new guidelines that charge animal use committees with review of research programs and inspection of animal laboratories. Animal welfarists are disappointed on several counts: committee's layperson member is not required to be an animal advocate, institution can apply for retroactive waiver from the guidelines, and guidelines do not have the force of law.

972. "Comment Opens on Animal Welfare Regs," *AA* 10 (September 1990):36.

Agriculture department has agreed to publish new regulations for dogs, cats, and primates used in laboratory research. Regulations would improve conditions for animals and were mandated by a 1985 amendment to Animal Welfare Act, but animal rights advocates fear they will be watered down.

973. Eskridge, Nancy K. "Researchers Concerned About Changes in Animal Care Policy," *Bioscience* 28 (June 1978):407–8.

National Institutes of Health has been instructed to turn into regulations the guidelines for care of laboratory animals. Some researchers fear new policies will enable animal rights advocates to learn more about their experiments, with object of harassing them. Federation of American Scientists, however, feels that animal experimenters overreact to every proposal for change, even when it is constructive.

974. Fields, Cheryl M. "Two University Groups Offer Guidelines on Use of Animals in Research," *Chron H Ed* 31 (December 11, 1985):7.

Association of American Universities and Association of American Medical Colleges recommend guidelines for institutions and researchers to follow in managing facilities that use animals. Also advises establishment of procedures to combat animal rights advocates and activities.

975. Fox, Jeffrey L. "Changes in Animal Care Policy Proposed," *Science* 224 (April 27, 1984):364–65.

National Institutes of Health has proposed new guidelines for treatment of lab animals. Researchers are worried new guidelines will be too costly, animal welfarists say the guidelines do not address inherent conflict of interest among animal care committee members who review experiment proposals.

976. Havemann, Judith. "Animal Rules Uncage Scientists' Complaints: Proposed U.S. Standards Require Bigger Pens, Regular Exercise," *WP* 9 July 1989:A1.

    Disagreement between animal rights activists and scientists over cost and effectiveness of implementing new animal welfare regulations in the research laboratory.

977. Holden, Constance. "Animal Regulations: So Far, So Good," *Science* 238 (November 13, 1987):880–82.

    A decade of new regulations by federal funding agencies in care and treatment of laboratory animals was ushered in by Silver Spring monkeys affair. Scientists say animal research will be more costly, but they are worried about animal rights movement, which they believe is made up of people who anthropomorphize animals but have little contact with them.

978. Holden, Constance. "New Animal Regulations Causing Scientists Pain and Distress," *Science* 233 (August 8, 1986):619.

    Scientists complain complying with new federal regulations for care and use of lab animals will cost them too much money. Seventy-five to 100 small research institutions have been forced out of the animal business. Animal rights organizations supporting these new regulations must pass the litmus test by lobbying as hard for funds to implement the rules as they did to pass them.

979. Holden, Constance. "PHS Revises Rules on Animal Research," *Science* 228 (May 17, 1985):830.

    Public Health Service has revised its policy on laboratory animals. Requires every institution must have an animal care committee, be accredited by the American Association of Laboratory Animal Accreditation and provide federal government with details about care and use of animals, facilities, staffing, and staff training.

980. "Laboratories Must Abide by NIH Animal Care Rules," *Bioscience* 28 (February 1978):148.

Summary of new National Institutes of Health laboratory animal care rules.

981. McDonald, Kim. "Agency to Press for Stricter Rules on Lab Animals," *Chron H Ed* 28 (April 11, 1984):1+.

Public Health Service will publish new rules for humane care of laboratory animals and distribute them to 22,000 research institutions. Researchers fear requirement to have one person outside institution serve on animal care committees will result in unqualified people's judgment of their work. Animal rights activists say this is already done in human experiments, and lab animals should be accorded the same level of concern.

982. McDonald, Kim. "New Animal Care Rules Could Force Small Institutions to Curtail Research," *Chron H Ed* 28 (June 13, 1984):16.

National Institutes of Health will hold hearings in Kansas City, Missouri; Boston; and Seattle on new regulations for animal labs. Scientists fear their independence is threatened and new regulations will cost more money than institutions can afford.

983. McDonald, Kim. "Researchers Say Moves to Protect Animals in Labs Would Hurt Biomedical Studies," *Chron H Ed* 23 (October 21, 1981):15–16.

University officials and researchers oppose tightened regulations to protect lab animals, saying humaneness cannot be legislated and such measures might obstruct efforts to eradicate human diseases and suffering. The regulations introduced in the House are in response to Silver Spring monkeys abuse case.

984. McDonald, Kim. "Rules on Animal Care Are Seen Penalizing Small Institutions," *Chron H Ed* 28 (May 16, 1984):1+.

Researchers fear new Public Health Service rules regulating treatment of lab animals will close down smaller research labs, which cannot afford cost of making changes.

985.  McDonald, Kim. "U.S. Announces More Stringent Standards for Treatment of Laboratory Animals," *Chron H Ed* 30 (May 15, 1985):10.

Public Health Service announces new standards for treatment of laboratory animals. John McArdle of the Humane Society of the U.S. criticizes standards, saying the institutions will still be policing themselves and individual researchers will still not be accountable.

986.  McGourty, Christine. "About Turn on Regulations," *Nature* 341 (September 7, 1989):6.

Agriculture department responds to thousands of complaints from animal researchers by revising regulations that would have improved the welfare of laboratory animals. Animal rights groups are angry and protest weakening of regulations.

987.  Miller, J. A. "Looking out for Animal Research," *Science News* 125 (April 21, 1984):247.

National Institutes of Health proposes several changes in lab animal welfare policy to head off more restrictive legislation from Congress.

988.  "NIH Proposes Changes in Animal Care and Use Policies," *Bioscience* 34 (July/August 1984):413.

National Institutes of Health proposes stricter animal welfare guidelines in use of laboratory animals, but animal rights groups feel too much responsibility still stays with individual researchers rather than their institutions.

989.  Reagan, Kinsey S. "Federal Regulation of Testing with Laboratory Animals: Future Directions," *Pace Environmental Law Review* 3,2 (1986):165–90.

Describes and analyzes major federal system of regulation of animal use in research and testing, including Animal Welfare Act, Public Health Services policies, and regulations applicable to animal testing of products required by Food and Drug Administration and Environmental Protection Agency. Suggests three ways to improve animal welfare regulation: alternatives, enforcement of existing regulations, and use of self-regulatory programs.

990. Sangeorge, Robert. "New EPA Rules Set to Reduce Harm to Laboratory Animals," *Los Angeles Daily Journal* 97 (August 30, 1984):3.

991. Winkler, Karen J. "Psychologists Adopt Guidelines for Use of Animals in Behavioral Research," *Chron H Ed* 31 (September 4, 1985):19.
     American Psychological Association (APA) follows examples of the Public Health Service and National Institutes of Health in voting to adopt new guidelines in care and use of laboratory animals. Approximately 3,000 of APA's 61,000 members use animals in behavioral research.

992. Wortman, Judith. "PHS Revises Its Lab Animal Welfare Policy," *Bioscience* 35 (July/August 1985):408.
     Public Health Service revises its Policy on Humane Care and Use of Laboratory Animals after conducting three public hearings and reviewing 270 letters.

## Animal Liberation Front

993. "Activists Free Animals from Pennsylvania Lab," *NYT* 29 July 1984:A18.
     Animal Liberation Front has raided University of Pennsylvania animal laboratories and taken three cats, two dogs, and eight pigeons.

994. "Activists Jailed: Wouldn't Talk to Grand Jury," *AA* 10 (October 1990):33.
     Activist Debra Young jailed for refusing to testify in a grand jury investigation of animal rights movement.

995. "Activists Take the Fifth in Grand Jury Probe," *AA* (July/August 1990):36–37.
     At least 7 California animal defenders are refusing to testify before a federal grand jury investigating Animal Liberation Front. Examines internal discord among animal rights groups.

996.  "ALF Sets Off Fireworks at Texas Tech," *AA* 9 (October 1989):40.
      Animal Liberation Front raids Texas Tech University Health Sciences Center and rescues five cats being used in sleep deprivation experiments by researcher John Orem.

997.  "Animal Activists Reportedly Probed," *LAT* 23 March 1990:I,29.
      Federal grand jury is reportedly probing the Animal Liberation Front in California and other states and has been taking testimony possibly as early as 1987.

998.  "Animal Grab," *WP* 30 August 1987:C6.
      Editorial condemns Band of Mercy's liberation of thirty-seven cats from Agricultural Research Center in Beltsville, Maryland. Says vigorous prosecution by federal government would have restraining effect on excesses of the animal rights movement.

999.  Banks, Sandy. "Rabbits Are Liberated a Second Time," *LAT* 20 February 1985:I,3.
      Ten rabbits stolen from the City of Hope research center and being held at the Napa Valley animal shelter as evidence were liberated again. The Animal Liberation Front, which claimed responsibility for the first theft, also did the second. The front left $10 to pay for padlock damage as well as a note thanking the shelter for "taking such good care of our friends."

1000. Beene, Richard. "Thirteen Dogs Used in Research are 'Liberated,' " *LAT* 1 February 1988:I,16.
      Animal Liberation Front takes thirteen beagles from University of California, Irvine, medical research labs. The dogs were being used to study effects of air pollution on the lungs. Head of the research team said they were "happy animals."

1001. Belcher, Jerry, and Steven B. Churm. "Animals Taken in Rescue at Research Lab," *LAT* 21 April 1985:I,1.
      Animal Liberation Front (ALF) broke into University of

California biology and psychology labs at Riverside and spirited away hundreds of animals, including monkeys, cats, rabbits, mice, and gerbils. Tapes and videos of experiments were also taken. ALF described rescued monkey as an infant whose eyes had been sutured closed in sight deprivation experiments. The dean of humanities and social sciences at the school said the monkey experiment was designed to develop "mobility aids" for the blind.

1002. Blakeslee, Sandra. "Animal Rights-Battle Joined on Animal Lib," *Nature* 315 (June 20, 1985):625.
Chronicles various laboratory break-ins by animal rights groups and says bill sponsored by assemblyman William Filante in California would stiffen penalties from misdemeanor to felony.

1003. "Bust the Cat Burglars," *WP* 1 January 1983:A16.
Editorial condemns Animal Liberation Front for liberating experimental cats at Howard University labs.

1004. Chavez, Stephanie. "Animal Rights Group Takes Credit for 'Freeing the Bunnies,' " *LAT* 19 April 1987:I,23.
Animal Liberation Front liberated from a breeding farm in San Bernardino, California, more than 100 rabbits destined for scientific research.

1005. "Chimps Stolen from Lab," *NYT* 9 December 1986:C14.
True Friends, an animal rights group, has stolen from SEMA, Inc., a medical lab in Rockville, Maryland, four baby chimpanzees slated for AIDS and hepatitis research.

1006. Clifton, Merritt. "Activists Take the Fifth in Grand Jury Probe," *AA* 10 (July/August 1990):36–37.
Investigation of Animal Liberation Front by a Sacramento grand jury leaves 7 animal rights activists uncertain of future legal action against them for refusing to testify.

1007. Dawson, Victoria. "Diseased Cats Taken from USDA Lab in Maryland," *WP* 25 August 1987:A1+.

Band of Mercy removed 27 cats, some infected with a parasitic disease, from agriculture department research facility in Beltsville, Maryland. People for the Ethical Treatment of Animals said cats were not scheduled to be treated but simply observed for dehydration, diarrhea, high fever, weakness, and inflammation of heart and liver.

1008.    Fintor, Lou. "Clearing of UC Riverside in Animal Case Expected," *LAT* 14 February 1986:I,32.

National Institutes of Health is expected to clear University of California, Riverside, of charges of animal cruelty made by animal rights activists. One NIH official said situation at Riverside was satisfactory on all counts.

1009.    Fintor, Lou, and Louis Sahagun. "Animal Rights Group May Have Hurt Monkey," *LAT* 28 February 1986:I,3.

Federal officials suggest animal rights activists may have injured a monkey they took in a raid on University of California, Riverside, animal labs. Activists deny allegation and say this lie shows how far researchers are willing to go to keep on torturing animals. Both National Institutes of Health and UC agree suturing the monkey's eyes shut may not have been the most appropriate way to conduct sleep derivation experiments.

1010.    Franklin, Ben. "Going to Extremes for Animal Rights," *NYT* 30 August 1987:D7.

Brief summary of activities of militant activists who remove animals from biomedical laboratories.

1011.    "Grand Jury Investigates ALF," *AV* 3 (March/April 1990):55.

Federal grand jury in Sacramento begins its investigation of Animal Liberation Front.

1012.    "Grand Jury Investigates Animal Liberation Front," *AV* 3 (December 1990):49.

Three California activists have been indicted on charges of burglary, theft, and criminal mischief after a 1986 break-in at University of Oregon animal laboratory.

All have pleaded not guilty. Grand jury has offered "deals" to various West Coast activists if they cooperate and inform on others in the movement.

1013. "Grand Jury Jails Animal Rights Activist," *AV* 9 (October 1990):56.
Nursing student and animal rights activist Debra Young jailed in Sacramento for refusing to answer questions in a grand jury session regarding animal rights movement.

1014. "Group Says It Rescued 260 Animals from Labs," *NYT* 21 April 1985:A22.
Animal Liberation Front removed twenty-one cats, thirty-five rabbits, thirty-eight pigeons, eighty rats, some gerbils and opossums, and one infant primate from a University of California research center at Riverside.

1015. Holden, Constance. "Animal Rightists Raid USDA Lab," *Science* 237 (September 4, 1987):1099.
Band of Mercy made off with twenty-eight cats infected with toxoplasmosis and eight miniature pigs at Protozoan Diseases Laboratory of Agricultural Research Center in Beltsville, Maryland. Catnappers say animals were suffering from dehydration, bloody diarrhea, and filthy housing conditions. Experiment's research leader characterizes these charges as fantasy.

1016. Holden, Constance. "Animal Stealer Convicted," *Science* 239 (January 29, 1988):458.
Roger Troen, 28-year-old graphics designer, was convicted of theft and burglary for his involvement in break-in at University of Oregon animal laboratories.

1017. Holden, Constance. "Beagle Theft at Irvine," *Science* 239 (February 12, 1988):722.
Animal Liberation Front broke into University of California, Irvine, and made off with thirteen beagles being used in air pollution experiments.

1018. Holden, Constance. "Centers Targeted by Activists," *Science* 232 (April 11, 1986):149.

Examines aftermath of animal liberation activities at University of Pennsylvania; City of Hope Medical Center, Duarte, California; University of California, Riverside; and Columbia University. Looks at grants that were or were not renewed, what happened to scientists involved in animal abuse allegations, and which institutions made changes to meet new lab animal treatment regulations.

1019.    Hoyt, John A. "Cat Burglars (letter)," *WP* 8 January 1983:A18.
President of Humane Society says not all lab animals are treated humanely and it would be better if *Post* editorial condemning lab break-in at Howard University instead looked seriously at issue of animal experimentation.

1020.    Ingiverson, Marshall. "Scientific Research vs. Animal Rights: Raids on Laboratories Point to Rising Militancy Among Protection Groups," *CSM* 25 April 1985:3.
Activities by Animal Liberation Front are increasing as group continues to break into labs, rescuing animals and sometimes vandalizing premises. Some recent raids include those against University of California, Riverside and City of Hope Medical Center in Duarte, Calfornia.

1021.    Lauer, Margaret. "Animal Rights Commandos," *Mother Jones* 8 (September/October 1983):9.
Animal Liberation Front's break-in at Howard University spurs researchers to take their case for animal experimentation to the public via press kits. It would be better if they and other research facilities made an effort to improve lab conditions for animals.

1022.    Malnic, Eric. "Animal Liberation Front: 'Deep Ecology,' " *LAT* 30 December 1984:I,1.
Malnic describes clandestine meeting with "Sandy," a member of Animal Liberation Front, an organization dedicated to eradication of vivisection and other forms of exploitation of animals. About 100 members, many of them vegetarians and all of them believing animals have inalienable rights, have carried out a dozen raids in the

past three years, liberating dogs, cats, monkeys, guinea pigs, and mice from research labs. "Sandy" said animal experiments are often cruel and unnecessary and inertia in scientific community is such that change by conventional methods such as legislation is unlikely.

1023. Malnic, Eric. "The Animal Liberation Front Uncages a Debate on Research," *WP* 30 December 1984:A11.

1024. Malnic, Eric. "City of Hope's Treatment of Animals Being Investigated," *LAT* 7 August 1985:II,1+.
National Institutes of Health froze funds to City of Hope research center in Duarte, California. Investigation of charges of neglect of laboratory animals made by People for the Ethical Treatment of Animals turned up ten major and ten minor "deficiencies" in the way animals were cared for. City of Hope officials minimized findings and were confident full funding would be restored.

1025. Malnic, Eric. "Doctor Calls Theft of Dogs Vigilantism," *LAT* 27 December 1983:II,1.
Researchers at Harbor-UCLA Medical Center call removal of twelve dogs used in heart research an act of frontier vigilantism, and comparing Animal Liberation Front (ALF) to the IRA, PLO, and SLA. ALF said it had made several raids during the Christmas holidays, because peace and goodwill are not just for humans but for all animals.

1026. Malnic, Eric. "Liberated Research Animals, Group Says: Harbor-UCLA Medical Center Verifies That Dogs Were Stolen," *LAT* 26 December 1983:II,1.

1027. Malnic, Eric. "Missing Lab Animals Found, Man Arrested," *LAT* 12 December 1984:I,3.
Police arrested Bruce Wayne Jodar for receiving stolen property and seized ten rabbits believed to have been taken from City of Hope research center in Duarte, California. Police were led to Jodar by rabbit breeder who said she was given the stolen rabbits by Jodar.

1028.   McFarland, Cole. "Portrait of a 'Terrorist,' " *AV* 3,1 (1990):40–41.
        Member of Animal Liberation Front and veteran of several animal rescues talks about why she became involved with the group and gives her thoughts on violence and economic sabotage.

1029.   "The Misguided," *LAT* 23 April 1985:II,4.
        Editorial condemns Animal Liberation Front and calls for police and local prosecutors to put an end to it.

1030.   Pardue, Leslie. "Band of Mercy Raids USDA Lab," *AA* 7 (November 1987):20–21.
        Band of Mercy removed thirty-seven cats and seven miniature pigs from agriculture department laboratories in Beltsville, Maryland. Animals had been infected with a parasitical disease by researchers and observed as they developed symptoms of dehydration, diarrhea, fever, and pneumonia.

1031.   Pennisi, Elizabeth. "Activists Attack in Arizona," *Nature* 338 (April 13, 1989):534.
        Animal Liberation Front removed 1,000 lab animals from University of Arizona research labs and caused thousands of dollars of damage to laboratories and equipment. Animals taken were being used in experiments studying heat stress, selenium-deficient diets, swine dysentery, and protein metabolism.

1032.   Ringle, Ken. "Cat Burglary: Animal Liberation Front Says It Staged Raid on Howard U Lab," *WP* 28 December 1982:B1+.
        Animal Liberation Front liberated three dozen cats from Howard University animal labs. Spokesperson for group says many of the animals were thin and had broken bones or surgical incisions. One cat found dead had been severely dehydrated.

1033.   Rosenberger, Jack. "Animal Rites," *Village Voice* 6 March 1990:30–39.

A look at controversy over animal rights, with a focus on animal experimentation and the activities of Animal Liberation Front.

1034.   Sagar, Mike. "Inhuman Bondage," *Rolling Stone* 24 March 1988:86–8+.

With help of several anonymous members of Animal Liberation Front, reporter re-creates what it's like to assemble and carry off a raid against an animal research laboratory. Explores motivations and personalities of organization's members, including a security systems expert, veterinarian, computer expert, librarian, hairdresser, and social worker.

1035.   Sahagun, Louis. "Thieves Got Goat Records, Doctor Says," *LAT* 17 August 1988:I,26.

Baby Fae surgeon Dr. Leonard Bailey says Animal Liberation Front (ALF), which stole seven dogs and medical records from Loma Linda University Medical Center did not get important records. ALF says records show Bailey had prior knowledge Baby Fae could not survive the baboon heart transplant.

1036.   Schneider, Keith. "Of Science and Sabotage," *NYT* 27 August 1987:B6.

Scientists at Beltsville Agricultural Research Center in Maryland are drawing up new security plans to prevent sabotage of animal experiments by animal rights groups.

1037.   Schneider, Keith. "Theft of Infected Cats Spurs an Alert," *NYT* 25 August 1987:A14.

Cats infected with *Toxoplasma gondii*, a parasite that can be transmitted to humans, were taken from Beltsville Agricultural Research Center in Maryland by animal rights group Band of Mercy.

1038.   Smith, David Christian. "Animal Liberator: Rights Radical Talks About 'Underground' Activities Against Cruelty," *CSM* 15 October 1990:13.

Member of Animal Liberation Front describes herself as

a regular person with a regular job who has chosen to oc-
casionally do things that are felonies. Talks about principles, procedures, goals, and structure of her organization.

1039. Specter, Michael. "Animal Research Labs Increasingly
Besieged: Violence, Threats from Activists Force
Institutions to Tighten Security," *WP* 30 May 1989:A1+.
Survey of recent break-ins in animal labs across coun-
try and price tag to researchers.

1040. Stein, M. L. "No Qualms About Anonymous Interview:
Reporter, Editor Defend Publication of Interview with
Masked Members of Animal Rights Group Who
Admitted to a String of Crimes," *Editor and Publisher* 121
(March 5, 1988):13–14.
Interview with Animal Liberation Front members who
admit to theft and vandalism at medical research facilities
while rescuing animals. Reporter who conducted inter-
view and newspaper editor who ran story defend their
decisions to do so.

1041. Sun, Marjorie. "NCI Tightens Security After Bomb
Threat," *Science* 226 (December 14, 1984):1296.
National Cancer Institute in Bethesda, Maryland,
tightened security after bomb threat from an unknown
source. Officials are concerned about violence from
Animal Liberation Front.

1042. "Thirteen Beagles Stolen from Researchers," *NYT* 2
February 1988:C4.
Animal Liberation Front removes thirteen beagles
being used in air pollution and tracheotomy studies at
University of California, Irvine.

1043. "Value of Two Dolphins Set Free in '77 at Issue in Hawaii
Case," *NYT* 8 March 1982:A14.
Steve Sipman and Kenneth LeVasseur were convicted
for releasing two dolphins being used in communications
experiments in Honolulu. Sipman was ordered to pay for
value of dolphin, although the value has not yet been de-

cided. Sipman maintains dolphins should not be treated or evaluated as if they were property.

1044. "Velucci Arrested for ALF Action," *AA* 10 (December 1990):43.

Cres Velucci, cofounder of the National Foundation for Animal Law, was arrested in connection with Animal Liberation Front's raid on University of Oregon.

1045. Warren, Peter M. "Animals Used in Labs Stolen," *LAT* 10 December 1984:II,1.

Animal Liberation Front (ALF) removed more than 100 animals including thirty-six dogs, twelve cats, twenty-eight mice, twelve rabbits, and eighteen rats that were being used in lung cancer and emphysema research at City of Hope Medical Center in Duarte, California. City of Hope officials say they run a first-class facility, but ALF cites soiled floors, rusting cages, and fetid air as well as animals found with bloated stomachs, with multiple tumors, and standing in water.

1046. Weil, Martin. "A 'Sea Dog' Claimed by Liberators," *WP* 29 December 1982:C3.

Animal Liberation Front (ALF) took experimental dog from the U.S. Navy research lab in Bethesda, Maryland, saying the animal had been badly chewed up by larger dogs because of overcrowding. ALF is also protesting excessive amount of research on animals and failure of Congress to pass legislation that would reduce duplicative experiments.

## Important Cases

### Silver Spring Monkeys

1047. Anderson, Alun. "Silver Spring Monkeys: And Then There Were Four," *Nature* 346 (July 12, 1990):94.

Despite congressman's efforts to negotiate future treatment for remaining Silver Spring monkeys, National

Institutes of Health OK's experiments and euthanization of one. Animal rights activists and scientists involved in the affair denounce one another's motives.

1048.   Anderson, Alun. "Valuable Data Claim," *Nature* 343 (February 15, 1990):581.
Researchers are claiming the last experiment performed on Billy, one of the Silver Spring monkeys, has produced "surprising and important results." Neal Barnard, president of Physicians Committee for Responsible Medicine, disagrees and maintains nothing new has been learned. Barnard believes experiment was done for public relations and political reasons, not scientific ones.

1049.   Anderson, Christopher. "Fight over Maryland Monkeys," *Nature* 343 ( January 25, 1990):297.
National Institutes of Health (NIH) performed invasive surgery on one of the last Silver Spring monkeys and then killed him. Critics say experiment had no scientific value and was done only to justify NIH's keeping the monkeys all these years rather than releasing them to a sanctuary. Physicians Committee for Responsible Medicine filed a complaint with Health and Human Services Office of Scientific Integrity and intends to request congressional oversight hearings.

1050.   Barnard, Neal D. "The Case of the Silver Spring Monkeys," *WP* 25 February 1990:B3.
Historical account of Silver Spring monkeys affair, with update about National Institutes of Health's recent permission allowing scientists to perform invasive surgery on the remaining monkeys.

1051.   Barnard, Neal D. "Scientific Fraud and the Silver Spring Monkeys," *AA* 10 (October 1990):50–51.
Questionable experiments are proposed for three more of the Silver Spring monkeys, in spite of Congress's call to the National Institutes of Health to release the animals for rehabilitation.

1052. Barnes, Donald J. "Using Monkeys in Vain Attempts to Improve the Human Condition (letter)," *WP* 18 April 1987:A21.

Director of the National Anti-Vivisection Society disagrees with the *Washington Post* editorial that lauded the Supreme Court decision to deny standing to animal advocates suing on behalf of a group of abused monkeys. As a former animal experimenter himself, he challenges newspaper's credibility, saying it has merely adopted biomedical litany that the ends justifies the means.

1053. Brisbane, Arthur S. "HHS Sanction Against Animal Research Upheld," *WP* 16 June 1984:B3.

U.S. Department of Health and Human Services has upheld termination of a grant to researcher Edward Taub. Grant was originally revoked in 1981, when animal rights activists developed evidence Taub was mistreating the experimental monkeys in his care at a lab in Silver Spring, Maryland.

1054. Carlson, Peter. "The Great Silver Spring Monkey Debate," *WP Magazine* 24 February 1991:14–19+.

A comprehensive look at the raid on Edward Taub's lab in Silver Spring, Maryland, in 1981, which catapulted controversial issue of animal experimentation into the public eye.

1055. "Fifteen Monkeys Cause a Stir," *NYT* 29 June 1986:A24.

Several members of Congress protest National Institutes of Health decision to move fifteen Silver Spring monkeys to primate center in Louisiana despite a letter signed by 300 congresspeople asking agency to release monkeys to a sanctuary in Texas.

1056. Heneson, Nancy. "Cruelty to Animals: The State Versus the Scientist," *New Scientist* 92 (December 3, 1981): 672–74.

Silver Spring monkeys used in stroke research lived in filthy conditions with open wounds on their arms and were left without food for days. Paper shuffling, buck-passing, a reductionist mentality, and failure of Animal Welfare Act were the causes.

1057. Herbert, W. "Animal Cruelty Verdict Reversed," *Science News* 124 (August 20, 1983):118.

Conviction of cruelty charges in Silver Spring monkey case is overturned.

1058. Herbert, W. "Verdict: Researchers 16, Anti-Vivisectionists 1," *Science News* 122 (July 17, 1982):37.

Sixteen counts of animal cruelty are overturned in Silver spring monkey case, one still up in the air.

1059. Holden, Constance. "High Court Spurns Animal Rights Plea," *Science* 236 (April 17, 1987):252.

Supreme Court denies standing to animal rights groups seeking custody of Silver Spring monkeys.

1060. Holden, Constance. "Monkey Researcher's Cruelty Verdict Reversed," *Science* 221 (August 26, 1983):839.

Researcher Edward Taub had his cruelty conviction overturned by Maryland's state appeals court. In spite of that, he feels his career is destroyed.

1061. Holden, Constance. "NIH Transfers Disputed Monkeys to Regional Primate Center," *Science* 233 (July 11, 1986):154.

Silver Spring monkeys were transferred from National Institutes of Health (NIH) to Delta Regional Primate Center run by Tulane University. Animal welfarists and 306 members of Congress want the animals sent to a sanctuary in Texas, but NIH won't agree.

1062. Holden, Constance. "Police Seize Primates at NIH-Funded Lab," *Science* 214 (October 2, 1981):32–33.

Montgomery County police in Silver Spring, Maryland, raided the laboratory of Edward Taub, a researcher who uses crab-eating macaques to study rehabilitation of stroke victims. Four scientists admitted into the lab by volunteer and cofounder of People for the

Ethical Treatment of Animals Alex Pacheco signed affidavits confirming appalling condition of facilities, neglect of the animals, and lack of rudimentary veterinary care.

1063. Holden, Constance. "Researcher Charged with Cruelty to Monkeys," *Science* 214 (October 9, 1981):165.
Edward Taub, a researcher charged with violation of Maryland's Animal Cruelty Law, fears his reputation will be ruined by animal rights setup.

1064. Holden, Constance. "Scientist Convicted for Monkey Neglect," *Science* 214 (December 11, 1981):1218–20.

1065. Holden, Constance. "Taub Appeal Set," *Science* 216 (June 18, 1982):1299.
Edward Taub has appealed on charges of cruelty to Silver Spring monkeys and will ask for a jury trial. He's running out of money, but has garnered $13,000 in contributions from fellow scientists for his defense.

1066. Judge, Mark G. "Primates Get the Shaft," *Progressive* 50 (October 1986):16–17.

1067. Kehrer, Daniel. "The Monkey Snatchers," *Science Digest* 90 (April 1982):12–4+.
Retelling of the Silver Spring Monkeys affair from point of view sympathetic to researcher Edward Taub.

1068. Kilpatrick, James J. "Caged in Poolesville," *WP* 12 May 1986:A15.
Although Congress has appealed for release of seventeen monkeys used in stroke experiments and now being held at a Poolesville, Maryland, facility, head of National Institutes of Health James Wyngaarden has refused to cooperate.

1069. Kilpatrick, James J. "Why Can't They Just Let Those Monkeys Go," *WP* 27 May 1986:A21.
Pleads for release of Silver Spring monkeys to a pri-

mate sanctuary. Such a gesture shouldn't be looked at as putting all future animal experimentation in jeopardy; it is simply that these fifteen monkeys have served their medical purpose and should now be allowed to live in peace.

1070.   "Lab Animals and the Law," *WP* 7 April 1987:A16.

Editorial praising Supreme Court decision to refuse to review court of appeals decision denying standing to International Primate Protection League and People for the Ethical Treatment of Animals, which asked to be named guardians of Silver Spring monkeys.

1071.   LaFranchi, Howard. "Animal Research Debate Heats Up," *CSM* 10 March 1989:8.

Update of status of Silver Spring monkeys affair and review of arguments on value of animal research.

1072.   Lauter, David. "Dr. Taub's Animal House: Laboratory Experimentation," *National Law Journal* (July 5, 1982):11.

1073.   Leary, Warren E. "Lawsuit Planned to Halt Killing of Lab Monkeys," *NYT* 18 January 1990:A23.

People for the Ethical Treatment of Animals and Physicians Committee for Responsible Medicine said they would go to court to keep National Institutes of Health from putting several of the Silver Spring monkeys to death.

1074.   Newkirk, Ingrid. "NIH Can Let Those Monkeys Go (letter)," *WP* 31 May 1986:A21.

Director of People for the Ethical Treatment of Animals says National Institutes of Health has found one excuse after another to avoid complying with an appeal from 307 congresspeople to release Silver Spring monkeys to a primate sanctuary.

1075.   "NIH Suspends Funding of Researcher Charged with Animal Cruelty," *Bioscience* 31 (November 1981):714.

Summary of events leading up to cruelty charges against researcher Edward Taub for his neglect of experi-

mental monkeys and suspension of National Institutes of
Health funding for violation of its guidelines in care and
use of lab animals.

1076. "NIH to Kill the Silver Spring Monkeys," *AA* 10 (May
1990):39.
National Institutes of Health, despite numerous in-
junctions brought by People for the Ethical Treatment of
Animals and the Physicians' Committee for Responsible
Medicine, plans to anesthetize seven remaining Silver
Spring monkeys, saw open their heads, insert electrodes
into their brains, and measure nerve response as they die.

1077. Noah, Timothy. "Have You Hugged Your Lab Animal
Today? Monkey Business," *New Republic* 186 (June 2,
1982):20–23.
Defense of Edward Taub and his experiments on
Silver Spring monkeys.

1078. Reidinger, Paul. "Monkey Business: No Standing for
Activists," *American Bar Association Journal* 76 (July 1990):85.
Animal rights groups argue for standing in the Silver
Spring monkeys case on bases that they have a long-
standing, sincere commitment to animal rights and that if
they aren't given standing, the monkeys would be unrep-
resented in ensuing legal proceedings. Louisiana's Fifth
Circuit Court rejected these arguments.

1079. Reinhold, Robert. "Fate of Monkeys, Deformed for
Science, Causes Human Hurt After Six Years," *NYT* 23
May 1987:B8.
Dr. Peter Gerone of Delta Regional Primate Research
Center wants to euthanize eight of the fourteen Silver
Spring monkeys in spite of congressional support to send
them to a refuge at animal rights activists' expense. Review
of history and present status of Silver Spring monkeys.

1080. Rowan, Andrew N. "The Silver Spring 17," *International
Journal of the Studies of Animal Problems* 3 (July/September
1982):219–27.

1081.  Saperstein, Saundra. "Cruelty Decision Reversed," *WP* 11 August 1983:C1.
Maryland Court of Appeals overturned animal cruelty conviction against researcher Edward Taub. The court found state anticruelty law didn't apply, because treatment of animals in federally funded projects falls under Animal Welfare Act.

1082.  Scott, Janny. "For Simians, It's out of the Limelight to Isolated Lives," *LAT* 15 November 1987:I,3.
Five of the macaque monkeys used in surgical experiments that left them partially paralyzed are now being observed by San Diego animal behaviorists to see if they can be re-socialized.

1083.  Smith, Lynn. "Animal Researcher Burned in Effigy," *LAT* 29 August 1983:II,3.
About 200 animal rights advocates protested outside the American Psychological Association conference at Anaheim Convention Center against Edward Taub, former head of a Silver Spring, Maryland research lab. Taub, a speaker at the conference, had been convicted in 1981 of cruelty to the monkeys he used in spinal injury research.

1084.  "Taub Animal Cruelty Trial Sparks Guideline Review," *Bioscience* 32 (January 1982):15.
National Institutes of Health expects to see increasing awareness and sensitivity on part of public and scientific community as result of Edward Taub affair but continues to defend animal experimentation as the root of all medical progress. Agriculture department which had inspected Taub's lab just before the raid, says it is redefining performance standards for inspectors.

1085.  "Warning on 15 Lab Monkeys," *NYT* 28 May 1986:A16.
Fifty-eight senators and 256 representatives have asked secretary of health and human services department to release Silver Spring monkeys to a private animal sanctuary that has offered free care.

## Important Cases

### University of Pennsylvania Baboon Studies

1086.  Amatniek, Joan C. "Militant Animal Rights Protesters and Aid Cutoff Alarm Researchers," *Chron H Ed* 30 (July 31, 1985):1.

Health and human services department secretary suspends funds for brain injury experiments on baboons at University of Pennsylvania after demonstrations and sit-ins by animal rights activists. Researchers see this as a betrayal while animal rights activists celebrate it as a victory and turning point.

1087.  Amatniek, Joan C. "NIH to Withhold Its Support from Research on Baboons at U of P," *Chron H Ed* 31 (October 16, 1985):8.

National Institutes of Health will not resume funding of baboon experiments at University of Pennsylvania until university animal labs meet new standards for care and treatment of research animals.

1088.  Amatniek, Joan C. "Scientists at Penn are Reprimanded for Baboon Studies," *Chron H Ed* 31 (October 2, 1985):19.

After release of an ad hoc committee report charging two University of Pennsylvania scientists with not fulfilling their responsibilities of supervision and training, the University of Pennsylvania reprimands the pair who had directed baboon head trauma experiments.

1089.  "Animal Rights Group Fights Baboon Research," *NYT* 29 April 1985:A12.

Pennsylvania Animal Rights Coalition calls for an end to experiments in head injury research on baboons at University of Pennsylvania.

1090.  "Animal Rights Group in a College Office," *NYT* 16 July 1985:A8.

A hundred animal rights activists seize an office at National Institutes of Health to protest funding of University of Pennsylvania animal research laboratories.

1091.   Clarke, Maxine. "Animals in Research: U.S. Rules to Be
        Made Tighter," *Nature* 317 (September 12, 1985):103.
        Agriculture department is charging University of
        Pennsylvania with violations of Animal Welfare Act dur-
        ing its head injury experiments with baboons. Violations
        include operating without adequate anesthesia for the an-
        imals, unsanitary lab conditions, and improper postoper-
        ative care. Events reflect problem of weak laboratory an-
        imal welfare regulations.

1092.   Clarke, Maxine. "Primate Research: NIH Withdraws
        Support," *Nature* 317 (October 3, 1985):375.
        National Institutes of Health withdraws financial sup-
        port from University of Pennsylvania baboon experi-
        ments because of violations of animal care guidelines.

1093.   Culliton, Barbara J. "HHS Halts Animal Experiment,"
        *Science* 229 (August 2, 1985):447–48.
        National Institutes of Health holds up re-funding of
        baboon experiments at University of Pennsylvania until
        allegations of abuse are investigated. Animal rights move-
        ment has spurred efforts to ensure proper treatment of
        lab animals among scientific community, some of whom
        admit there's room for improvement.

1094.   Edwards, Rob. "Video of Animal Pain Shatters
        Researcher," *New Statesman* 108 (November 23, 1984):6.
        Professor James Hume Adams of Glasgow University
        has been performing postmortem examinations on pri-
        mate brains from University of Pennsylvania baboon ex-
        periments. Videos of how those experiments were con-
        ducted shocked him, and he wants assurance that
        practices at UP have improved or his department will
        withdraw from the work.

1095.   Fox, Jeffrey L. "Lab Break-in Stirs Animal Welfare
        Debate," *Science* 224 ( June 22, 1984):1319–20.
        Videos of baboon experiments taken from University
        of Pennsylvania by Animal Liberation Front are "embar-
        rassing to disastrous." Animal welfarists are outraged, but

scientists continue to justify the experiments. National Institutes of Health officials say they need more data before they can declare the baboons were abused.

1096. Katches, Mark. "Animal Rights Protesters Settle in for Second Night at NIH," *WP* 17 July 1985:C3.
Eighty animal rights demonstrators spend their second night at National Institutes of Health (NIH) to protest funding of brain trauma experiments on baboons at University of Pennsylvania. Dr. William Raub, NIH director, said the demand was nonnegotiable.

1097. Katches, Mark. "HHS Secretary Suspends Funding of Pennsylvania Brain-Trauma Experiments," *WP* 19 July 1985:A10.
U.S. Department of Health and Human Services Secretary Margaret Heckler ordered National Institutes of Health (NIH) to suspend funding of University of Pennsylvania baboon head injury experiments. Animal rights activists occupying NIH headquarters in Washington claimed victory and ended their four-day sit-in.

1098. Katches, Mark, and Eve Zibart. "Animal Rights Activists Stage Sit-in at NIH to Protest Experiments," *WP* 16 July 1985:D3.
Ninety animal welfare activists staged a sit-in at National Institutes of Health in Washington to protest continued funding of brain trauma experiments on baboons at University of Pennsylvania.

1099. Kilpatrick, James J. "Brutality and Laughter in the Lab," *WP* 23 July 1985:A15.
Video of brain experiments on baboons at University of Pennsylvania is shocking. Researchers and lab assistants are shown as they taunt and torment animals. Applauds health and human service secretary's suspension of funding and hopes Congress cancels it permanently.

1100.    "Penn Agrees to a Fine to Settle Animal Case," *NYT* 19 November 1985:A20.

University of Pennsylvania has agreed to pay a $4,000 fine for violating Animal Welfare Act in its treatment of baboons used in head injury research.

1101.    "Penn Is Told to Review Labs and End Abuses to Animals," *NYT* 5 October 1985:7.

Health and human services department tells University of Pennsylvania to review its procedures and policies and to open its animal laboratories to federal inspections. Funding for the baboon studies will remain suspended indefinitely.

1102.    "Research Using Animals Is Ordered Halted," *NYT* 19 July 1985:A8.

Health and human services secretary suspended grant money to University of Pennsylvania for research on head injuries using primates. Head of National Institutes of Health watched many hours of videotapes and indicated the animal lab failed to comply with standards for care of lab animals.

1103.    "Restoration of Funds in Head Injury Research Asked," *NYT* 26 July 1985:A8.

Head injury victims ask federal government to restore funds for University of Pennsylvania research using baboons.

1104.    Sun, Marjorie. "USDA Fines Pennsylvania Animal Laboratory," *Science* 230 (October 25, 1985):423.

Agriculture department fines University of Pennsylvania for abusing baboons at university's head injury clinic. National Institutes of Health suspended funds for baboon experiments after videos of the experiments were made public by Animal Liberation Front.

1105.    Weil, Robert. "Inhuman Bondage: The Untold Story of a Midnight Raid That Doomed a Lab and Sent

Reverberations Through the Scientific Community,"
*Omni* 9 (November 1986):64–71.

## Important Cases

## Other

1106. "Activist's Plea Terminates Attempted Murder Trial,"
*WSJ* 18 April 1990:A9.
Fran Trutt, accused of attempted murder of president
of U.S. Surgical, pleads no contest.

1107. Altman, Lawrence K. "Federal Financing of Animal
Research Halted at Columbia," *NYT* 3 February
1986:A1.
National Institutes of Health director suspended research funds for many animal studies at Columbia
University, because the university's programs failed to
meet standards for animal welfare and safety. Columbia
was cited for deficiencies in several areas: insufficient
number of veterinarians, lack of sterility of areas where
animals recover from surgery, and inadequate housing for
dogs under quarantine.

1108. Barnard, Neal. "Cleaning Up U.S. Surgical," *AA* 9
(September 1989):44–45.
Animal rights activists and doctors join in opposition
to U.S. Surgical's use of dogs for demonstrating surgical
staplers. Suggests hospitals and doctors purchase staples
from four other surgical supply companies, which don't
use animals to sell the product.

1109. "Basic Research on Breathing Is Target of Animal Rights
Attack," *Chemical and Engineering News* 68 (May 7,
1990):16–21.
Describes researcher John Orem's breathing experiments on cats. Animal rights activists disagree his experiments will lead to cures for human problems, saying that
after fifteen years, his work has still produced no useful
results.

1110.   Beardsley, Tim. "Animal Welfare: Tip-Off Leads to NIH Ban," *Nature* 318 (February 13, 1986):524.

National Institutes of Health staged an unannounced inspection of Columbia University animal labs and found deficiencies in veterinary care, sterility of postoperative areas, and quarters for dogs. Funds were suspended until facilities improved. Unannounced inspections at other facilities can be expected.

1111.   "Bomb Suspect's Driver Says He Was Informer," *NYT* 13 January 1989:B2.

Marc Mead, who drove Fran Trutt to U.S. Surgical headquarters armed with a bomb, admits to being a paid informer cooperating with police and U.S. Surgical.

1112.   "Cat Skull Crushing Experiments Halted," *AA* 9 (January 1989):26–27.

University of Cincinnati research project funded by National Institutes of Health for past fourteen years with almost $1 million has been canceled after bad publicity and pressure from animal rights activists and medical professionals. Project involved shooting cats with .22-caliber cartridges and immersing into liquid nitrogen the heads of those who survived.

1113.   Clifton, Merritt. "Bombs and Bombast," *AA* 9 (February 1989):28–29.

Reviews Fran Trutt case and how animal rights groups are reacting to it. Suggests possibility Trutt was set up so as to discredit animal rights movement.

1114.   Clifton, Merritt. "Informant Paid by U.S. Surgical Reveals Bombing Attempt Was a Setup," *AA* 9 (March 1989):26.

Marc Mead, an employee of anti-animal-rights consulting firm, was paid to spy on Fran Trutt and encourage her to buy four pipe bombs and plant them in parking lot of U.S. Surgical Corp.

1115. Fintor, Lou. "Columbia U Loses Animal Research Aid," *LAT* 1 February 1986:A2.

Federal funding was suspended at Columbia University when a surprise government investigation found the school in violation of animal research guidelines. Money will remain suspended on vertebrate research above level of rodents until school corrects deficiencies.

1116. Gwynne, Peter, and Stephen G. Michaud. "Cat Fight: American Museum of Natural History Cat Behavior Experiments," *Newsweek* 88 (November 8, 1976):100.

Animal rights activist Henry Spira spearheads protest against New York museum and two of its researchers who are studying sexual behavior of cats by surgically interfering with their brains, smell organs, and penises.

1117. "Hello Mary Lou, Goodbye Trutt," *AA* 9 (April 1988):28.

Mary Lou Sapone and Marc Mead of Perceptions International, a private security firm, were reportedly paid by U.S. Surgical to spy on animal rights groups, befriending Fran Trutt and helping her buy and plant a bomb at U.S. Surgical's parking lot.

1118. "Hiding Behind Dead Babies," *AA* 10 (May 1990):36.

Animal researchers Adrian Morrison of the University of Pennsylvania and John Orem of Texas Tech claim their work is valuable to the understanding of sudden infant death syndrome; animal rights activists and some medical experts deny their claim.

1119. Holden, Constance. "Universities Fight Animal Activists," *Science* 243 (January 6, 1989):17–19.

Scientists are angry with Cornell University administrators for giving in to animal rights pressure and turning down a government grant for research using cats in drug addiction studies. Suggests universities adopt an offensive posture in these matters, citing specific institutions that waged a successful battle against animal rights protests.

1120.  Howe, Marvine. "Advocate for Animals Pleads Guilty in
       Bomb Case," *NYT* 15 July 1989:29.
       Fran Trutt pleaded guilty to possessing bombs in her
       New York apartment. She says she was only trying to
       scare owner of U.S. Surgical, a Connecticut company
       that uses live dogs in demonstrating its surgical staples.
       The two men who provided Trutt with the bombs
       pleaded guilty to charge of conspiracy.

1121.  Johnson, Kirk. "Connecticut Arrest Underlines Split
       Within the Animal Rights Movement," *NYT* 13
       November 1988:40.
       Trutt case points up different approaches of groups
       and individuals in animal rights movement. Some are
       willing to work toward changing attitudes over the long
       haul; others want action now and are willing to perform
       acts of civil disobedience to get it. Most advocates, how-
       ever, condemn violence, believing it is not only a tactical
       mistake but has no place in a peaceful movement whose
       goal is humane treatment of animals.

1122.  Lyall, Sarah. "But Are Some More Equal Than Others?"
       *NYT* 29 January 1989:IV,E24.
       Cornell University researcher is switching from cats to
       rats in barbiturate addiction experiments, and the ques-
       tion is why animal rights people don't make as much of a
       fuss over rats as they do over cats.

1123.  Lyall, Sarah. "Scientist Gives Up Grant to Do Research
       on Cats," *NYT* 22 November 1988:B1+.
       Professor Michiko Okamoto of Cornell University has
       given up a $600,000 federal grant in fourteen-year pro-
       ject studying barbiturate addiction in cats. The action
       was brought about by pressure from animal rights groups
       who question value of her work. Several biomedical re-
       searchers in academia feel Cornell should have supported
       Prof. Okamoto and find the affair a threat to academic
       freedom.

1124.  McDonald, Kim. "NIH Citing New Rules on Animal

Care, Halts Some Research Aid to Columbia U," *Chron H Ed* 31 (February 12, 1986):6.

National Institutes of Health bars Columbia University from using funds to do certain types of animal research after unannounced visit there showed violations of new federal rules regarding treatment of laboratory animals. Scientists worry small research institutions may have to shut down if they cannot afford to make changes necessary to meet new regulations, but animal advocates say if an institution can't do research properly, it shouldn't do it at all, because the data collected will be useless and a waste of taxpayer money.

1125. McFadden, Robert D. "Animal Rights Advocate Held in Bombing Attempt," *NYT* 12 November 1988:29.

Fran Stephanie Trutt was arrested as she was planting a bomb in parking lot of U.S. Surgical, a company that uses live dogs to demonstrate its surgical staples to salespersons and doctors. She was charged with attempted murder, possessing explosives, and manufacturing a bomb. Animal rights organizations deny any connection with her.

1126. Morgan, Thomas. "Two New York Men Charged by U.S. in Bomb Scheme," *NYT* 28 January 1989:30.

Student from Queens College and bank teller from Flushing, neither connected with the animal rights movement, were arrested and charged with providing Fran Trutt with bombs and a gun.

1127. Oakie, Susan. "Cornell Cat Case Shows Clout of Animal Rights Movement: School Forced Researcher to Reject Drug-Abuse Grant," *WP* 23 November 1988:A3.

Researcher at Cornell who uses cats in drug experiments refused a grant from the federal government under pressure from university administration and animal rights groups. Scientists are up in arms, saying such precedent jeopardizes all research.

1128. Raloff, J. "NIH Limits Animal Studies at Columbia," *Science News* 129 (February 8, 1986):85.

1129.  Ravo, Nick. "Animal Rights Groups Infiltrated by Informers," *NYT* 26 January 1989:B1.

U.S. Surgical Corp. admits it paid informers to infiltrate animal rights organizations since early in the '80s. President Leon Hirsch said many animal rights groups are terrorist, and the company had to protect itself.

1130.  Regan, Tom. "Misplaced Trust," *AV* 3,1 (1990):18–25.

Account of Fran Trutt case and the web of sabotage, betrayal, intrigue, infiltration, and conspiracy surrounding it.

1131.  "A Serious Case of Puppy Love," *Time* 132 (November 28, 1988):24.

Fran Stephanie Trutt, 33-year-old substitute teacher, was caught planting a pipe bomb in the parking lot of U.S. Surgical, a company that uses live dogs in demonstrating surgical staples. Animal rights activists disavowed Trutt and wondered if she was set up by an agent provocateur to give animal rights movement a bad name.

1132.  "Thwarting an Animal Rights Attack," *Newsweek* 112 (November 28, 1988):47.

Police were waiting for Fran Stephanie Trutt when she placed a pipe bomb near parking space of founder of U.S. Surgical, a company that uses dogs for demonstrating surgical staples. Animal rights groups repudiated Trutt and condemned violence as unrepresentative of their cause.

1133.  "Tomasson, Robert E. "Suit Seeks a U.S. Inquiry on Cruelty to Dogs," *NYT* 8 December 1981:B11.

Friends of Animals (FoA) filed a suit in Federal District Court in New Haven in attempt to stop use of dogs by U.S. Surgical Corp. in its demonstrations of surgical staple guns. FoA said federal law was violated, because the dogs are obtained from unapproved dealers and are not properly anesthetized during stapling procedure.

1134.  "TSU Shuts Down Cat Lab at Cornell," *AA* 9 (March 1989):22–23.

Researcher using animals in drug addiction studies at Cornell University returns $700,000 grant and terminates fourteen-year study under pressure from animal rights group Trans-Species Unlimited.

1135.  "Update on the Trutt Trial," *AV* 3 (March/April 1990):54.
Fran Trutt, accused of trying to kill the chairman of U.S. Surgical Corp., is scheduled to go on trial in April.

1136.  Wade, Nicholas. "Animal Rights: NIH Cat Sex Study Brings Grief to NY Museum," *Science* 194 (October 8, 1976):162–67.
At New York American Museum of Natural History, a twenty-year study of cats' sexual behavior triggers protests from animal rights/welfare people and general public. Examines charges against museum and its defense.

1137.  Waldholz, Michael. "Animal Activists Sue U.S. Surgical Over Proxy Matter," *WSJ* 17 April 1989:B5A.
New England Anti-Vivisection Society sued U.S. Surgical, charging company's proxy material was fake and misleading. The company claims dogs used in demonstrations of its suture stapler are all obtained from licensed dealers, but activists say they may be lost, abandoned, or stolen pets.

1138.  Waldholz, Michael. "U.S. Surgical's Work on Dogs Stirs Up Town," *WSJ* 3 December 1981:B31.
U.S. Surgical's salespeople have used about 1,000 dogs to demonstrate suture staplers to physicians. The company says it is licensed by agriculture department and the state as a research and teaching facility. Animal rights groups dispute need for live animals in the demonstrations, and some in the community are alarmed, because some of the dogs used may have been pets that mysteriously disappeared from their home and their owner.

## Military Experiments

1139. Barnard, Neal D. *Animals in Military Wound Research and Training.* Washington, DC: Physicians Committee for Responsible Medicine, 1988.

   Military researchers continue to use animals in "wound labs" to help students learn how to perform surgery on injured soldiers, yet animals can't replicate human anatomy or physiology. Traditional method of supervised, hands-on surgical training on humans' is best way to learn.

1140. Brisbane, Arthur S. "Animal Crusaders Briefed on Jail," *WP* 10 June 1984:B9.

   People for the Ethical Treatment of Animals held a civil disobedience workshop in Silver Spring, Maryland, on how to protest defense department's shooting of animals in wound experiments. After appealing to Congress and the courts, activists feel civil disobedience is their last resort.

1141. Brown, Chip. "Weinberger Is Butt of Animal Protest," *WP* 5 October 1983:A1.

   In front of defense Secretary Caspar Weinberger's house, eight goats accompanied by activists from People for the Ethical Treatment of Animals protested against military wound experiments on animals. Activists offered Weinberger a basket of squash and Indian corn as thanks for banning the use of dogs.

1142. Budkie, Michael. "Military Animal Abuse," *AA* 10 (September 1990):38.

   Military experiments involve 540,000 animals annually, with a cost of $110 million. Some congresspeople are calling for hearings.

1143. "Compromise Is Reached in Army Animal Surgery," *NYT* 20 November 1983:A26.

   Congress has barred military from using cats and dogs in wound surgical training but instead will allow use of goats and pigs. People for the Ethical Treatment of Animals protests, saying just because an animal isn't "cute" doesn't mean it's OK to shoot it.

1144. "Court Order Forces Army to Free Dogs," *LAT* 14 October 1989:I,34.

Nineteen greyhounds scheduled to have their hind legs broken and studied by army researchers were released to Marin Humane Society by court order.

1145. "Defense Research on Dogs, Cats Stirs Dispute," *Chemical and Engineering News* 62 (October 8, 1984):6.

Defense Secretary Weinberger bans use of dogs and cats in military research but after protests from researchers, seems about to change his mind.

1146. Fox, Jeffrey L. "Ban on Shooting Animals for Research Is Lifted," *Science* 223 (10 February 1984):568.

Military program to study gunshot wounds in live animals has been reinstated on orders from Secretary Caspar Weinberger. Researchers will use pigs and goats instead of dogs and cats.

1147. "In the Doghouse: Protest Halts Animal Killings," *Time* 122 (August 8, 1983):38.

Animal rights campaign succeeds in convincing defense Secretary Weinberger to cancel wound experiments on pigs and dogs and to review use of all animals in military research.

1148. Moore, Molly. "Sale of Dogs for Army Experiment Probed: More Than a Dozen Greyhounds Were Obtained for Research Without Owners' Approval," *WP* 9 October 1989:E1.

Army's use of illegally obtained greyhounds in experiments has led to congressional investigation of military's procurement of dogs.

1149. "Navy Dolphin Use Expands Despite Failures," *AA* (April 1989):29.

The Navy is capturing dolphins and using them to guard submarine bases in Washington State. So far, forty-four dolphins have died, and many suffer from anorexia, stomach ulcers, and heart failure.

1150.   Newman, Barry. "No Banana Republic, U.S. Struggles to End a Monkey Embargo," *WSJ* 26 March 1981:1.
        Bangladesh has decided to ban selling monkeys to U.S. dealers after International Primate Protection League informed them U.S. government was using monkeys in neutron and atomic bomb experiments rather than medical research.

1151.   "Pentagon Revises Itself: No Shooting of Dogs," *NYT* 27 July 1983:A1+.
        Pentagon's wound laboratory had planned to shoot eighty dogs at close range this year so medical students could learn how to treat combat wounds. After animal rights and congressional protests, defense Secretary Weinberger canceled plan. Use of other animals in experiments by defense department, however, continues.

1152.   Richburg, Keith B. "Army, Air Force Cease Tests on Dogs and Cats," *WP* 4 October 1984:A17.
        Air Force and Army officials have decided to ban use of dogs and cats in biomedical and clinical research, but animal rights organizations are suspicious. Decision came after a review ordered by Secretary Weinberger and a public outcry against wound experiments using dogs.

1153.   Richburg, Keith B. "Pentagon Switches Signals on Lab Use of Animals," *WP* 9 October 1984:A17.
        Defense department reverses its recent policy to ban animals in research. Confusion and bureaucratic blunders left Pentagon officials scrambling for an explanation to their contradictory announcements.

1154.   Saperstein, Saundra. "Weinberger Halts School's Plan to Shoot Dogs," *WP* 27 July 1983:C1+.
        Representative Tom Lantos, after an appeal from

People for Ethical Treatment of Animals, circulated a letter on Capitol Hill protesting planned shooting of eighty dogs at military medical school in Bethesda, Maryland with high-powered weapons. Defense Secretary Weinberger canceled project after reading a description of it in the newspaper.

1155. Schochet, Barry. "Dog Days in D.C.," *LAT* 7 August 1983:IV,5.

A rare example of sanity prevailed in Washington when Congress and defense Secretary Weinberger acted with lightning speed to cancel wound experiments on dogs in a military research institute. This is highly unusual, because most animal protection bills introduced in Congress become watered down or are too weak to do the job correctly.

1156. "Stopping the War on Animals," *AA* 10 (October 1990):29–30.

Congressional inquiry into military experiments on animals set for October. Records show the military used more than 142,000 animals in 1988.

1157. Wade, Nicholas. "India Bans Monkey Export: U.S. May Have Breached Accord," *Science* 199 (January 20, 1978): 280–81.

India bans further export of rhesus monkeys to U.S. after disclosure that some were being used in weapons-related radiation experiments, a use that is expressly in violation of agreement between U.S. and India.

## Genetic Experiments

1158. "Animal Cruelty Charged in Growth Gene Work," *Chemical and Engineering News* 62 (October 8, 1984):5.

Humane Society and Foundation on Economic Trends file suit in United States District court to halt experiments involving human genetic transfers to pigs and sheep.

1159.  Beardsley, Tim. "Genetic Manipulation: Rifkin Strikes Against Gene Transfer Experiments," *Nature* 311 (October 11, 1984):495.

Jeremy Rifkin of the Foundation on Economic Trends teams up with Humane Society of United States to halt gene transfer experiments with sheep and pigs by filing suit in district court. Suit claims experiments are a violation of ethical canons of civilization and a new form of cruelty to animals.

1160.  Crawford, Mark. "Religious Groups Join Animal Patent Battle," *Science* 237 (July 31, 1987):480–81.

Fourteen animal welfare groups, thirteen farm groups, and five religious denominations are questioning experiments that would alter animals genetically to produce more profitable livestock. Farmers want a moratorium until farm animal gene pool can be assessed and royalties understood; religious leaders question morality of it all.

1161.  Fox, Jeffrey L. "Rifkin Takes Aim at USDA Animal Research," *Science* 226 (October 19, 1984):321.

Jeremy Rifkin and the Humane Society have filed a lawsuit to prevent genetic engineering research on animals at the agriculture department in Beltsville, Maryland facility. They object to experiments on both economic and ethical grounds.

1162.  Fox, Jeffrey L. "USDA Animal Research Under Fire," *Bioscience* 35 (January 1985):6–7.

Jeremy Rifkin of the Foundation on Economic Trends and Michael Fox of the Humane Society filed a lawsuit to stop agriculture department's gene transfer experiments on animals on environmental, economic, and ethical grounds.

1163.  Hart, Kathleen. "Making Mythical Monsters," *Progressive* 54 (March 1990):22.

Genetic manipulation and patenting of animals are being resisted by animal rights groups and other groups.

1164. "Lawsuit Challenges Patenting of Animals," *NYT* 30 July 1988:34.

Coalition of animal rights groups filed a lawsuit, hoping to stop the Patent and Trademark Office from issuing patents on animals bred by genetic engineering.

1165. Tangley, Laura. "RAC Rejects Rifkin's Proposals," *Bioscience* 35 (January 1985):7.

Jeremy Rifkin and Humane Society protest to Recombinant DNA Advisory Committee against agriculture department effort to transfer human genes to pigs and sheep.

1166. Wheeler, David L. "Grant Patents on Animals? An Ethical and Legal Battle Looms," *Chron H Ed* 33 (March 25, 1987):1.

Ethical, economic, and legal issues surrounding scientists' desire to research and patent genetic experiments on animals.

1167. No entry.

## Consumer Product and Toxicity Tests

1168. "Animal Rights Group Protest at Revlon," *Women's Wear Daily* 153 (February 23, 1987):6.

1169. "Avon Drops Draize," *AV* 2 (August 2, 1989):67.

Avon announces it will drop the Draize eye irritancy test used on rabbits to determine product safety. The company denied this action was a result of campaign mounted by People for the Ethical Treatment of Animals, which included demonstrations and obtaining stockholder vote on a proxy asking for data on company's animal testing practices.

1170. "Benetton Feels the Pressure," *AV* 2 (February 1989):76.

Activists in U.S., Canada, and Europe protest at Benetton retail stores against the company's use of animals in testing of new personal care products.

1171.   "Carme Boycott Continues," *AA* 10 (December 1990):47.
        Animal rights groups boycott cosmetic company
        Carme after it was acquired by International Research
        and Development Corporation, which uses animals in its
        product testing.

1172.   *Cosmetic Tests on Animals.* Clarks Summit, PA: Society for
        Animal Rights, 1978.
        Description of toxicity tests done using animals, who
        determines if the tests must be done and what kind, the
        brutality of the LD-50 and Draize tests, and their lack of
        scientific validity.

1173.   "Draize Test May Be Made More Humane," *Science News*
        118 (October 25, 1980):262–63.
        Because it's so cruel, rabbits hate it and so do techni-
        cians who administer the Draize Test to them. Now a
        coalition of protesters are pressuring industrial and gov-
        ernment animal testing labs to use more humane meth-
        ods.

1174.   "E.P.A. Moves to Trim Animal Deaths in Tests," *NYT* 30
        August 1984:A21.
        Environmental Protection Agency (EPA) announced
        new guidelines to discourage extensive use of animals in
        product testing. Dr. McArdle of the Humane Society
        would like to see EPA go further by not accepting docu-
        mentation based on animal testing.

1175.   Feder, Barnaby J. "Research Looks Away from Labora-
        tory Animals," *NYT* 29 January 1989:IV, E24.
        Animal rights movement is starting to have some effect
        on use of animals in research and product safety testing.
        Benetton, Noxell, and other companies have stopped
        using animals in cosmetics safety testing, and Cornell
        University recently returned a grant that would have
        funded barbiturate addiction testing in cats.

1176.   Freeman, Laurie. "Animal Uproar," *Advertising Age* 26
        February 1990:S1–2.

Animal rights groups continue to boycott and protest against cosmetics companies that use animals in testing, but some companies, such as Revlon, Mary Kay, and Avon, have listened and stopped. Product safety testing methods are not usually part of advertising strategy, but those companies that use anticruelty marketing tactics in the 1990s may reap huge benefits.

1177. "Group Accuses Gillette Company of Animal Cruelty in Tests," *WSJ* 26 September 1986:40.

Animal rights groups boycott Gillette products after videotapes and photographs are released showing technicians' putting shaving cream into rabbit's eyes and force-feeding them deodorant.

1178. "Group Charges Gillette Abuses Lab Animals," *Chemical and Engineering News* 64 (October 6, 1986):5.

Animal rights groups play videotapes of animal suffering in Gillette labs taken by a former employee of the company. Calls for boycott of Gillette products until firm stops using animals in testing.

1179. "Industry Responds to Product Testing Campaigns," *AA* 9 (October 1989):40+.

Revlon, Avon, Fabergé, Mary Kay, and Amway are eliminating product safety testing on animals.

1180. Koenig, Richard. "Companies Begin to Use Fewer Animals When Testing New Consumer Products," *WSJ* 19 May 1986:45.

Some animal protectionists and corporations are drawing closer together as industries attempt to either reduce use of animals in product safety testing or modify tests to be more humane. Now some industries force-feed caustic chemicals to only ten rats instead of forty, and they allow rabbits to blink after having irritants placed in their eyes.

1181. Krizmanic, Judy. "Avon Halts Animal Testing on Its Products," *Vegetarian Times* 145 (September 1989):12.

Under pressure from People for the Ethical Treatment of Animals and other animal rights groups, Avon Products has announced it will stop using animals to test for product safety and will switch to alternative methods. Revlon and Mary Kay have also agreed to end animal testing.

1182. Kullberg, John F. "Force Feeding (letter)," *WSJ* 10 June 1986:29.

President of the American Society for the Prevention of Cruelty to Animals says U.S. Food and Drug Administration (FDA) no longer requires LD-50 test, but companies continue to use it anyway. FDA should take a stronger stance and tell companies the LD-50 will not enhance their chances for product approval.

1183. "NJ and MD Ban Draize Eye Test," *AV* 2 (February 1989):75.

A ban on the use of the Draize eye irritancy test on rabbits passed unanimously by the New Jersey Assembly. Maryland passed a similar bill, but it was not signed by the governor.

1184. Norman, Colin. "FDA Amending Regulations to Reduce LD-50 Testing," *Science* 225 (September 7, 1984):1005.

1185. People for the Ethical Treatment of Animals. *Shopping Guide for Caring Consumers.* Washington, DC: PETA, 1990.

List of more than 250 companies that do not test their products on animals.

1186. Rich, Susan. "Encouraging Corporate Responsibility," *AA* 8 (September/October 1988):24.

Propelled by various animal rights groups, 750,000 stockholders in seven major cosmetics and household products companies voted in favor of proposals designed to investigate ways in which their companies use animals in product testing. Although proposal was not carried, enough votes were garnered to allow reintroduction at later date.

1187. Smith, David Christian. "Animal Testing Feels the Heat," *CSM* 15 October 1990:12–13.

Animal rights movement is starting to make a dent with the public in use of animals for product safety testing. Polls show public condemns such use and would purchase noncruelty products if available. Cosmetic companies are also heeding animal rights pressure. Revlon and Avon are now using Eyetex, a toxicity test that uses cell cultures instead of live animals.

1188. Sun, Marjorie. "Lots of Talk About LD-50," *Science* 222 (December 9, 1983):1106.

Animal rights advocates and scientists agree LD-50 test used to test product safety is outdated and has limited value. Federal regulations do not demand such tests, and U.S. Food and Drug Administration would prefer other kinds of testing. Environmental Protection Agency and Department of Transportation still mandate the LD-50 in modified form. It's not clear how many animals are killed from LD-50 testing each year, but it could number in the millions.

1189. Thompson, Richard C. "Reducing the Need for Animal Testing," *FDA Consumer* 22 (February 1988):15–17.

U.S. Food and Drug Administration does not specifically require LD-50 or Draize test but asks for best available means for determining safety of consumer products. For many industries, that often translates into animal testing even though alternatives are now available. Office of Technology Assessment report calls for replacement, reduction and refinement of animal testing.

1190. Ward, Adrienne. "Consumers at Odds with Animal Testing," *Advertising Age* 26 February 1990:S2.

Gallup poll shows majority interviewed were against testing on animals but did not know if products they used were or were not tested on animals.

1191. White, George. "Cosmetics: Advocates Have Racked Up Major Victories Against the Industry Giants," *LAT* 3 December 1989:D1.

Influence of animal rights movement on a number of cosmetics firms, which have stopped testing on animals— Avon, Revlon, Christian Dior.

1192. White, George. "How Carme Went from Ethical Icon to Enemy," *LAT* 3 December 1989:D7.

Carme doesn't test on animals, but the company that wants to buy Carme—International Research and Development—does. People for the Ethical Treatment of Animals launches attack and boycott of Carme, a company it once praised.

## Animal Use in Educational Settings

1193. "Apple Drops T.V. Ads Starring Animal Activists," *Vegetarian Times* 126 (February 1988):14.

1194. Barinaga, Marcia. "Activists Infiltrate Stanford," *Nature* 338 (April 6, 1989):449.

In a private letter to the university administration, Stanford University biology faculty criticize course on animal rights. Instructors of the course, Kim Sturla and Lisa Giraud of Peninsula Humane Society, obtained a copy of the letter, released it to the public, and demanded an apology.

1195. Barinaga, Marcia. "Frog Liberationists Croak Up," *Nature* 332 (April 21, 1988):672.

California law gives elementary and secondary school students the right to refuse to perform animal dissection.

1196. Barnard, Neal D. "Barbara Orlans: On Research Reforms and Regulations," *AA* 9 (May 1989):7–10+.

Interview with Barbara Orlans, a scientist who worked at National Institutes of Health and witnessed science fair projects involving crude, highly invasive, and scientifically invalid student projects on small mammals. Such projects only teach students the wrong thing—that anything goes in the name of science. Orlans calls for standards and legislation that would define pain, invasiveness, and so on.

Humane people within the scientific community are starting to speak up.

1197. Barnard, Neal D. "Dog Days in Medical School," *AA* 9 (April 1988):42–43.

More and more medical schools are dropping "dog labs,"—the use of dogs to demonstrate to students certain physiological or surgical principles. Barnard evaluates lectures, computer programs, and videotapes used by some medical schools as alternatives to live dogs.

1198. Brownley, Nancie, and Heather McGiffin, eds. *Animals in Education: Use of Animals in High School Biology Classes and Animal Fairs.* Washington, DC: Institute for the Study of Animal Problems, 1980. Available from ERIC (ED206508).

Proceedings of conference on use of animals in classroom and science fairs. Sixteen essays by educators, psychologists, and veterinarians representing both the pro and con arguments.

1199. DeRosa, Bell. "Moving Against Dissection," *AA* 8 (September/October 1988):42–43.

1200. "Dissection Debated in Maine," *NYT* 28 August 1988:A42.

Animal rights groups urge school districts to allow students to choose alternatives, such as videotapes and computer simulation, to dissection in the classroom.

1201. "Dissection Lab Animal Dealers Exposed," *AA* 10 (September 1990):37.

People for the Ethical Treatment of Animals and Friends of Animals expose Wise & Leach, animal dealers with evidence of cruel treatment of animals put to death and sold for dissection.

1202. Fishlock, Diana J. "Anti-Vivisectionist Students are Refusing to Harm Animals in Classes, Laboratories," *Chron H Ed* 33 (July 15, 1987):33–34.

Growing number of students are unwilling to use live

animals in the classroom. Focuses on specific cases and how they were resolved.

1203.   Graham, Pat. "Know Your Rights and Refuse," *AV* 2 (August 1989):88–89.

When Jennifer Graham refused to dissect a frog in biology class and took the issue to court, she was inundated by letters and calls from many other students who agreed with her position. Jennifer's mother felt the need for a hotline to inform students of their rights under First Amendment, provide advice on difficulties involved in taking a stand against dissection, and suggest how to approach school officials in resolving the conflict.

1204.   Hecht, Jeff. "A Lesson to Be Avoided: Dissection Classes May Be Sending Out the Wrong Message," *New Scientist* 126 (May 19, 1990):70.

Daughter's repulsion at dissection in biology class triggers author's belief that the way we teach biology may be turning kids off to science. Believes schools could teach animal physiology much more effectively with color graphics and computer simulations than with dissections and at the same time avoid perception that biomedical science is gruesome or sadistic.

1205.   Henig, Robin Marantz. "Animal Welfare Groups Press for Limits on High School Research," *Bioscience* 29 (November 1979):651–53.

Washington conference entitled "The Use of Animals in High School Biology Classes" was attended by both scientists and animal welfarists. Strained civility between two groups gave way to name-calling as discussion progressed. A number of issues, however, did receive attention if not resolution: what should and should not be allowed in science fairs and classrooms regarding painful experimentation on animals.

1206.   Hentoff, Nat. "The High Cost of Speaking up for Animals," *WP* 18 February 1989:A25.

Explains how Nedim Buyukmihci, tenured professor of

ophthalmology at University of California, Davis, and a cofounder of Association of Veterinarians for Animal Rights, faces dismissal from his position because of encouraging use of alternatives to live, healthy dogs in teaching eye surgery. Buyukmihci is suing the university in federal court for violation of his First and Fourteenth Amendment rights.

1207. Herzog, Harold A. "Discussing Animal Rights and Animal Research in the Classroom," *Teaching Psychology* 17 (April 1990):90–94.

Reviews two philosophical arguments for animal rights and describes exercises he uses in his college psychology classes to encourage discussion of animal experimentation. Students pretend they are part of an animal care committee and evaluate specific proposals for experiments using animals.

1208. Holden, Constance. "Apples, Frogs, and Animal Rights," *Science* 238 (December 4, 1987):1345.

Apple Computer Co. pulled a television advertisement featuring Jennifer Graham, a teen who asked to be allowed to earn a biology grade using computer simulation program instead of dissecting a frog. The company withdrew the commercial after receiving protests from biomedical community, which claimed the ad was antivivisection propaganda.

1209. Holden, Constance. "NASA Student Rat Project Questioned," *Science* 217 (July 30, 1982):425.

Head of NASA's life sciences division, worried about animal rights advocacy, questions plan to send arthritic rats into space as part of a student project. After consulting with arthritis experts, concludes project has no scientific validity.

1210. King, Peter H. "A Schoolgirl Sets out to Dissect an Old Tradition," *LAT* 1 May 1987:I,3.

The tradition of dissecting a frog in biology class is

being challenged by 15-year-old sophomore Jennifer Graham of Victor Valley High School in Victorville, California. Graham believes she can learn as much or more from computer graphics or models. School officials disagree, and although they have retreated from their original position of giving Graham a failing grade, they insist her refusal to dissect will have to be noted on her transcript. Jennifer and her lawyer reject decision and say she will sue school district under civil rights law.

1211.   Moment, Gairdner B. "Humane Treatment and Rational Discrimination," *Bioscience* 29 (October 1979):571.

Discusses guidelines to help science instructors convince their students of importance of animal experimentation and overcome their reluctance to participate in it.

1212.   Murphy, Kim. "Judge Jumps to Conclusions: Find Naturally Dead Frog," *LAT* 2 August 1988:I,3+.

U.S. district court judge makes compromise by ruling teenager Jennifer Graham can earn biology grade by identifying photographs of a deceased frog that died naturally, rather than having to dissect one killed on purpose. Graham's lawyers are skeptical, but school officials think it an excellent idea.

1213.   Orlans, F. Barbara. "Should Students Harm or Destroy Animal Life?" *American Biology Teacher* 50 (January 1988):6+.

1214.   Palca, Joseph. "Guidelines Off," *Nature* 319 (February 6, 1986):440.

The National Academy of Sciences rejected new guidelines drawn up by the National Science Teachers Association for use of animals in the classroom. Guidelines would have allowed surgery under supervision and experimentation that causes pain.

1215.   Richmond, Gail, Manfred Engelmann, and Lawrence R. Krupka. "The Animal Research Controversy: Exploring Student Attitudes," *American Biology Teacher* 52 (November/December 1990):467–71.

1216. Robeznieks, Andis. "Teen Takes a Leap for Animalkind," *Vegetarian Times* 121 (September 1987):7+.

Fifteen-year-old Jennifer Graham, a high school student in Victorville, California, has taken to court her objection to dissecting a frog. In addition to her lawsuit, she has testified before the state legislature in support of a student's right to refuse.

1217. Santopoalo, Tina. "Stop Condoning Cruelty to Animals," *American Biology Teacher* 47 (November/December 1985):454.

1218. Sieber, Joan E. "Students' and Scientists' Attitudes on Animal Research," *American Biology Teacher* 48 (February 1986):85–91.

1219. Sobel, Dava. "The Truth About Black Beauty," *Omni* 9 (March 1987):27.

Halvor N. Christensen, emeritus professor of biological chemistry at Michigan Medical School, is afraid children's literature that portrays animals sentimentally and unrealistically will result in antiscience attitude and opposition to animal experimentation. Writers of children's books should strive for biological honesty, avoid gabby animals, and alert children to presence of fantasy by mixing in some toys around animal characters.

1220. "Student Who Sued School Isn't Required to Cut Frog," *NYT* 3 August 1988:A8.

Federal district court judge dismissed the lawsuit against a California school district by 16-year-old Jennifer Graham, who refused to dissect a frog in biology class and had her grade lowered from A to B for doing so.

1221. Sun, Marjorie. "Science Teachers to Ban Testing Harmful to Animals," *Science* 209 (August 15, 1980):791.

National Association of Biology Teachers and National Science Teachers Association have adopted guidelines that ban classroom experiments harming animals. Action spurred by pressure from animal welfare groups and from fear of proposed legislation in several states that would be even more restrictive in the use of live animals.

1222. "Teen's Objection to Dissection Pays Off," *Vegetarian Times* 147 (November 1989):13.

With the help of the American Civil Liberties Union, 16-year-old Maggie McCool convinced school board of Ley High School in Woodstown, New Jersey, to allow students to perform alternative assignments in place of dissection in biology class.

1223. Uzych, Leo. "Animals in the Classroom," *Hastings Center Report* 18 (August/September 1988):3.

Dearth of regulations on animal experimentation in our nation's schools is striking, because so many animals are used annually. Discusses Maine's regulations to govern proper treatment of animals used in elementary and secondary schools.

1224. Wells, Ken. "If the Star Witness Croaks Will the Case Then Be Dismissed," *WSJ* 6 November 1989:A1+.

Jennifer Graham has sued Victorville, California, School District, because her refusal to dissect a frog on moral grounds led to a lowering of her grade. Spurred on by the Graham case, California legislature has passed a law allowing students to choose alternative projects in place of dissection. Researchers fear the law will teach students it is wrong to use animals in research.

## Alternatives to Animal Experimentation

1225. "Alternatives to Animals," *Futurist* 20 ( July/August 1986): 35–6.

Office of Technology Assessment says although all animal use cannot be fully replaced by alternatives, some modifications can be made in existing animal tests to reduce number of animals used and to make tests more humane.

1226. Boffey, Philip M. "Animals in Lab: Protests Accelerate,

But Use Is Dropping; Economics Cited as Chief Reason for Sharp Decline," *NYT* 27 October 1981:C1+.

Although animal welfare groups are putting pressure on laboratories that use animals in research and testing, the cost of buying and maintaining lab animals is also leading scientists to design nonanimal experiments. Scientists are switching to tissue cultures, computer models, and other techniques that are cheaper.

1227.  Brown, Kitty. "Alternatives to Animal Tests and Other Cruelties," *MS* 10 (December 1981):45.

Neither the U.S. Food and Drug Administration nor the Consumer Product and Safety Commission mandates use of animals to test for product safety, but companies often use animals as protection against being sued. Cosmetic industry beginning to respond to public pressure by setting up research centers to develop alternative testing in place of animals.

1228.  Budiansky, Stephen. "Animal Experimentation: Alternatives Neglected," *Nature* 315 (May 2, 1985):9.

National Academy of Sciences study says National Institutes of Health discourages researchers from developing nonanimal models of human disease and physiology by withholding funding. Researchers working with nonanimal or "unconventional" systems are reviewed by ad hoc committees not always sympathetic to nontraditional models of research. As biological understanding shifts more to molecular level, the best model is not always a whole organism, but rather an analogue of the fundamental biological principle involved.

1229.  Caras, Roger. "We Must Find Alternatives to Animals in Research," *Newsweek* 112 (December 26, 1988):57.

ABC-TV news reporter thinks finding alternatives is answer to getting animals out of research laboratories.

1230.  Dagani, Ron. "In Vitro Methods May Offer Alternatives to Animal Testing," *Chemical and Engineering News* 62 (Novem-ber 12, 1984):25–28.

Trend among researchers is under way to detect potentially toxic substances without using live animals in testing.

1231.  Davis, Donald A. "Is There an Alternative?" *Drug and Cosmetics Industry* 133 (July 1983):23.

It's a delusion to think alternatives to animals exist for testing the safety of products. The sacrifice of mice, rabbits, and lab rats is price that must be paid to achieve assurance of safety in products we buy and use.

1232.  Davis, Donald A. "New Life for Lab Animals?" *Drug and Cosmetics Industry* 139 (July 1986):19+.

Alternatives to animal testing are not available and won't be anytime soon. Animal rights activists may have had some victories, but completely eliminating animal testing is unlikely.

1233.  Davis, Donald A. "Premature Activism," *Drug and Cosmetics Industry* 142 (April 1988):22.

There are no reliable alternatives for animal tests that animal rights advocates are having banned. The ultimate guinea pigs will be humans.

1234.  "FDLI on Animal Testing," *Drug and Cosmetics Industry* 135 (November 1984):42.

U.S. Food and Drug Administration announces establishment of animal research committee for developing alternatives to animal research. Animal rights pressure, lack of efficiency, and high cost of animal studies are reasons for the initiative.

1235.  Feder, Barnaby J. "Beyond White Rats and Rabbits: New Techniques Reduce the Number of Animals Needed to Test the Safety of New Drugs and Other Products," *NYT* 28 February 1988:C1+.

Researchers say pressure from animal rights groups only partly responsible for their shift to nonanimal testing of products for safety. Rising costs of animal use in the laboratory and emergence of scientifically acceptable alternatives are also driving forces.

1236. Franklin, Ben. "Cosmetic Unit Aids Research," *NYT* 23 September 1981:C12.

Cosmetics industry gives a $1-million grant to Johns Hopkins University to find laboratory alternatives to the use of animals in product safety testing.

1237. Gallup, Gordon G., and Susan D. Suarez. "Alternatives to the Use of Animals in Psychological Research," *American Psychologist* 40 (October 1985):1104–11.

Assesses alternatives to animal experiments suggested by animal rights advocates and concludes there are no viable alternatives to use of live organisms in behavioral research.

1238. Goldemberg, Robert L. "Alternative Testing and the Eye," *Drug and Cosmetics Industry* 139 (July 1986):14–16.

Controversy is generated at Cosmetics Chemists conference about alternatives to use of animals in product safety testing.

1239. Goodwin, Michael. "The Easing of Creaturely Pain," *NYT* 1 March 1981:E20.

Animal welfare groups are winning several battles. Avon and Revlon have committed money to find alternatives to animal testing of cosmetics and household products after pressure from coalition of 400 animal welfare groups.

1240. "Grant by Revlon Seeks Humane Test for Cosmetics," *NYT* 24 December 1980:B3.

Revlon announces a $750,000 three-year grant to Rockefeller University to develop alternatives to using animals in product safety testing.

1241. Henderson, Keith. "Reducing Animal Testing: Congressional Report Offers List of Alternatives but Warns Against a Complete Ban on Such Experiments," *CSM* 4 February 1986:6.

Office of Technology Assessment report, "Alternatives to Animal Use in Research, Testing, and Education," says much testing and experimentation on animals is unnecessary and poorly regulated and ignores available alternatives. Recommends an increased use of cell cultures, micro-organisms, and computer simulation, as well as better collection and distribution of existing data.

1242.   Heneson, Nancy. "American Agencies Denounce LD50 Test," *New Scientist* 100 (November 17, 1983):475.

At a meeting on toxicity testing, sponsored by U.S. Food and Drug Administration (FDA), it became clear neither FDA nor Environmental Protection Agency has a statute requiring companies to use LD-50 test for proof of product safety. Still, industry is unwilling to abandon the test.

1243.   Holden, Constance. "Industry Toxicologists Keen on Reducing Animal Use," *Science* 236 (April 17, 1987):252.

Spurred on by animal welfare movement, major manufacturers of drugs, pesticides, and the like met informally to assess progress in their efforts to reduce use of animals in product safety testing.

1244.   Holden, Constance. "New Focus on Replacing Animals in the Lab," *Science* 215 (January 1, 1982):35–38.

Animal rights people don't realize it's not always possible to use alternatives for whole-animal testing; however, the best possibilities for alternatives are mathematical models and the cultivation of living material in culture. Animal welfare/rights movement has raised consciousness of researchers working with animals, but it is of less importance in alternatives' gaining popularity than economic and scientific imperatives.

1245.   "Hurting Rabbits," *NYT* 30 May 1982:A33.

Researchers at Rockefeller University say preliminary data from attempts to find replacements for animal testing are encouraging. It is hoped Draize test, which involves placing chemicals in rabbits' eyes can be eliminated, but researchers caution it may take seven to nine years.

1246.   Jefferson, David J. "Toxicologist Gets Trapped Between Science, Commerce," *WSJ* 21 February 1990:B2.

Eyetex, a nonanimal test for product safety testing, can replace Draize test, which uses rabbits, but it is receiving cool reception from some in the scientific community.

1247. "Johns Hopkins Is Selected as Site for Center for Animal Test Alternatives," *Drug and Cosmetics Industry* 129 (November 1981):42+.

1248. Knobelsdorff, Kerry Elizabeth. "Trying to Move away from Animal Testing," *CSM* 5 October 1987:16.

The LD-50 (Lethal Dose 50%) method of testing involves force-feeding chemical substances to a group of 40–100 animals until half of them die. U.S. Food and Drug Administration discourages use of this test, and toxicologist Gerhard Zbinden has condemned it as wasteful and not necessarily meaningful for humans. Nonanimal alternatives are available, yet companies continue to use LD-50. Animal rights activists say it is hard to bring about change when dealing with the inertia of tradition.

1249. "Lab Animal Tests Decline Thanks to New Technology and Animal Rights Efforts," *WSJ* 8 September 1988:1.

New and cheaper technology plus pressure from animal rights advocates has made corporations turn to nonanimal testing for product safety.

1250. McDonald, Kim. "Researchers Test Alternatives to the Use of Live Animals in Judging Safety of New Products," *Chron H Ed* 32 (May 14, 1986):6–8.

Alternatives to use of animals in product safety testing exist, but establishing their value scientifically can take up to fifteen years. Animal rights advocates believe improved accuracy of alternatives protects the public better than animal testing does, but they don't believe that cosmetics industry has made developing and establishing alternatives a priority.

1251. McDonald, Kim. "Some Research Will Always Require

Live Animals, Congressional Study Concludes," *Chron H Ed* 31 (February 12, 1986):4.

A 440-page report by Office of Technology Assessment, "Alternatives to Animal Use in Research, Testing, and Education," concludes use of some animals will always be necessary in research but suggests ways to reduce their numbers by using available and viable alternatives, developing new ones, and eliminating duplicative experiments.

1252. "A Mild Rhubarb at SCC Conference," *Drug and Cosmetics Industry* 139 (July 1986):36–7.

Scientific Conference of the Society of Cosmetics Chemists turns into a controversial session as some scientists in audience challenge research of those presenting new developments in alternatives to animal testing.

1253. Muller, Carrie. "Animal Test Alternatives: Rockefeller, Johns Hopkins Utilize Separate Routes," *Drug and Cosmetics Industry* 136 (April 1985):36–41+.

Two research centers follow different paths in their search for alternatives to using animals to test for product safety.

1254. Palca, Joseph. "Animal Welfare: OTA Squares Circles of Dissent," *Nature* 319 (February 6, 1986):440.

Office of Technology Assessment has issued a $425,000, two-year report on use of animals and alternatives to animals in research. Concludes that the U.S. lags behind other countries in protecting laboratory animals and that although live animals are necessary for some experiments, alternatives are available for many others.

1255. Petersen, Iver. "Meeting Offers Hope for Fewer Animal Tests," *NYT* 12 April 1987:A31.

Meeting sponsored by Mobil Oil Corp. saw scientists from many research organizations come together to discuss alternative tests in place of use of animals, including bacteria and cell cultures. Some animal rights activists see this as a breakthrough.

1256. "Policies on Animal Use in Research Studied," *Chemical and Engineering News* 64 (February 10, 1986):23.
Office of Technology Assessment identifies policy issues on use of animals in research, including dissemination of research data, use of existing and development of better alternatives, more restriction on use of animals, provision of better statistics on animal use, establishment of minimal policy for animal use by federal agencies, and improvement of Animal Welfare Act.

1257. Pratt, Dallas. *Alternatives to Pain in Experiments on Animals.* New York: Argus Archives, 1980.
Sequel to *Painful Experiments on Animals,* this book describes experiments that cause animals pain and distress and suggests specific alternatives to them that would reduce suffering or eliminate use of animals altogether. Challenges scientists to think about an animal's pain when designing and doing experiments and to seriously consider using alternatives he presents.

1258. "Progress in Nonanimal Cosmetic Irritancy Test," *Chemical and Engineering News* 60 (October 11, 1982):7–8.
Rockefeller University scientists are correlating Draize test data with uptake of radioactive uridine or light microscopic observation cell cultures in effort to find an alternative to the Draize testing.

1259. "Revlon Project Shows Promise for Draize Test Alternative," *Drug and Cosmetics Industry* 133 (July 1983):44+.
Rockefeller University researchers are in process of developing a replacement for Draize funded by $1-million grant from Revlon.

1260. Richards, Robin. "Animal Test Alternatives: A Progress Report," *Drug and Cosmetics Industry* 132 (April 1983):30–32.
Specific details about several alternatives under development.

1261. Richards, Robin. "A Status Report on Animal Test Alternatives, Part II," *Drug and Cosmetics Industry* 132 (May 1983):42–46.

Looks at House and Senate bills as well as state legislative initiatives that would affect product safety testing on animals, especially the Draize and LD-50 tests.

1262. Rowan, Andrew N. "Laboratory Animals and Alternatives in the '80s," *International Journal for the Studies of Animal Problems* 1 (May/June 1980):162–69.

1263. Rowan, Andrew N. "The LD50 (Median Lethal Dose): The Beginning of the End," *International Journal for the Studies of Animal Problems* 4 (January 1983):4–7.

1264. Smith, R. Jeffrey. "Revlon Funds Animal Test Research," *Science* 211 (January 16, 1981):260.

Revlon responds to protests and boycotts by committing $750,000 to find alternatives to Draize test.

1265. Starr, Douglas, ed. by Dick Teresi. "Good News for Lab Animals," *Omni* 4 (July 1982):35.

Examines drug and cosmetics industries' new interest in developing alternatives to Draize test as a response to animal advocates' pressure.

1266. United States. Congress. House. *Alternatives to Animal Use in Research and Testing.* Hearing before the Subcommittee on Science, Research, and Technology of the Committee on Science and Technology, House of Representatives, 99th Cong., 2nd Sess., May 6, 1986. Washington, DC: U.S. Government Printing Office, 1986, Y4.Sci2:99/130.

1267. United States. Congress. Office of Technology Assessment. *Alternatives to Animal Use in Research, Testing, and Education.* Washington, DC: U.S. Government Printing Office, 1986, Y3.T22/2:2 An5.

Study from Office of Technology Assessment analyzes scientific, regulatory, economic, and ethical considerations involved in using alternatives to animals in biomedical and behavioral research. Includes an overview of federal, state, and institutional regulation of use of animals in this country and ten other countries.

1268. Walton, Susan. "Choosing More Models for Biomedical Research," *Bioscience* 35 (July/August 1985):406–7.
Because of economic cost of using animals in research and criticism from animal rights groups, scientists look at alternative models. Asks National Institutes of Health to give greater funding consideration to research using nonanimal models.

1269. Webster, Bayard. "Lab Animals Use May Be Cut," *NYT* 3 June 1983:A19.
Drastic reduction in number of animals used in medical and drug testing may be possible by using in vitro methods instead. Both Draize and LD-50 tests, which claim the lives of thousands of animals each year, might be eliminated.

## Scientific Validity of Animal Experimentation

1270. "Addicted by Yale," *AA* 9 (May 1989):21–23.
At Yale University, monkeys are forced to become addicts and are observed when drug is withdrawn, yet those who work with drug addicts say drug treatment programs have proved far more effective than animal research. Drug rehabilitation programs remain severely underfunded and have long waiting lists while millions of dollars are spent on animal addiction experiments.

1271. Barnard, Neal D. "Animal Experiments in Stroke Research," *AA* 10 (December 1990):50–51.
Reviews debate among medical researchers over usefulness and relevance of animal experimentation in human stroke research. Some maintain treatments used in animals have not proved effective in humans. Money and time are being wasted on studying strokes in animals that could be spent on studies of strokes in humans.

1272.  Barnard, Neal D. "Longer Life Expectancy: Who Gets the Credit," *AA* 9 (May 1989):45+.

Animal experiments have played virtually no role in increased human longevity. Real decline in early mortality has come from better diets, improvement in hygiene, and prevention rather than curing of disease. Decline will continue if we focus on a preventive life-style that includes eliminating tobacco smoking and avoiding high-fat, low-fiber diets associated with 40–60 percent of all cancers, instead of focusing on research on induced cancers in lab animals.

1273.  Barnard, Neal D. "A Look at Cancer Research," *AA* 9 (March 1989):40.

Cancer research using animals is unkind not only to animals but also to the humans it is supposed to help. Nonanimal tests are more accurate, less costly, and less time-consuming. Preventive medicine that includes a vegetarian diet can also help decrease death rates from cancer of colon, breast, and prostate. As death rates from cancer continue to increase, medical research must move away from nonproductive use of animal models and shift to alternative modes as well as prevention education.

1274.  Barnard, Neal D. "Studying the AIDS Epidemic," *AA* 9 (July/August 1989):43+.

Chimpanzees, the animal model preferred by AIDS researchers, can harbor human immunovirus but not develop the disease. Prevention of the disease by education, counseling, and persuasion is a more useful approach, and epidemiological and in vitro studies have done much to provide information on the disease.

1275.  Barnard, Neal D. "The Truth About Heart Research," *AA* 9 (February 1989):49.

Using animals in heart research may have led to erroneous conclusions about safety of artificial-heart operations. Species differences can lead to dangerously wrong conclusions or knowledge that cannot be applied clinically to humans. The sacrifice of hundreds of animals may be a hindrance to medical progress.

1276. Bauer, Don. "Cruel Science: A Few Strong Words for Dr. White," *AV* 2 (June 1989):55.

Animal advocate interrupts award ceremony to condemn Dr. Robert J. White, whose experiments on grafting the heads of live animals to the bodies of others were described as so horrifying "they seem to reach the limits of scientific depravity."

1277. Kaufman, Stephen. "The First to Fall," *AV* 2 (June 1989):54.

Animal researchers are campaigning hard to defend their livelihood by disputing those who say their work is inappropriate or irrelevant to human health. Animal rights activists have the upper hand, however, since they can point to clear examples of waste in cancer, psychiatry, toxicity, and addiction research.

1278. Kaufman, Stephen. "How Useful Are Animal Models?" *AA* 10 (September 1990):18–19.

Diseases in animal models have little if any relevance to analogous human diseases. Uses study of colon cancer in rats as an example.

1279. Kuker-Reines, Brandon. "Animal Testing: New Controversy Over Old Problem," *Family Health* 12 (March 1980):44.

Animal testing is not only cruel but also maybe misleading. Some scientists now believe what cures disease in animals may not do so in humans and vice versa. Is it possible the cure for human cancer lies at the bottom of some reject pile because it gave cancer to a rat?

1280. Regan, Tom. "A Question of Honor: Part I," *AV* 3 (March/April 1990):62–63.

Examines scientific fraud and misconduct in biomedical research.

1281. Regan, Tom. "A Question of Honor: Part II," *AV* 3 (August 1990):12–16.

Part II of an investigative article that looks at scientific misconduct and fraud, focusing on some recent, well-publicized cases.

1282. Rowan, Andrew N. "Primate Testing: Adequate Alternatives (letter)," *Science* 199 (March 3, 1978):934.

Explains why use of primates in U.S. for drug testing and toxicology may be scientifically questionable. Some primates have very different metabolic rates from humans, so their use in certain studies is inappropriate.

1283. Roy, Suzanne E. "Medical Progress and the Animals," *AV* 2 (June 1989):49–50.

Reliance on animal models may actually impede medical progress. Some scientists are now recognizing danger inherent in using animal models to study human disease and are switching to use of human cells rather than animal cells because of mechanistic differences among species.

1284. Stewart, Les. "Anti-Vivisection: The Pro Health Solution," *AV* 2 (June 1989):46–48.

Human disease can't be replicated in animals, because there are too many variables in experimental conditions and too many differences between animals and humans. As the incidence of cancer, diabetes, birth defects, and other health problems increases and researchers increasingly depend on animal experimentation for answers, humans become as great losers as do laboratory animals.

1285. Stoller, Kenneth P. "Rats! to Animal Models," *AV* 2 (June 1989):84–85.

Drugs and new chemical products tested for safety in animals do not guarantee safety for humans. Experiments on rats to test safety of saccharin didn't take into account vital differences between rats and humans and are example of why extrapolating data from animals to humans is futile. Yet animal testing continues to be used for political and legal reasons.

1286. Stoller, Kenneth P. "The Secret of NIH," *AV* 2 (June 1989):56–58.

Examples cited of "morally and informationally bankrupt" animal experiments funded by National Institutes of Health that cost millions of dollars: baboons are immersed in scalding water, live dogs cooked in microwave ovens, and monkeys shocked repeatedly in drug addiction studies. In the meantime urgent health and social needs such as drug rehabilitation centers and homeless shelters go unfunded.

1287. Stone, Jeremy J. "Political Misuse of Science," *Bioscience* 28 (February 1978):83.

Editorial chastises two scientists who engaged in a frivolous experiment on rats to prove a political point.

1288. Tiger, Steven. "Misplaced Priorities," *AV* 2 (June 1989): 52–53.

Investing federal monies in biomedical research has the least efficiency in improving human health and saving lives. Medical intervention or clinical application of research data is least important of four factors that determine state of health. According to the Centers for Disease Control, life-style (51 percent), environment (20 percent), and biologic inheritance (19 percent), are more important.

## Animal Researchers' Response

1289. Anderson, Christopher. "Industry Fights Back," *Nature* 347 (October 11, 1990):505.

Biomedical industry says $17–$25 million a year needed to counter animal rights campaigns. Establishes new organization to serve as umbrella group for counterattack activities. Targets high school teachers and students in an education campaign.

1290.   "Animal Day," *Science* 240 (April 29, 1988):596.
        Foundation for Biomedical Research held a press con-
        ference with celebrity speakers to thank laboratory ani-
        mals and combat animal rights annual World Laboratory
        Animal Liberation Day.

1291.   "Animals' Advocates Seen as 'Terrorists' by Health
        Secretary," *NYT* 8 June 1990:A10.
        U.S. Department of Health and Human Services
        Secretary Louis Sullivan calls press conference to de-
        nounce animal rights activists who plan to march to the
        Capitol over the weekend.

1292.   "Animals and Medical Research," *WP* 18 April
        1984:A26.
        Editorial applauds researchers fighting back by having
        patients and their families testify to benefits received from
        animal experimentation. The more the public knows
        about such benefits, the more it will favor research on an-
        imals. At the same time, researchers should be sure they
        treat their laboratory animals humanely or they will have
        more intrusive supervision imposed upon them.

1293.   "Animals and Sickness," *WSJ* 24 April 1989:A14.
        Editorial criticizes animal rights movement and its ac-
        tivities. Praises scientific community for launching a
        counterattack campaign.

1294.   "Animals in Research," *Journal of the American Medical
        Association* 259 (April 1, 1988):2007–8.
        Plea to American physicians, scientists, and veterinari-
        ans to assume a prominent role in defending use of ani-
        mals in biomedical research. Whenever these groups
        have banded together to give the public information, an-
        imal rights promoters have lost ground.

1295.   Baum, Rudy M. "Biomedical Researchers Work to
        Counter Animal Rights Agenda," *Chemical and Engineering
        News* 68 (May 7, 1990):9–24.
        Biomedical researchers are mobilizing to counter ani-

mal rights movement's effort to curtail animal experimentation. Looks at researcher's side of the argument on issues like Draize and LD-50 tests, alternatives, federal agency guidelines for treatment of lab animals, and lab animal care in today's research centers. Outlines strategies for winning the public's support.

1296. Baum, Rudy M. "Researchers Take Aim at Animal Rights Activists," *Chemical and Engineering News* 68 (February 26, 1990):6.

At a symposium on use of animals in research held at Association for the Advancement of Science's annual meeting, speakers called for aggressive campaign to counteract efforts of animal rights movement.

1297. Breo, Dennis L. "Animal Rights vs. Research? A Question of the Nation's Scientific Literacy," *Journal of the American Medical Association* 264 (November 21, 1990):2564–65.

Researchers are leaving field of animal experimentation, because they're being physically intimidated by animal rights activists. Scientists need to band together to make it socially acceptable to stand up and defend animal experimentation. American Medical Association joins the crusade along with American Veterinary Medical Association.

1298. Chen, Edwin. "Sullivan Blasts 'Terrorist' Acts Against Labs," *LAT* 3 April 1990:A4.

An audience of experimental biologists applauded U.S. Department of Health and Human Services Secretary Louis Sullivan's vow to explore ways to guarantee adequate punishment for break-ins, bomb threats, arson, and theft at animal research labs. He says only a countercampaign can turn public opinion around in support of animal experimentation.

1299. Cohen, Carl. "The Case for the Use of Animals in Biomedical Research," *New England Journal of Medicine* 315 (October 2, 1986):865–70.

Animal experimentation does not violate rights of animals, nor does it impose much avoidable suffering on sentient creatures. If we ban the use of animals in research, we will have to experiment on humans instead. We should encourage increased, wide, and imaginative use of animals.

1300. Culliton, Barbara J. "Nobelists Back Animal Research," *Science* 244 (May 5, 1989):524.

1301. Dalton, R. "Waging War on the Animal Rights Lobby: Tired of Being Defenseless Targets of Animal Rights Protesters, Scientists are Fighting Back and Winning," *Scientist* 3,3 (1989):1+.

1302. Davis, Donald A. "Too Passive a Defense," *Drug and Cosmetics Industry* 134 (February 1984):31.
      Animal experimenters have not done anything to defend themselves or their work and have capitulated to animal rights advocates. Calls for industry to start presenting its case to the public.

1303. Drogin, Bob. "Medical Field Defends Use of Animals in Lab," *LAT* 22 April 1989:I,1.
      Medical school deans, research scientists, patient advocacy groups, secretary of health and human services, and national drug policy director joined together today to condemn animal rights opposition to use of animals in research.

1304. Erickson, Deborah. "Blood Feud," *Scientific American* 262 (June 1990):17–18.
      Outlines ways animal research community plans to thwart animal rights movement: get laws passed making lab break-ins a federal crime, send scientists around the country to speak positively about animal experimentation, put on television ads promoting animal experimentation, and review all grants to a university that ends a research project under animal rights pressure.

1305. "Flattery Will Get Them Nowhere," *AA* 10 (December 1990):46–47.

American Medical Association (AMA) and three animal researchers—Michael Carey, John Orem, and Adrian Morrison—gather in Washington to denounce the animal rights movement. Several animal rights and consumer groups responded to the AMA in a press conference, including the Physicians Committee for Responsible Medicine, the Medical Research Modernization Committee, and the Disabled and Incurably Ill for Alternatives to Animal Research.

1306. Gladwell, Malcolm. "Sullivan Assails Animal-Rights Movement," *WP* 8 June 1990:A5.
U.S. Department of Health and Human Services Secretary Louis Sullivan condemns animal rights movement in press conference several days before animal advocates are to rally at the Capitol.

1307. Goldsmith, Marsha F. "Nobel Laureates Call for Speaking out on Need for Animals in Research," *Journal of the American Medical Association* 262 (November 17, 1989): 2647–48.

1308. Goodwin, Frederick K. "Animal Research vs. Humane Use: The Struggle to Sustain Our Research Advances: Part I," *FASEB Journal* 3 (November 1989):2455.
Administrator of alcohol, drug abuse, and mental health administration makes it his special cause to promote use of animals in biomedical research. In this interview, he alerts his colleagues and members of Congress to dangers of animal rights movement.

1309. Goodwin, Frederick K. "Animal Research vs. Humane Use: The Struggle to Sustain Our Research Advances: Part II," *FASEB Journal* 3 (December 1989):2563–64.
Scientists are traditionally not good at defending themselves against anti-intellectual movements. Scientists need media training to learn same techniques politicians use. Scientists should not let a colleague be isolated during an attack by animal rights promoters. There is a need to create incentives for full-time scientists to step out of the labs and clinics and engage in public relations on this issue.

1310. Holden, Constance. "Activists Call for Procter and Gamble Boycott," *Science* 246 (October 13, 1989):215.

Animal rights activists uncover memo from Procter and Gamble officials, which recommends a $17.5-million program be launched to educate public about importance of using animals in research.

1311. Holden, Constance. "A Preemptive Strike for Animal Research," *Science* 244 (April 28, 1989):415–16.

New York University led new aggressive strategy in fighting animal rights movement by preempting an impending protest against animal experimenter Ron Wood. The university called a press conference in which well-known scientific and medical experts condemned the movement. Other activities included an advertising campaign by Foundation for Biomedical Research, an American Medical Association educational program, and formation of faculty-student groups that support animal research.

1312. Holden, Constance. "Scientists Start Fund to Fight Anti-Vivisectionists," *Science* 215 (February 5, 1982):640.

Group of neuroscientists have established Biomedical Research Defense Fund to fight aggressiveness of animal rights movement.

1313. Karpati, Ron. "A Scientist: 'I Am the Enemy,' " *Newsweek* 114 (December 18, 1989):12–13.

Pediatrician involved in immunological research says scientists have been apathetic to dangers of animal rights movement; they must now rouse themselves to protect future of medical research against a vocal and misdirected minority. Lists future health catastrophes if animal rights is allowed to win out.

1314. Koshland, Daniel E. "Animal Rights and Animal Wrongs," *Science* 243 (March 10, 1990):1253.

Animal rights groups' goal is not to prevent cruelty, but to abolish animal research altogether. Scientists must speak out in the media and at public gatherings often, in favor of animal experimentation.

1315. Loeb, Jerod M., et al. "Human vs. Animal Rights," *Journal of the American Medical Association* 262 (November 17, 1989):2716–20.
Summary of the "White Paper on Animal Research," an American Medical Association document alerting its membership to the danger to biomedical research from animal rights movement.

1316. Mervis, J. "United States Officials Defend Animal Research: Under Attack by Animal Rights Campaigners, Federal Health Agencies Counter with a Vigorous Drive to Gain Public Support," *Scientist* 4,1 (1990):1.

1317. Nicoll, Charles S., and Sharon M. Russell. "Analysis of Animal Rights Literature Reveals the Underlying Motives of the Movement: Ammunition for Counter Offensive by Scientists," *Endocrinology* 127 (September 1990):985–89.
Editorial analyzes books listed by bibliographer Charles R. Magel as "important books on animal rights." Concludes animal rights activists are obsessed mainly with animal experimentation and not other issues such as farm animals. Animal rights activities are anti-intellectual, antiscience, and aimed only at those who wish to acquire new knowledge.

1318. Ojeda, Sergio R. "Animal Rights and the Inertia of the Scientific Community," *Endocrinology* 126 (February 1990):677–79.
Interprets animal rights agenda from endocrinologist's point of view and calls for closing ranks and presenting a united and active front by organizations such as American Medical Association, Society for Neuroscience, and Endocrine Society.

1319. Pennisi, Elizabeth. "Neuroscience Society Fights for Animals in Research: At the Annual Meeting Members Learned How to Strike Back Against Animal Rights Extremists," *Scientist* 3,2 (1989):5+.

1320.   Schwarz, Richard H. "Animal Research: A Position Statement by the Associated Medical Schools of New York," *Science* 244 (June 9, 1989):1128.

1321.   Vaughan, Christopher. "Animal Research: Ten Years Under Siege," *Bioscience* 38 (January 1988):10–13.
Explains animal rights philosophy from vivisector's point of view. Concludes society will always value humans more than animals. Researchers need to communicate better about animal experimentation, since many in general public are scientifically ignorant.

1322.   Wheeler, David L. "Scientists Urged to Use Strong Measures to Counter Animal Rights Movement," *Chron H Ed* 33 (February 25, 1987):12.
American Medical Association speaker told researchers attending American Association for the Advancement of Science annual meeting to counter animal rights movement by lobbying for appropriate legislation.

# AUTHOR AND EDITOR INDEX

(Numbers in this index refer to entry numbers)

Adams, Brook, 116
Adams, Carol J., 376
Adler, Jerry, 717
Ahlers, Julia, 185
Ali, Cairo Fatima, 718
Allen, Don W., 335
Altman, Lawrence K., 1107
Amatniek, Joan C., 1086–1088
Amato, Paul R., 377
Amory, Cleveland, 607
Anchel, Marjorie, 556
Anderson, Alun, 1047–1048
Anderson, Christopher, 117, 668,
    719, 892–893, 969–970,
    1049, 1289
Aoki, Elizabeth N., 471–472
Armstrong, Susan B., 186
Astor, Gerald, 119
Auxter, Thomas, 448

Baer, Debbie, 9
Balzar, John, 720
Banks, Sandy, 999
Barinaga, Marcia, 721,
    1194–1195
Barker, Bob, 722
Barker, Leigh, 3
Barnard, Neal D., 723,
    1050–1051, 1108, 1139,
    1196–1197, 1271–1275
Barnes, Deborah M., 724
Barnes, Donald J., 669, 725–726,
    1052
Barnes, Fred, 336, 727
Bartlett, Kim, 4, 120, 187, 380
Batten, Peter, 670
Bauer, Don, 1276
Baughman, Michael, 543

Baum, Rudy M., 1295–1296
Bauston, Lorri, 121
Beardsley, Tim, 728, 899, 971,
    1110, 1159
Bebee, Charles N., 381
Beck, Melinda, 487
Beene, Richard, 729, 1000
Begley, Sharon, 636, 730, 777
Behar, Richard, 5
Belcher, Jerry, 1001
Belkin, Lisa, 488
Bennett, Richard E., 473
Bennon, Rhonda, 337
Benson, John, 188
Berkman, Meredith, 489
Berman, Louis A., 449
Berry, Rynn J., 382
Bishop, Katherine, 6, 122, 544
Blakeslee, Sandra, 1002
Blaz, Michael, 383
Bleiberg, Robert M., 7, 8
Blum, Deborah, 731
Boffey, Philip M., 732, 1226
Booth, William, 608
Bowd, Alan D., 874–875
Boyce, John R., 189
Bradshaw, Patricia, 490
Brebner, Sue, 9
Breedy, Kevin J., 10
Breo, Dennis L., 1297
Bresnick, Peter Haskell, 734
Briggs, Anna C., 735
Brisbane, Arthur S., 1053, 1140
Broad, William J., 900
Brody, Mimi, 901
Brooks, S., 11
Brooks, Tad, 636
Brown, Chip, 1141
Brown, Elizabeth A., 491

Brown, George E., 902
Brown, Kitty, 1227
Brown, Larry, 384
Brown, Scott, 532
Browne, Malcolm W., 12
Brownlee, Shannon, 672
Brownley, Nancie, 1198
Budiansky, Stephen, 736, 1228
Budkie, Michael (A.), 737, 1142
Burch, Robert W., 190
Burghardt, Gordon M., 876
Burgos, Javier, 738
Butler, J. George, 492
Buyukmihci, Ned, 903

Callen, Paulette, 13, 385
Callicott, J. Baird, 191
Cantor, Aviva, 14
Caras, Roger, 1229
Carlsen, Spence, 15
Carlson, Peter, 1054
Carone, Jack, 16–18
Carson, Gerald, 19
Causey, A. S., 638
Cave, George P., 192–194,
    739
Cebik, L.B., 195
Chambers, Tate, 907
Charlton, Linda, 740
Chase, Marcelle P., 20
Chavez, Stephanie, 1004
Chen, Edwin, 1298
Chinnici, Madeline, 908
Christopher, Kristen, 561
Chui, Glennda, 741
Churm, Steven B., 1001
Citron, Alan, 742
Clark, Stephen R.L., 197–199
Clarke, Maxine, 1091–1092
Clarke, Paul A.B., 21
Clifton, Merritt, 22–24, 125–127,
    386–388, 494–499, 609–610,
    639–640, 673, 909, 1006,
    1113–1114
Clingerman, Karen J., 200,
    338–339, 743–744
Clooney, Francis X., 450

Close, Sandy, 201
Coats, David, 389
Cocroft, Anne, 562
Cohen, Carl, 1299
Cohen, Henry, 910
Cohen, Murray J., 745
Cornell, Marly, 130–131
Cottingham, John, 202
Coulbourn, Keith, 706
Cowen, Robert C., 746
Cowley, Geoffrey, 747
Crawford, Mark, 1160
Culliton, Barbara J., 1093, 1300
Curtis, Patricia, 748

Dagani, Ron, 1230
Dalton, R., 1301
Daniel, Michelle D., 341
Darlin, Damon, 25
Davidoff, Donald [Donna] J., 26
Davis, Donald A., 1231–1233,
    1302
Davis, Karen, 27, 132
Davis, Michael, 203
Dawkins, Marian Stamp, 28–29
Dawson, Victoria 1007
Dean, Tom, 391
Deats, Paula, 133
DeBakey, Michael E., 563
DeCapo, Thomas A., 30
de Kok, Wim, 500
Denton, Herbert H., 501
Derby, Pat, 675
DeRosa, Bell, 1199
DeSilver, Drew, 134, 749
Devenport, J. A., 750
Devenport, L. D., 750
Devine, Philip E., 451
Dewsbury, D. A., 751
Diamond, Cora, 452
Dichter, Anita, 342
Dines, Sheila, 676
Dodds, W. Jean, 752
Doherty, Shawn, 677
Dolan, Maura, 641
Dombrowski, Daniel A.,
    204–205, 453–454

Dommer, Luke, 611–612, 642–644
Donahue, Thomas J., 31
Donnelley, Strachan, 206–207, 877
Donnelly, William L., 32
Donovan, Josephine, 33
Dorschner, John, 564
Dresser, Rebecca, 912–913
Drogin, Bob, 1303
Dudek, Ronald D., 914
Dukes, Esther F., 915
Dunayer, Eric, 565–566
Dunayer, Joan, 566
Dunkerly, Rick, 208
Duvin, Edward S., 567–568
Dyer, Judith, 455

Earl, Christopher, 569
Ecenbarger, William, 135
Eckholm, Erik, 754
Edwards, Rob, 1094
Eftink, B., 393
Elliot, Robert, 209–210
Ellis, Gary B., 755
Elshtain, Jean Bethke, 34
Engel, Margaret, 570
Engelmann, Manfred, 1215
Engelmayer, Paul A., 678
Erber, Cynthia, 32
Erickson, Deborah, 1304
Eskridge, Nancy K., 973

Fabiano, Franco, 343
Falkin, Larry, 916
Fallows, James, 35
Favre, David S., 344, 646, 917
Feder, Barnaby J., 394, 1175, 1235
Feeney, Dennis M., 757
Feldon, Leah, 713
Feral, Priscilla, 758
Festing, Sally, 759
Fields, Cheryl M., 760–761, 918–920, 974
Finsen, Lawrence, 36

Fintor, Lou, 1008–1009, 1115
Fisher, John A., 211
Fishlock, Diana J., 1202
Flick, Larry, 136
Fogelson, Gail, 571
Foltz, Kim, 502
Forbes, Dana, 137
Foster, Catherine, 395–396
Fox, Jeffrey L., 572–573, 762, 921–922, 975, 1095, 1146, 1161–1162
Fox, Michael A., 212–214, 878–879
Fox, Michael W., 37, 397–399, 680, 763, 880
Francione, Gary L., 345, 574, 647, 764–765, 923–924
Francis, Leslie Pickering, 215
Frank, Jonny, 400
Frankel, Glenn, 504
Franklin, Ben, 1010, 1236
Frazier, Claude A., 766
Free, Ann Cottrell, 401
Freeman, Laurie, 1176
Freese, Betsy, 402
Frey, R. G., 216–220, 456
Friedman, Ruth, 38, 767
Fritsch, Jane, 681–685

Gallistel, C. R., 768
Gallup, Gordon G., 769, 1237
Galvin, Robert W., 346
Garment, Suzanne, 138
Gaylin, Willard, 881
Gendin, Sidney, 882
Gerson, Ben, 347
Gibson, Robert W., 509
Giraud, Raymond, 221
Gladwell, Malcolm, 1306
Gleason, Sean J., 222, 339
Glover, Mark, 510
Gluckstein, Fritz P., 770–773
Godlovitch, Ruth, 39
Godlovitch, Stanley, 39
Goldemberg, Robert L., 1238
Goldman, Ari L., 575
Goldsmith, Marsha F., 1307

Goodall, Jane, 774
Goodkin, Susan L., 348
Goodman, Walter, 775
Goodpaster, Kenneth E., 223, 313
Goodwin, Frederick K., 1308–1309
Goodwin, Michael, 1239
Gornery, Greg, 511
Graham, Pat, 1203
Grandin, Temple, 403
Grant, Gordon, 613
Greanville, David Patrice, 40–44, 576, 614, 648
Greenberg, Daniel S., 776
Greenfield, Meg, 45
Griswold, Charles, Jr., 224
Groller, Ingrid, 46
Grunow, Steve, 577
Gruson, Lindsay, 686
Gunn, Alastair S., 225
Gwynne, Peter, 777, 1116

Hager, Mary, 717, 730
Hampton, Aubrey, 139
Hanauer, Gary, 687
Handley, Virginia, 404
Harris, John, 39
Harris, Ron, 546
Harris, Scott, 547
Harrison, Barbara Grizzuti, 778
Harriston, Keith, 47
Hart, Kathleen, 1163
Hartshorne, Charles, 226
Harvard University's Office of Government and Community Affairs, 48
Hatch, Orrin G., 779
Havemann, Judith, 976
Haworth, Lawrence, 227
Hazlett, Thomas, 780
Hecht, Jeff, 1204
Heffernan, Nancy, 925
Henderson, Keith, 1241
Heneson, Nancy, 1056, 1242
Henig, Robin Marantz, 781, 1205

Henry, Neil, 689
Hentoff, Nat, 350, 649, 1206
Herbert, W., 578, 1057–1058
Herrington, Alice, 579, 690–691
Hershaft, Alex, 228
Herzog, Harold A., Jr., 876, 1207
Heston, Charlton, 782
Hettinger, Edwin C., 783
Hewitt, Bill, 692
Hibbert, Bob, 405
Hillinger, Charles, 406
Hines, Cathleen, 907
Hirsch, James, 512
Hitchens, Christopher, 49
Hoch, David, 229, 926
Hochswender, Woody, 513
Hoff, Christine, 784
Hogshire, Jim, 140
Holden, Constance, 141, 351, 407, 785, 927, 977–979, 1015–1018, 1059–1065, 1119, 1208–1209, 1243–1244, 1310–1312
Holton, A. Camille, 352
Hoover, Eleanor, 713
House, Charles, 475
Houston, Paul, 928
Howe, Marvine, 1120
Hoyt, John A., 1019
Hunt, Mary, 230
Husack, Douglas N., 231

Iacobbo, Karen, 142–144
Iacobbo, Michael, 142–144
Iglehart, John K., 786–787
Ingiverson, Marshall, 929, 1020
Isen, Susan, 457

Jackson, Christine M., 51
Jacobs, Rabbi Sidney J., 232–233
James, Carollyn, 409
Jamieson, Dale, 234–236, 788
Jefferson, David J., 1246
Johnson, Dirk, 548
Johnson, Edward, 237–238
Johnson, Kirk, 1121

Johnson, Lawrence E., 239
Johnson, Lisa M., 789
Jones, Arthur, 145
Jones, Gary E., 240–241
Jordan, Debra, 693
Joyce, Christopher, 930
Judge, Mark G., 1066
Juergensmeyer, Mark, 230

Kagan, Connie, 790
Kahrl, William, 53
Kalechofsky, Roberta, 458, 791
Kapleau, Philip, 459
Karpati, Ron, 1313
Kasindorf, Jeanie, 514
Katches, Mark, 1097–1098
Katz, Susan, 730
Kaufman, Stephen, 1277–1278
Kehrer, Daniel, 1067
Kelling, Vanessa, 146–147, 581
Kelly, Jeffrey A., 792, 883
Kennedy, Donald, 793
Kevles, Betty Ann, 794–796
Kilpatrick, James J., 1068–1069,
    1099
King, Peter H., 1210
Kirkpatrick, Jay D., 619
Kislak, Paula, 54
Knight, Jerry, 410
Knobelsdorff, Kerry Elizabeth,
    931, 1248
Koenig, Richard, 1180
Kopperud, Steve, 411
Koshland, Daniel E., 1314
Krauthammer, Charles, 797
Krawiec, Richard, 55
Krizmanic, Judy, 1181
Krupka, Lawrence R., 1215
Kuker-Reines, Brandon,
    798–799, 1279
Kullberg, John F., 582, 694, 932,
    1182
Kuntz, Phil, 353

LaFranchi, Howard, 1071
LaGanga, Maria (L.), 515–516

Lamb, David, 242
Landes, Susan Sperling, 800
Langley, Gil, 801
Larson, Jean A., 744
Lauer, Margaret, 148, 1021
Lauter, David, 1072
Lawson, Carol, 517
Leary, Warren E., 1073
Leavitt, Emily S., 354
Leccese, Michael, 802
Leepson, Marc, 56
Lehman, Hugh, 243
Lesco, Philip A., 244
Levey, Gerald S., 803
Levin, Michael E., 245–246
Levy, Claudia, 933
Lewis, Jennifer, 650
Lewis, Patricia Brazeel, 934–935
Linck, Peter, 936
Linneman, Judith Ann, 412
Linzey, Rev. Andrew, 21, 187,
    247–249
Loeb, Jerod M., 1315
Loew, Franklin M., 804
Logsdon, Gene, 414
Loop, Michael S., 583
Lopatto, David, 805
Lorch, Donatella, 695
Loring, Murray, 344
Lowry, Jon, 250
Lutes, Christopher, 189
Lyall, Sarah, 937, 1122–1123

Macauley, David 57–58,
    415–416
McCabe, Jane, 810
McCarthy, Coleman, 63–64, 158,
    424–425, 521, 586, 651–652,
    698
McCarthy, Richard F., 473
McCloskey, H. J., 884
McDonald, Jay, 255
McDonald, Karen L., 939
McDonald, Kim, 587, 811–813,
    940–941, 981–985, 1124,
    1250–1251
McDonald-Lewis, Mary, 16–18

McDonough, Yona Zeldis, 522
McFadden, Robert D., 1125
McFarland, Cole, 159–160, 251,
 256–257, 653, 699–701, 1028
McGiffin, Heather, 1198
McGinnis, Terri, 588
McGourty, Christine, 986
McGuire, Richard, 426
Mackay-Smith, Anne, 806
Magel, Charles R., 59–60, 251
Maggitti, Phil, 61–62, 149–156,
 696–697
Magner, Denise K., 807
Malnic, Eric, 1022–1027
Mann, Judy, 518
March, B. E., 808
Marcotte, Paul, 157
Margolis, Joseph, 252
Martin, Douglas, 519
Martin, Phillip W.D., 48
Martin, Rafe, 253
Marx, Linda, 692
Mason, Jim, 417–422, 520, 584,
 620
Masonis, Robert J., 938
Masri, Al-Hafiz B.A., 254
Mayes, Dorothy, 423
Meade, Bill, 702
Medlock, Aaron, 814
Mervis, J., 1316
Messett, Marci, 942
Metz, Holly, 943
Michaud, Stephen G., 1116
Midgley, Mary, 65, 258–259
Miller, Harlan, 260
Miller, J. A., 987
Miller, Neal E., 815
Miller, Peter, 261
Mills, Eric, 703–704
Mishkin, Barbara, 816
Mitric, Joan McQueeney, 818
Moll, Lucy, 820
Moment, Gairdner B., 1211
Monticone, George T., 263
Moore, Mary Tyler, 66
Moore, Molly, 1148
Moran, Victoria, 67–70, 429, 524

Moretti, Daniel S., 356
Moretti, Laura A., 71–72,
 161–163
Morgan, Thomas, 1126
Morris, Desmond, 73
Morris, Edward K., 789
Morrison, Lynn, 803
Morse, Mel, 74
Moseley, Ray Edward, 264
Moss, Thomas, 821
Mouras, Belton P., 75–76, 822
Mrazek, Robert J., 589–590
Muirhead, Sarah, 430
Muller, Carrie, 1253
Mulvaney, Kieran, 621, 705
Murphy, Kim, 1212
Muscatine, Alison, 823

Narveson, Jan, 265, 460
Nelson, James A., 266–267
Nelson, John O., 268
Nevin, David, 164
Newkirk, Ingrid, 77, 269, 824,
 1074
Newman, Alan, 825
Newman, Barry, 1150
Newman, Edward, 591
Newmann, Holly, 654
Nicoll, Charles S., 1317
Noah, Timothy, 1077
Nolan, Kathleen, 207
Norman, Colin, 1184
Norman, Michael, 655
Norman, Richard, 215
Norton, Bryan G., 270

Oakes, John B., 525–526
Oakie, Susan, 1127
O'Barry, Richard, 706
Ojeda, Sergio R., 1318
Olsen, Gretchen, 646
O'Neill, Molly 432
Orlans, F. Barbara, 752,
 1213
Ost, David E., 271

Pacelle, Wayne, 167–169, 622, 656–658, 828
Palca, Joseph, 1214, 1254
Pardue, Leslie, 433, 1030
Park, Ava, 79
Partridge, Ernest, 272
Partridge, Sonia A., 377
Passamano, Russell J., 551
Paterson, David, 80
Paterson, R. W. K., 273
Pavelock, Lisa A., 945
Pennisi, Elizabeth, 1031, 1319
Peppu, S. S. Rama Rao, 274
Perry, Clifton, 241
Perry, Nancy, 707
Petersen, Iver, 1255
Pierce, Christine, 275
Povilitis, Anthony J., 276
Pratt, Dallas, 830, 1257
Pritzker, Karen, 172


Quade, Vicki, 357
Quigley, Cheryl Ann, 831


Rabe, Marsha, 660
Rachels, James, 277
Raloff, J., 1128
Ravo, Nick, 1129
Reagan, Kinsey S., 989
Reed, J. D., 532
Regan, Susan, 173
Regan, Tom, 82–83, 174–176, 278–291, 358, 461–464, 533, 832, 886, 1130, 1280–1281
Regenstein, Lewis, 661
Reid, T. R., 552
Reidinger, Paul, 1078
Reinhold, Robert, 833, 1079
Rich, Susan, 1186
Richards, Robin, 1260–1261
Richards, Stewart, 465
Richburg, Keith B., 477, 1152–1153
Richmond, Gail Manfred Engelmann, 1215

Richter, Paul, 534
Rikleen, Lauren Stiller, 359
Ringle, Ken, 1032
Ritvo, Harriet, 834
Robbins, John, 434–436
Robbins, William, 177
Roberti, David, 593
Robeznieks, Andis, 1216
Rodd, Rosemary, 887
Rogers, Bonnie, 835
Rollin, Bernard E., 84–85, 292, 836–837, 888
Rosen, Steven, 293, 466
Rosen, Yereth, 536
Rosenberger, Jack, 1033
Rosenfeld, Albert, 838
Rosner, Fred, 839
Ross, Elizabeth, 478, 950
Ross, Kenneth D., 360
Rottenberg, Dan, 178
Rowan, Andrew N., 837, 840–841, 889, 1080, 1262–1263, 1282
Roy, Suzanne E., 1283
Ruesch, Hans, 842
Russell, Sharon M., 1317
Russow, Lilly-Marlene, 294
Ryder, Richard D., 80, 86


Sachs, Andrea, 532
Sagar, Mike, 1034
Sahagun, Louis, 594, 1009, 1035
Salisbury, David F., 710, 843
Salt, Henry, 87
Sammut-Tovar, Dorothy, 88
Sangeorge, Robert, 990
Santopoalo, Tina, 1217
Saperstein, Saundra, 1081, 1154
Sapolsky, Harvey M., 844
Sapontzis, Steve F., 295–302, 845
Satchell, Michael, 624, 663
Sayre, Kenneth M., 313
Schall, James V., 303
Schmidt, William E., 625, 711
Schneider, Keith, 479, 712, 1036–1037

Schochet, Barry, 1155
Schuster, Lynda, 437
Schwartz, Richard H., 467
Schwartz, Sheila, 89
Schwarz, Richard H., 1320
Scott, Janny, 1082
Seligman, Daniel, 90
Shapiro, Jeremy, 847
Shapiro, Kenneth J., 848
Shenon, Philip, 92
Shepard, Paul, 304
Sherman, Jeffrey, 180
Shiflett, Dave, 553
Shulman, Seth, 952
Sieber, Joan E., 1218
Siegel, Steve, 93
Siepp, Catherine, 361
Sikora, R. I., 305
Silas, Faye A., 598
Simpson, James R., 85
Sinclair, Ward, 480
Singer, Peter, 94–97, 291,
    306–315, 421–422, 468–469,
    849–850, 890
Sitomer, Curtis J., 316, 362
Slicer, Deborah, 891
Smith, David Christian, 1038,
    1187
Smith, Lucinda, 713
Smith, Lynn, 1083
Smith, R. Jeffrey, 1264
Smith, Rod, 438–440
Smollar, David, 851
Sobel, Dava, 1219
Solomon, Jolie, 537
Solomon, Wendy E., 626
Sommer, Mark, 181, 481
Specter, Michael, 1039
Sperling, Susan, 98
Spickard, J.W., 99
Spiegel, Marjorie, 100–101
Sprigge, T. L. S., 317
Squadrito, Kathy, 318
Stafford, Tim, 319
Stange, Mary Zeiss, 538
Starr, Douglas, 102, 1265
Stein, Benjamin J., 104, 852

Stein, M. L., 1040
Stein, Mark A., 406
Steinbock, Bonnie, 320
Steinmetz, Johanna, 441
Sternberg, Mary, 321
Stevens, Christine, 363, 853–854,
    953
Stevenson, Richard W., 855
Stewart, James B., 364
Stewart, Les, 1284
Stille, Alexander, 954
Stinnet, Caskie, 105
Stockwell, John, 322
Stoller, Kenneth P., 665,
    1285–1286
Stone, Jeremy J., 1287
Stott, John R. W., 323
Stuchell, Dana, 739
Sturla, Kim, 88
Suarez, Susan D., 769, 1237
Subar, Lorin M., 955
Sujithammaraksa, Roongtham,
    324
Sumner, L. W., 470
Sun, Marjorie, 599, 856–857,
    956–958, 1041, 1104, 1188,
    1221
Sunlin, Mark, 106
Swan, Christopher, 442, 714
Swanson, Janice C., 222, 339, 365
Swinehart, C., 443


Tangley, Laura, 1165
Taylor, Paul W., 325
Taylor, Ronald B., 627–628
Teresi, Dick, 799, 1265
Thomas, Brenda L., 959
Thomas, H. S., 444
Thomas-Lester, Avis, 47
Thompson, Richard C., 1189
Tiger, Steven, 1288
Tischler, Joyce S., 366, 482
Tobias, Michael, 326
Tomasson, Robert E., 1133
Torrey, Lee, 859
Trachtenberg, Jeffrey A., 539

Trebay, Guy, 540
Trimmingham, Scott, 630
Trizzino, Jeannie, 861
Troiano, Linda, 110
Trull, Frankie L., 601
Tyrrell, R. Emmett, Jr., 111

United States Congress,
    367–370, 483, 555, 602,
    960–965, 1266–1267
Unti, Bernard, 182
Uzych, Leo, 1223

Valentine, Paul W., 183
Van De Veer, Donald, 327
Vaughan, Christopher, 1321
Vetri, Kristi, 603

Wade, Nicholas, 863, 1136, 1157
Waldholz, Michael, 1137–1138
Walker, Alice, 184
Wall, James, 328
Walton, Susan, 864, 1268
Ward, Adrienne, 1190
Warren, Peter M., 1045
Watson, Richard A., 329
Webster, Bayard, 634, 865, 1269
Weil, Martin, 1046
Weil, Robert, 1105
Weintraub, Daniel M., 666

Weiss, Laura B., 966
Wells, Ken, 715, 1224
Wheeler, David L., 967, 1166, 1322
White, George, 1191–1192
White, James E., 330
White, Kenneth, 604–605
White, MacDonald, 606
Willard, L. Duane, 331
Williams, Meredith, 332
Williams, William H., 260
Willman, Michelle L., 446
Winkler, Karen J., 991
Winters, Mary A., 372
Wise, Stephen, 373
Wise, Stuart M., 484
Woldenberg, Susan, 635
Wolinsky, Leo C., 447
Worsnop, Richard L., 869–870
Wortman, Judith, 871, 992
Wright, Robert, 113
Wynne-Tyson, Jon, 114

Yen, Marianne, 541
Young, Thomas, 334

Zak, Stephen (Steven), 115, 374,
    872
Zawistowski, Stephen, 716
Zelezny, John, 375
Zibert, Eve, 1098
Zurvalec, Lori A., 968

# SUBJECT INDEX

(Numbers in this index refer to entry numbers)

Acquired Immune Deficiency Syndrome, 633, 727, 1005, 1274
activists and activism, 9, 53, 68, 75–77, 98, 102, 107, 116–184, 349, 353, 393, 514, 994–995, 1006, 1013; *See also* organizations (animal rights)
Adams, James Hume, 1094
adult education classes, 70
Agricultural Research Center (Beltsville, MD), 998, 1007, 1015, 1030, 1036–1037, 1161
Agriculture Department, U. S., 388, 632, 910, 934, 1104, 1138; and Animal Welfare Act, 359, 477, 679, 684, 871, 915, 940, 972, 1091; and Improved Standards for Laboratory Animals, 915, 938; and Pet Theft Act, 947; face-branding of cows, 476, 479–480; gene transfer experiments, 1162, 1165; inspectors of animal facilities, 477, 854, 856, 933, 940, 1084; regulations, 969–970, 972, 986
ahimsa, 256, 293, 326
AIDS. *See* Acquired Immune Deficiency Syndrome
Air Force, U.S. and animal experiments, 1152
Alaskan Natives, 501, 528, 536
Ally (chimpanzee), 833
alternatives to animal expermentation, 200, 730, 735, 779, 785, 790, 841, 864, 872, 894, 900, 907, 927, 941, 953, 956–958, 966, 989, 1197, 1225–1269, 1295. *See also* Draize Eye Test; LD-50 Test

*Alternatives to Animal Use in Research, Testing, and Education*, 1241, 1251, 1267
American Association for the Advancement of Science, 1296, 1322
American Association of Laboratory Animal Accreditation, 979
American Bar Association, Animal Protection Committee, 350
American Civil Liberties Union, 371, 1222
American Farm Bureau Federation, 430, 934
American Horse Protection Association, 712
American Horse Shows Association, 712
American Humane Association, 667, 713
American Institute of Biological Sciences, 871, 934–935
American Kennel Club, 566
American Medical Association, 1297, 1305, 1311, 1315, 1318, 1322
American Museum of Natural History (NY), 1116, 1136
American Physiological Society, 934
American Psychological Association, 751, 760–761, 828, 991, 1083
American Society for the Prevention of Cruelty to Animals, 125, 172, 394, 579, 582, 677
American Veterinary Medical Association, 1297

Amory, Cleveland, 66, 137, 149, 175, 178
Amway Co., 1179
*Ancient Mariner,* 204
Anderson, Loni, 507
animal care and use committees, 764, 899, 908, 923, 950, 979, 981, 1207
animal experimentation, 2, 4, 19, 34–37, 46, 48, 53–54, 56, 62, 74, 81, 84, 88, 96, 115, 128, 141, 207, 717–872, 1106–1138; agency rules, regulations, and policies, 969–992; alternatives, 1225–1269; animal care committees, 764, 899, 908, 923, 950, 979, 981, 1207; Animal Liberation Front, 993–1046; animal shelter animals, 556–558, 561–563, 569–570, 572–573, 575, 578, 582–583, 585, 587, 589–591, 593–596, 598–603, 606, 947–948, 958; bibliography, 743–744, 767, 770–773; consumer product and toxicity testing, 1168–1192; defense of, 1289–1322; genetic experiments, 1158–1165; in education, 1193–1224; law and legislation, 354–356, 572, 598, 892–968; military experiments, 1139–1157; philosophy, ethics, and religion, 200, 206, 244, 246, 255, 278, 300, 873–891; public relations, 789; scientific validity of, 806, 1270–1288; Silver Spring monkeys, 1047–1085; University of Pennsylvania baboon studies, 1086–1105
Animal Legal Defense League, 157, 350, 943
Animal Liberation Front, 8, 103, 122, 681, 785, 796, 806, 827, 993–1046

animal models (in research), 839–840, 1274, 1278, 1283, 1285; funding for, 724, 799, 1228, 1268
Animal Protection Institute, 128
Animal Research Facilities Protection Act of 1989, 896, 951
Animal Rights International, 108
Animal Rights Law Clinic, 103
*Animal Rights Law Reporter,* 364
animal rights literature, 95, 1317
Animal Rights March (Washington, D.C., 1990), 47, 109, 423
animal sacrifice, 257, 886
animal sanctuaries. *See* Black Beauty Farm, Farm Sanctuary, Living Free, Primarily Primates
animal shelters and pounds, 564, 567–568, 576–577, 579–581, 604–605; and animal experimentation, 556–558, 561–563, 569–570, 572–573, 575, 578, 582–583, 585, 587, 589–591, 593–596, 598–603, 606, 947–948, 958. *See also* cats; companion animals; dogs
animal suffering. *See* pain and animals
Animal Welfare Act, 115, 352, 367, 785, 837, 896, 898, 903, 910, 930, 932, 936, 943, 953, 955, 972, 989, 1091, 1100, 1256; animal care committees, 899, 923; congressional hearings, 368–369, 962–963; enforcement, 359, 477, 679, 684, 871, 915, 933, 940, 943, 962; Improved Standards for Laboratory Animals, 899, 915, 938, 962; Information Dissemination and Research Accountability Act, 922; Pet Theft Act, 947

Animals Farm Home, 592
anthropocentricity, 12, 106, 229, 889
anthropomorphism, 258
anti-cruelty statutes (state), 916, 939
antinomy and animals, 959
Antonovich, Inc., 534
Apple Computer Co., 1193, 1208
aquatic theme parks, 687, 692, 705–706
Aquinas, Thomas, 291
Aristotle, 21, 291
armadilloes, 795
Army, U.S. and animal experiments, 798, 1143–1144, 1148, 1152
arts and animals, 116, 130–131, 179
ASPCA. *See* American Society for the Prevention of Cruelty to Animals
Aspen (CO), ban on fur, 545–548, 552–553
Associated Medical Schools of New York, 1320
Association of American Medical Colleges, 934, 974
Association of American Universities, 974
Association of Veterinarians for Animal Rights, 173, 565,
attitudes toward animals, 39, 86, 97, 259, 800, 808
Attorneys for Animal Rights, 92
Avon Co., 1169, 1176, 1179, 1181, 1187, 1191, 1239

B-52s, 171, 181
baboons, 786, 794, 1035, 1086–1105, 1286
Baby Fae, 794, 1035
Bailey, Leonard, 1035
Baker, Robert, 678
Band of Mercy, 998, 1007, 1015, 1030, 1037
Barker, Bob, 499, 713, 742

Barnard, Neal, 1048
Barnes, Donald, 96, 108, 162
Barth, Karl, 319, 328
Bates, Tom, 472
beagles, 1017, 1042
bears, 137, 639
beavers, 500
Bell, Charles, 768
Benetton Co., 1170, 1175
Bernstein, Madeline, 172
Berosini, Bobby, 668
Betty, 171
Bible, 208, 319, 323, 513
bibliography (animal rights/welfare), 26, 59–60; animal experimentation, 743–744, 767, 770–773; farm animals, 381; legislation and regulation, 20, 338–339, 365; magazine and journals, 38; philosophy and ethics, 20, 200, 222, 230; vegetarianism, 455
Big Bang Theory, 171
Billy (monkey), 1048
Biomedical Research Defense Fund, 1312
*The Bird Business,* 710
birds, 125, 609, 635, 710; banding, 634
Black Beauty Farm (animal sanctuary), 137, 175
Blass, Bill, 122, 507, 513
*Bloom County,* 122, 167
Boston University, 587
Breathed, Berke, 122, 167
Brown, George E., 854, 902
Buddhism and animals, 244, 253, 293, 459, 886
buffaloes, 636
bull fighting, 699
bulls, 257, 699
Burger King, 395–396, 427
Burnet, Nancy, 151
Burnett, Carol Lyn, 183
burros, 137
Bush, George, (President), 651
business investment and animal rights, 32, 50, 67

Buyukmihci, Nedim, 173, 1206

Callicott, J. Baird, 237
calves, veal boycott, 395–396,
    427; veal production, 403,
    411, 445, 471–472, 483
Cambridge Committee for
    Responsible Research, 905
Cambridge, MA (animal experi-
    mentation), 895, 897, 904–
    906, 930–931, 950, 952, 967
cancer research, 1273
Caplan, Arthur, 52
Carey, Michael, 1305
Carlisle, Belinda, 507
Carme Co., 1171, 1192
carriage trade. *See* horse-
    carriage trade
Carson, Rachel, 105
Cate, Dexter, 146
Catholicism and animals, 145,
    196, 321–322, 886
cats, 155, 366, 560, 565, 619; in
    animal experimentation,
    948, 969, 972, 993, 1001,
    1007, 1014–1015, 1030,
    1032, 1037, 1045, 1109,
    1112, 1116, 1119, 1122–
    1123, 1127, 1134, 1136,
    1143, 1145–1146, 1152. *See
    also* animal shelters and
    pounds; companion animals
CEASE. *See* Citizens to End
    Animal Suffering and
    Exploitation
Centers for Disease Control,
    1288
Central Park, NYC, 695; zoo,
    691, 714
cetaceans, 372, 630
Chicago Meat Board, 388
chickens, 257, 391–392, 394,
    434, 478. *See also* cockfight-
    ing
children and animals, 745, 1219
Chimp Rehabilitation Program,
    133

chimpanzees, 137, 329; and
    organ transplants, 877, 881;
    as endangered species, 608,
    629, 633; in animal experi-
    mentation, 608, 629, 633,
    762, 774, 833, 864, 1005,
    1274; in movies, 713; in
    transit, 740; in zoos, 709
chinchillas, 500
Chivers, Eileen, 133
Christensen, Halvor, 1219
Christian Dior, 1191
*Christian Science Monitor,* 11
Christianity and animals, 187,
    189, 196, 247–249, 255, 303,
    321–322, 328, 450, 886;
    Bible, 208, 319, 323
circuses, 74, 200, 675, 677, 697
Citizens to End Animal Suffer-
    ing and Exploitation, 946
City of Hope Medical Center
    (Duarte, CA), 835, 999,
    1018, 1020, 1024, 1027,
    1045
civil disobedience, 16–18, 1140
Clark, Faria, 50
Clark, Stephen, 188
Coalition to End Animal
    Suffering, 478
Coalition to Protect Animals in
    Entertainment, 151
Cock and Bull awards, 128
cockfighting, 667, 678, 689, 702
Coe, Sue, 116, 131
Columbia University, 1018, 1107,
    1110, 1115, 1124, 1128
Committee to Abolish Sport
    Hunting, 161, 168
companion animals, 84, 338,
    354, 556–606, 960
conferences and meetings (ani-
    mal rights/welfare), 80, 92,
    347, 834, 1205
Confucianism and animals, 886
Congressional Friends of
    Animals, 351
Connecticut Humane Society,
    129

Consumer Product and Safety Commission, 1227
consumer product and toxicity testing, 36, 81, 964, 1168–1192, 1227, 1230–1231, 1236, 1238–1240, 1242–1243, 1245–1246, 1248–1250, 1253. *See also* Draize Eye Test; LD-50 test
Consumer Product Safety Act, 948, 964
contraception for wildlife, 618–619, 626
Cornell University, 1119, 1122–23, 1127, 1134
cosmetics industry, 53, 1168–1172, 1176, 1179, 1181, 1186–1187, 1191–1192, 1227, 1231–1234, 1236, 1238–1240, 1247, 1250, 1252–1253, 1259–1261. *See also* Avon Co.; Bennetton Co.; Carme Co.; Fabergé Co.; Gillette Co.; Mary Kay Co.; Noxell Co.; Revlon
cows, 121, 404, 179, 877; and branding, 474, 476, 479–480. *See also* calves
coyotes, 137, 610, 632
Cruelty to Animals Act (United Kingdom), 854
Culture and Animals Foundation, 130

Darwin, Edwin, 277, 291, 836
Day, Doris, 119
"dead piles," 121. *See also* "downers"
DeBakey, Michael, 105, 590, 596, 606, 727
*Declaration Against Speciesism,* 808
deep ecology, 272

deer, 619, 657, 660, 665
Delta Regional Primate Center, 1061, 1079
Denver Livestock Exchange Building, 388
Descartes, Rene, 202, 259, 292
Detroit zoo, 709
Deukmejian, George, 720
Disabled and Incurably Ill for Alternatives to Animal Research, 1305
disabled persons and animals, 615–616, 757, 1305
dissection (animals), 155, 908, 1195, 1200–1201, 1203–1204, 1208, 1210, 1212, 1216, 1220, 1222, 1224
dogs, 155, 329, 366, 559, 565, 571, 592, 664; and dog-fighting, 88, 678, 716; in animal experimentation, 561, 586, 720, 768, 835, 928, 948, 969, 972, 993, 1000, 1017, 1025–1026, 1035, 1042, 1045–1046, 1108, 1110, 1120, 1125, 1131–1132, 1137–1138, 1143–1148, 1151–1152, 1154–1155, 1197, 1286. *See also* animal shelters and pounds; companion animals
Dole, Robert, 753, 854, 932, 934, 957
dolphins, 76, 140, 146, 163, 429, 609, 621, 701; in experiments, 946, 1043, 1149; in marine parks, 672, 692, 705–706
Dommer, Luke, 161, 168
Donaldson, James, 126
Doris Day Pet Foundation, 119
Dorman, Francelle, 647, 649
Dornan, Robert, 336
"downers," 404. *See also* "dead piles"

Draize Eye Test, 56, 148, 730,
    853, 1169, 1172–1173, 1183,
    1189, 1245–1246,
    1258–1259, 1261,
    1264–1265, 1269, 1295
drifnets 609, 635
Dunda (elephant), 681–685

eagles, 632
Earth Day, 605
economics and animal rights, 85,
    90
education about animal rights,
    70, 88–89, 255
elephants, 137, 681–685
Emory University, 812
endangered species, 7, 96, 294,
    303; and hunting, 653, 661;
    and taxpayers, 654; chim-
    panzees, 608, 629, 633
Endocrine Society, 1318
The Enlightenment, 221
entertainment industry and ani-
    mals, 255, 667–716, 713
environment and animal rights,
    24, 37, 40, 110, 185, 270,
    272, 294, 313, 611; factory-
    farming, 62, 397; fur trap-
    ping, 495; green party, 4, 41;
    hunting, 644; land ethic,
    185, 191, 237; meat-eating,
    419, 435
Eskimos. See Alaskan Natives
ethics and animal rights, 185–
    334, 747, 840, 901; animal
    experimentation, 873–891;
    bibliography, 20, 200, 222,
    230; factory farming and
    vegetarianism, 448–470
Exene of X, 171
exotic animal trade, 620
exotic game ranches, 651, 653,
    662
exotic pets, 88
Eyetex, 1187, 1246

Fabergé Co., 1179
factory-farming, 4, 35, 37, 39, 46,
    53, 56, 62, 74, 88, 96, 121,
    132, 141, 255, 354, 376–484;
    and environment, 397, 435
    bibliography, 381
fake fur, 523, 538
Falk, Peter, 153
Farm Animal Reform Movement,
    388, 428
Farm Freedom Fighters, 392
Farm Sanctuary (animal sanctu-
    ary), 121, 132, 433
fashion industry, 39, 255. See also
    fur industry; trappers and
    trapping
Fauci, Anthony, 727
Federation of American
    Scientists, 973
Feinberg, Joel, 210
feminism and animal rights,
    14, 33, 41; and fur, 522;
    and vegetarianism, 376,
    380
Feral, Priscilla, 154
Filante bill (CA), 558, 600,
    1002
fish and fishing, 384, 429, 609,
    635, 700–701
Flipper (dolphin), 692, 706
Foundation for Biomedical
    Research, 855, 1290, 1311
Foundation on Economic
    Trends, 1158–1159, 1162
Fox, Michael A., 283, 312
Fox, Michael W., 141, 164, 407,
    409, 1162
Francione, Gary, 52
Freedom of Information Act,
    737, 937
Frey, R.L., 198, 236, 284
Friends of Animals, 154, 691,
    1133, 1201
frogs and dissection, 155, 1195,
    1203, 1208, 1210, 1212,
    1216, 1220, 1224

Fund for Animals, 66, 108, 133,
  149, 175, 178, 343, 613
fund-raising, 107, 123, 136
fur-farming, 500
Fur Free Friday, 499, 515
fur industry, 19, 81, 485–555,
  622. *See also* trappers and
  trapping; leghold traps
Fur Information Council of
  America, 533
Fur Vault, Inc., 534


Galileo Syndrome, 776
Gallistel, C.R., 880, 882–883
Gallup, Gordon G., 875
game ranches. *See* exotic game
  ranches
Geach, Peter, 273
geese, 410, 441
genetic experiments, 1158–1166
Gentle World, 166
gerbils, 1001, 1014
Gerone, Peter, 1079
Gillette Co., 1177–1178
giraffes, 620
Giraud, Lisa, 1194
goats, 137, 257, 592, 613, 619,
  677; and animal experimentation, 1141, 1143, 1146
Goldman, Roger, 52
gorillas, 329, 714
Graham, Jennifer, 1203, 1208,
  1210, 1212, 1216, 1220,
  1224
grand jury and animal rights
  activists, 349, 994–995, 997,
  1006, 1011–1013
Great American Meatout, 424,
  428, 431
Green Party, 4, 41
Greenpeace, 133
greyhounds, 707, 1144, 1148
Griswold, Charles, 269
Guadalcanal Diary, 171


*Halacha*, 232
Handley, Virginia, 133

Harbor-UCLA Medical Center,
  1025–1026
harp seals. *See* seals
*Harper's Magazine*, 42
Harrods department store, 504
Hartshorne, Charles, 205
Harvard University, 587, 812,
  897, 905, 967
Health Research Extension Act,
  870
heart research, 1025, 1275
heat and cold injuries in
  humans, 798
*Heaven's Gate*, 667
Heckler, Margaret, 786, 1097
Heflin, Howell, 896, 951
Heidegger, Martin 192
Helms, Jesse, 896, 951
Helping Hands, 615–616
hepatitis research, 1005
Herrera, 513
Herrington, Alice, 654
Hicks, Brad, 179
Hinduism and animals, 274, 293,
  886
Hirsch, Leon, 1129. *See also* U.S.
  Surgical Company
Hitt, Jack, 52
Hobbes, Thomas, 21
Hodel, Donald P., 624
Holzer, Mark, 364
horses, 592; carriage trade,
  673, 695, 698; in movies,
  667; racing, 74, 696; rid-
  ing, 200; rodeos, 74, 708;
  Tennessee Walking, 712;
  wild, 619, 623–625,
  627–628, 631
Howard, James, 407
Howard University, 806, 1003,
  1019, 1021, 1032
Humane Farming Association,
  108
Humane Farming Initiative
  (MA), 481
Humane Society Institute for the
  Study of Animal Problems,
  141

Humane Society of Rochester, 479
Humane Society of the United
    States, 124, 394, 403, 407,
    409, 441, 476, 608, 618, 626,
    633, 678, 682, 689, 1158–
    1159, 1161–1162, 1165, 1174
hunter harassment, 645, 655,
    659; laws, 647, 649, 652, 656
hunters and hunting, 4, 46, 54,
    62, 88, 125, 150, 168, 607,
    612, 618, 626, 636–666


IACAUCs. *See* animal care and
    use committees
Immuno Corporation, 371
Improved Standards for
    Laboratory Animals Act, 22,
    853, 899, 902, 915, 926, 934,
    938, 962, 965
In Defense of Animals, 617
Information Dissemination and
    Research Accountability Act,
    921–922
Institute for Behavioral Research,
    352, 942, 955
international activities (animal
    rights), 86, 316, 335
International League for Animal
    Rights, 335
International Primate Protection
    League, 352, 371, 942, 955,
    1070, 1150
International Research and De-
    velopment Corp, 1171, 1192
Iroquois Brands Limited, 410, 441
Islam and animals, 254, 886


Jainism and animals, 293, 326, 886
Jane Goodall Institute, 608, 633
Jodar, Bruce Wayne, 1027
John Paul II, Pope, 196
Johns Hopkins University, 1236,
    1247, 1253
Johnson, Hugh, 430
Johnson, Samuel, 759
Jones, Howard, 171

*Journal of Medical Primology*,
    371
Judaism and animals, 232–233,
    449, 458, 467, 886


Kant, Immanuel, 21, 279, 291
karma, Doctrine of, 256
Kennedy, Donald, 741, 847
Kevles, Betty Ann, 722
King, Martin Luther, 71
Koran. *See* Qur'an
Kullberg, John, 677


Labor Day Pigeon Shoot
    (Hegins, PA), 669, 671, 676,
    686, 688, 694
LaBudde, Sam, 140, 163
Lancaster Stockyards, 433
land ethic, 185, 191, 237
Landers, Ann, 128, 735
Lantos, Tom, 1154
Larson, Sandy, 144
LaRussa, Elaine and Tony, 127
law and legislation, 52, 84, 278,
    335–375, 400, 574, 581, 597,
    702; animal experimenta-
    tion, 732, 821, 837, 839,
    853–854, 883, 892–968,
    1261; animal shelters,
    557–558, 569, 572–573, 575,
    578, 583, 585, 587, 589–591,
    593–595, 598–603; bibliogra-
    phy, 20, 338–339, 365; facto-
    ry farming, 471–484; fur
    industry and trapping,
    542–555; horses, 623,
    627–628, 673, 695; hunter
    harassment statutes, 647,
    649, 652, 656; hunting, 641,
    650; whales, 621, 630
Lazare, Bobbi, 147
Lazarian Society for Animals,
    145
LD-50 test, 56, 148, 730, 853,
    1172, 1182, 1184,
    1188–1189, 1242, 1248,

1261, 1263, 1269, 1295
leather and leather industry, 46,
    415
leghold traps, 63, 355, 492, 510,
    525–526, 544, 549–551,
    554–555. *See also* fur indus-
    try; trappers and trapping
leopards, 661
Leopold, Aldo, 191
LeVasseur, Kenneth, 1043
Levin, Michael, 314
Levy, Marc, 150
libel and slander lawsuits, 373
*Liberation of Life*, 255, 333
Linzey, Reverend Andrew, 187,
    316, 328
lions, 137, 620, 651, 662; moun-
    tain, 176, 500, 666
Living Free (animal sanctuary),
    147
Locke, John, 21, 318
Loma Linda University Medical
    Center, 1035
longevity (human), 1272
*Los Angeles Times*, 593
Lovenheim, Peter, 410
Lovich, Lene, 123, 171, 181
lung disease research, 835, 1045
Luxemborg, Rosa, 49
lynxes, 500

McArdle, John, 124, 182, 985,
    1174
McCabe, Katie, 117
McCarter, Thomas III, 125
McCarthy, Coleman, 120, 316
McCarthy, Justin, 592
McCartney, Linda, 159
McCay, Peggy, 152
McCloskey, H.J., 285
McCool, Maggie, 1222
McDonalds restaurant, 427
Macy's department store, 503,
    529
Madison, James, 21
Magel, Charles, 1317

Magendie, Francois, 768
Malone, Thomas E., 863
Maltison, Brother Victorian, 145
Marin County Humane Society
    (CA), 1144
marine and swim parks. *See*
    acquatic theme parks
martens, 500
Martha (monkey), 809
Marx, Karl, 21
Mary Kay Co., 1176, 1179, 1181
Mason, Jim, 96
Massachusetts Institute of Tech-
    nology, 587, 897, 905, 967
Mayo, Charles, 722
"Me Generation" and animals, 79
Mead, Marc, 1111, 1114, 1117
meat industry, 405, 443, 446
media and animal rights, 8, 10,
    11, 17, 42–44, 55, 68, 109
Medical Research Moderniza-
    tion Committee, 1305
medical schools, 1197, 1320
Melman, Larry "Bud", 181
Merchant, Natalie, 134, 171, 181
mice, 25, 155, 257, 910, 1001,
    1045, 1231
military experiments, 561, 586,
    798, 869–870, 1139–1157
Mill, John Stuart, 21
Miller, Bradley, 108
Ministries for Animals, 262
Mink Stole, 181
minks, 500, 518
Mobil Oil Corp., 1255
Mobilization for Animals, 118,
    813, 819, 857
monkeys, 257, 615–616, 620,
    802, 809, 823, 1001, 1009,
    1150, 1157, 1286; Silver
    Spring monkeys, 117, 935,
    1047–1085
Montaigne, 21
Moor-Jankowski, Jan, 371, 740
Morrison, Adrian, 1118, 1305
mousetraps, 25
movies and animals, 667, 713

Moyer, Bill, 23
Mud Lake Farmers Rabbit
    Committee, 343
mules, 667, 711
music and animals, 136, 171, 181


Narveson, Jan, 234, 286
NASA. *See* National Aeronautics
    and Space Administration
National Academy of
    Engineering, 728
National Academy of Sciences,
    728, 1214, 1228
National Aeronautics and Space
    Administration, 802, 1209
National Agricultural Library, 22
National Anti-Vivisection
    Society, 92, 103, 162
National Association of Biology
    Teachers, 1221
National Cancer Institute, 1041
National Foundation for Animal
    Law, 103, 1044
National Humane Education
    Society, 735
National Institutes of Health,
    183, 608, 732, 753, 785, 813,
    823, 826, 863, 900, 918–920,
    922, 973, 975, 980, 982,
    987–988, 991, 1008–1009,
    1024, 1047, 1049–1051, 1055,
    1061, 1068, 1073– 1076,
    1084, 1087, 1090, 1092–
    1093, 1095–1098, 1102, 1104,
    1107, 1110, 1112, 1124,
    1128, 1136, 1228, 1268, 1286
National Rifle Association, 525,
    647, 665
National Science Teachers
    Association, 1214, 1221
National Society for Medical
    Research, 781, 870
National Trappers Association,
    511
Native Americans, 278, 501. *See
    also* Alaskan Natives

Nazis, 723, 791
Neiman-Marcus, 560
New England Anti-Vivisection
    Society, 108, 144, 1137
New York Horse and Carriage
    Association, 695
*New York Times,* 11, 42
New York University, 1311
Newkirk, Ingrid, 5, 52
*Newsweek,* 42
Nilson, Greta, 710
Nim Chimsky (chimpanzee),
    833
Nobel laureates, 1307
non-violence, 3, 69, 72, 256,
    326
North American Vegetarian
    Society, 433
Noxell Co., 1175


O'Barry, Ric, 692
Okamoto, Michiko, 1123
Oneida Community (NY), 492
opossums, 257, 1014
opposition to animal rights, 61,
    64, 766
orangutans, 668
Oregon Ballot Measure, 543
Orem, John, 996, 1109, 1118,
    1305
organ transplants. *See*
    zenografts
organizations (animal rights),
    34, 48, 116–184, 352, 355,
    394
Orlans, F. Barbara, 1196
ostriches, 620
otters, 176
Owings, Margaret, 176
owls, 110
oxen, 257


Pacelle, Wayne, 108
Pacheco, Alex, 96, 117, 183,
    1062

pain and animals, 15, 27–29, 237, 273, 286, 315, 830, 836, 840, 872, 899, 901, 912, 928, 931, 941, 953, 1257

*Painful Experiments on Animals,* 1257

panthers, 680

papal encyclicals, 196

Paska, Alison, 616

pate, 410, 441

patriarchy, 14, 380

Pattycake (gorilla), 714

penguins, 128

Peninsula Humane Society (San Mateo, CA), 581, 1194

Pennsylvania Animal Rights Coalition, 1089

People for the Ethical Treatment of Animals, 5, 9, 51, 92, 117, 123, 136, 138, 156, 170–171, 181, 183, 668, 727, 855, 1007, 1024, 1062, 1070, 1073–1074, 1076, 1140–41, 1143, 1154, 1169, 1181, 1192, 1201

Perceptions International, 1117

Perdue, Frank, 394

Performing Animal Welfare Society, 668

pet stores, 559

Pet Theft Act, 583, 602, 909, 947–948

pets. *See* companion animals

Pfieffer, Linda, 133

philosophy and animal rights, 2, 52, 185–334, 448–470, 849, 873–891, bibliography, 20, 200, 222, 230

Phoenix, River, 123, 160, 181, 507

Physicians Committee for Responsible Medicine, 1048–1049, 1073, 1076, 1305

pigeons, 669, 671, 676, 686, 688, 694, 993, 1014

pigs, 121, 137, 155, 385, 436, 877, 1015, 1030, 1143, 1146–1147, 1158–1159, 1165

Plimpton, Martha, 180

political theory, 21

politics and animal rights, 10, 57–58, 727

polls. *See* public opinion polls

Pope, Alexander, 759

*Porkopolis,* 116

Porphyry, 454

pounds. *See* animal shelters and pounds

Prescott, Heidi, 652

Primarily Primates (animal sanctuary), 809

primates, 800, 812–813, 823, 857, 859, 933, 972, 1282

Probst, Marian, 149

Procter & Gamble Company, 103, 1310

*Project X,* 713

Psychologists for the Ethical Treatment of Animals, 143

public opinion polls, 46, 81; animal experimentation, 829, 858, 1187, 1190; hunting, 659

public relations, 789

puppy mills, 559, 597

Putting People First, 506

quail, 651

Qur'an, 254

rabbit drives, 343

rabbits, 155, 343, 665, 999, 1001, 1004, 1014, 1027, 1045, 1169, 1173, 1177, 1180, 1183, 1231, 1245–1246

raccoons, 500, 664

racism, 275

radio and animal rights, 142

Ralston Purina, 664

Rational Egoism, 194, 234, 286

rats, 802, 910, 1014, 1045, 1122, 1180, 1209, 1231, 1278–1279, 1285, 1287

Raub, William, 1096

*Reader's Digest, The,* 42

reform movements and animal
rights, 3, 13, 23, 71, 242,
308
Regan, Tom, 21, 96, 135, 210,
212, 214, 217–219, 235, 243,
265–266, 271–272, 307, 311,
325, 327, 424, 873, 885, 891
relativism, 889
religion and animal rights, 257,
293, 466, 886; Buddhism,
244, 253, 459; Christianity,
187, 189, 196, 208, 247–249,
255, 303, 319, 321–323, 328,
333, 450; Hinduism, 274;
Islam, 254; Jainism, 326;
Judaism, 232–233, 449, 458,
467
Research! America, 112
Research Modernization Act,
768, 821, 837, 882–883, 894,
900, 922
reverence for life, 328, 889
Revlon, 1168, 1176, 1179, 1181,
1187, 1191, 1239–1240,
1259, 1264
Rich, Susan, 156
Rifkin, Jeremy, 1159, 1162, 1165
roadkills, 614
Roberti bill (CA), 557–558, 591,
593, 599–600, 929
Roberts, Louise, 133
Rockefeller University, 1240,
1245, 1253, 1258–1259
rodeos, 19, 74, 690, 703–704,
708, 715
Romanes, G. J., 836
Rose, Charles, 896
Ross, Kenneth, 157
Rousseau, Jean-Jacques, 221
Rowland, Sandy, 133
Royal Canin Co., 664
Royal Society for the Prevention
of Cruelty to Animals
(United Kingdom), 80
rules, regulations, and policies
(animal experimentation),
969–992
Ryder, Richard, 96

San Diego Wild Animal Park,
681–685
Santeria, 257
Sapone, Mary Lou, 1117
Sapontzis, Steve, 267
Schopenhauer, Arthur, 291
Schweitzer, Albert, 21, 291, 328
science fair projects, 141, 781,
1196, 1198, 1205
Scientists Center for Animal
Welfare, 781
Scientists Group for Reform of
Animal Experimentation,
556
sea lions. See seals
Seabert, 622
seals, 66, 176, 200, 501, 519, 609,
622, 672
Seaworld, 705
SEMA, Inc., 933, 1005
sentimentality and animals, 259
sexism, 275
Shapiro, Ken, 143
shareholder proxy proposals, 30
sharks, 611, 701
Shaw, George Bernard, 139
sheep, 121, 1158–1159, 1165;
sheep industry, 387
shelters. See animal shelters and
pounds
sign language, 833
Sikhism and animals, 293
The Silent Spring, 105
Silver Spring monkeys, 336, 761,
916, 935, 977, 983, 1047–1085
Singer, Peter, 21, 158, 188, 212,
214–215, 240, 242, 245, 266,
275, 282, 329, 332, 547, 873,
891
Sipman, Steve, 1043
slaughterhouses, 116, 121, 132,
356, 385, 404, 425, 482, 696
slavery, 100–101
Smith, Robert, 336
Snyder, Gwenyth, 174
Society of Cosmetics Chemists,
1252
Society for Neuroscience, 1318

"soring", 712
spay/neuter clinics, 565
speciesism, 86, 275, 320, 808
Spinoza, Benedict, 259
Spira, Henry, 96, 108, 148, 394, 1116
Spring, Dona, 108
squirrels, 617, 665
Stamp, Marian Dawkins, 315
*Standards for Research with Animals*, 834
Stanford University, 741, 1194
State University of New York, Stony Brook, 937
Staub, Rusty, 507
Stenholm, Charles, 896
Sterling, Bill, 547, 553
stroke research, 1271
Student Action Corps for Animals, 155
Sturla, Kim, 1194
Suarez, Susan D., 875
Sullivan, Louis, 64, 1291, 1298, 1306
Supreme Court, U.S., 1052, 1059
Sydel's Egg Farm, 392
sympathy for animals, 211, 259

Taub, Edward, 761, 916, 955, 1053–54, 1060, 1062–1065, 1067, 1072, 1075, 1077, 1081, 1083–1084
television and animals, 43–44, 68
Tennessee Walking Horse, 712
terrorism and animal rights, 5, 64, 83, 91, 108, 345, 533, 1291, 1298
Texas Tech University Health Sciences Center (Lubbock), 996, 1118
Thalberg, Katherine, 547
toxicity testing. *See* consumer product and toxicity testing
toxoplasmosis, 1015, 1037
Trans Species Unlimited, 93, 433, 499, 503, 686, 1134

transportation of animals, 341, 356, 404, 482, 740
trappers and trapping, 4, 54, 62, 88, 150, 356, 492, 495, 497–498, 510–511, 542–544, 555. *See also* fur industry; leghold traps
Triangle Animal Awareness Week, 130
Troen, Roger, 1016
True Friends, 1005
Trutt, Fran Stephanie, 1106, 1111, 1113–1114, 1117, 1120–1121, 1125, 1130–1132, 1135
Tufts University, 587
Tulane University, 1061
Tule elk hunt, 103
turkeys, 121, 416, 447
turtles, 429, 609

U.S. Bureau of Land Management, 624, 627–628
U.S. Congress. Animal Welfare Caucus, 351
U.S. Congress. Hearings, 368–370, 483, 555, 602, 960–965, 1266
U.S. Congress. Office of Technology Assessment, 755, 1189, 1225, 1241, 1251, 1254, 1256, 1267
U.S. Defense Department, and animal experimentation, 561, 586, 870, 1140, 1151
U.S. Department of the Interior, 661
U.S. Environmental Protection Agency, and animal experimentation, 989–990, 1174; LD-50 test, 1188, 1242
U.S. Federal Bureau of Investigation, 6, 122, 406
U.S. Fish and Wildlife Service, 608, 633
U.S. Food and Drug Administration, 989, 1182, 1184, 1188–1189, 1227, 1234, 1242, 1248

U.S. Health and Human
Services, 941; animal experimentation guidelines, 971;
baboon experiments, 1097,
1101– 1102; Office of
Scientific Integrity, 1049;
Silver Spring monkeys,
1053, 1085
U.S. Justice Department, 893
U.S. National Park Service, 636
U.S. Navy, 613, 617, 946; and
animal experimentation,
1046, 1149
U.S. Public Health Services, 785,
979, 981, 984–985, 989,
991–992
U.S. Surgical Co., 1106, 1108,
1111, 1114, 1117, 1120,
1125, 1129, 1131–1133,
1135, 1137–1138
U. S. Transportation Depart-
ment, 1188
United Activists for Animal
Rights, 151, 713
*Universal Declaration of Rights of
Animals*, 213, 335, 808
University of Arizona, 1031
University of California;
Berkeley, 721, 862; Davis,
812, 1206; Irvine, 1000,
1017, 1042; Los Angeles,
742; Riverside, 827, 1001,
1008–1009, 1014, 1018,
1020
University of Cincinnati, 1112
University of Massachusetts, 587
University of Oregon, 1012,
1016, 1044
University of Pennsylvania, 993,
1018, (1118); baboon stud-
ies, 786, 1086–1105
University of Washington, 809
University of Wisconsin, 812
*Use of Animals in High School
Biology Classes*, 1205
utilitarianism, 229, 279, 282,
287, 332, 463–464, 469–470,
889, 891

Veal Calf Protection Act, 483,
948
veal calves. *See* calves
vegetarianism, 2, 4, 19, 56, 81,
90, 199–200, 205, 246, 278,
300, 314, 376–377, 380,
382–383, 401, 406, 448–470,
660, 749, 1273; bibliography, 455
Velucci, Cres, 1044
veterinarians, 37, 54, 62, 173,
292, 360, 565, 574, 903
Voltaire, 221, 291


Walden, Shelton, 142
Walgren, Doug, 956–957
Walk to Rome for Animal Rights
(1990), 322
Wall, Rev. James, 316
*Wall Street Journal*, 11
*Washington Post*, 401
*Washingtonian*, 117, 170
Watson, R.A., 276
Waxman, Henry, 896
Weinberger, Caspar, 613, 869,
1141, 1145–1147,
1151–1152, 1154–1155
whales and whaling, 609, 621,
630, 672, 705
White, Robert, 112, 1276
White Award, 112
*White Paper on Animal Research*
(American Medical Asso-
ciation), 1315
Whitehead, Alfred, 186
Wiedlin, Jane, 123, 181, 507
Wild Horse and Burro Act, 623,
628
wildlife, 2, 37, 338, 356, 419,
607–666, 670
Wildlife Legislative Fund of
America, 118
Wildlife Refuge Reform Act,
612, 948
wildlife refuges, 612, 650, 948
Wise and Leach Co., 1201
Wisket, John, 507

wolves, 128
women and animals. *See* feminism and animal rights
Wood, Ron, 1311
World Council of Churches, 255, 333
World Day for Laboratory Animals, 83, 742, 831
World Farm Animals Day, 388
World Laboratory Animal Liberation Day, 1290
World Laboratory Animal Liberation Week, 165, 861, 867–868
World Vegetarian Day, 388
World Wildlife Fund, 608, 633

Wyngaarden, James, 1068

xenografts, 765, 794, 877, 881, 885, 1035

Yale University, 660, 1270
Yellowstone National Park, 636
Young, Debra, 994, 1013

Zbinden, Gerhard, 1248
zoos, 46, 96, 620, 670, 679–685, 691, 693, 709, 714, 851
Zoroastrianism and animals, 293

# ABOUT THE AUTHOR

BETTINA MANZO earned a B.A. degree at Marywood College, a Master of Library Science at Florida State University, and an M.A. in history at the University of Wyoming. Ms. Manzo is a reference librarian at the College of William and Mary in Williamsburg, Virginia, and a Ph.D. candidate in the American Studies program at the college. Her scholarly interests center on the history of social reform movements and material culture in the United States.